KB184309

절대어휘
5100
③

저자

김호성 한국외국어대학교 대학원 영어과 석사 / 마일스톤 학원 원장

전진완 한국외국어대학교 대학원 영어과 석사 / (전) 정이조 영어학원 당산 캠퍼스 원장

백영실 Liberty University 졸업 / 정이조 영어학원 주니어 총괄 원장

고미선 New York State University at Buffalo 졸업 / 정이조 영어학원 총괄 원장

이나영 University of Arizona 졸업 / 이나영 영어학원 원장

박영은 The University of Auckland 졸업 / (전) 정이조 영어학원 강사

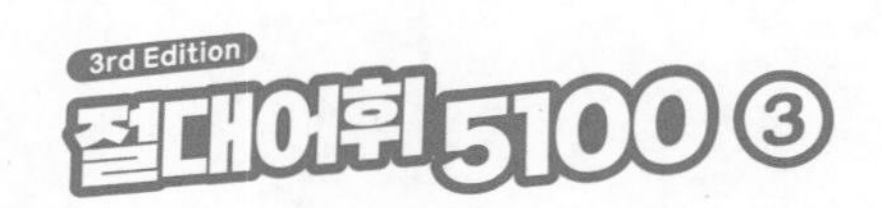

지은이 김호성, 전진완, 백영실, 고미선, 이나영, 박영은
펴낸이 정규도
펴낸곳 (주)다락원

초판 1쇄 발행 2008년 8월 18일
제2판 1쇄 발행 2015년 9월 14일
제3판 1쇄 발행 2024년 11월 21일

편집 김민아
디자인 구수정, 포레스트

다락원 경기도 파주시 문발로 211
내용문의 (02)736-2031 내선 504
구입문의 (02)736-2031 내선 250~252

Fax (02)732-2037
출판등록 1977년 9월 16일 제406-2008-000007호

ISBN 978-89-277-8081-6 54740
978-89-277-8078-6 54740(set)

http://www.darakwon.co.kr

다락원 홈페이지를 방문하시면 상세한 출판정보와 함께
동영상강좌, MP3 자료 등 다양한 어학 정보를 얻으실 수 있습니다.

DARAKWON

구성과 특징

절대어휘 5100 시리즈는

어휘 학습에 있어서 반복학습의 중요성을 강조합니다.
자기주도적인 어휘학습의 중요성을 강조합니다.
체계적인 단계별 학습의 중요성을 강조합니다.

1 | 단계별 30일 구성! 계획적인 어휘 학습

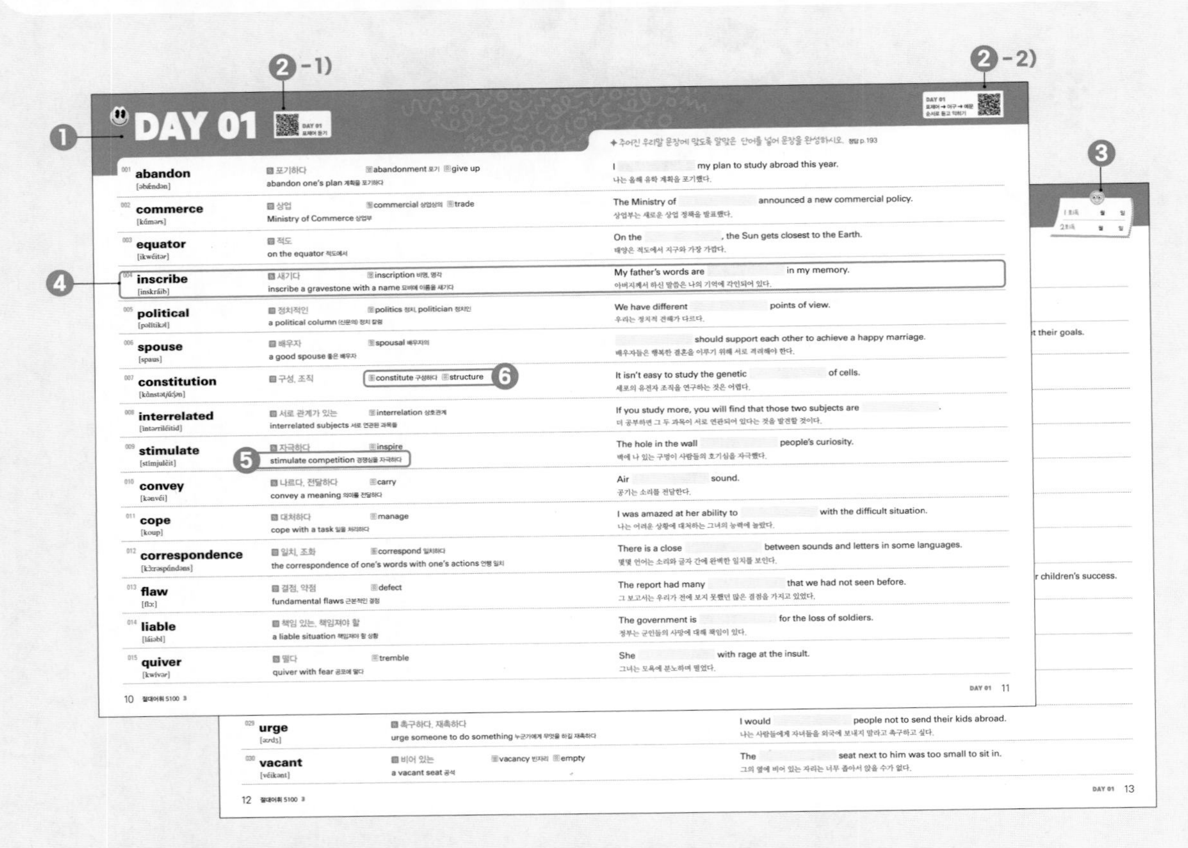

DAY 01

DAY 01 표제어 듣기

DAY 01 표제어 → 어구 → 예문 순서로 듣고 익히기

✦ 주어진 우리말 문장에 맞도록 알맞은 단어를 넣어 문장을 완성하시오. 정답 p.193

No.	Word	Meaning / Phrase	Related	Example
001	abandon [əbǽndən]	포기하다 abandon one's plan 계획을 포기하다	abandonment 포기 / give up	I ____ my plan to study abroad this year. 나는 올해 유학 계획을 포기했다.
002	commerce [kάmərs]	상업 Ministry of Commerce 상업부	commercial 상업상의 / trade	The Ministry of ____ announced a new commercial policy. 상업부는 새로운 상업 정책을 발표했다.
003	equator [ikwéitər]	적도 on the equator 적도에서		On the ____, the Sun gets closest to the Earth. 태양은 적도에서 지구와 가장 가깝다.
004	inscribe [inskráib]	새기다 inscribe a gravestone with a name 묘비에 이름을 새기다	inscription 비명, 명각	My father's words are ____ in my memory. 아버지께서 하신 말씀은 나의 기억에 각인되어 있다.
005	political [pəlítikəl]	정치적인 a political column (신문의) 정치 칼럼	politics 정치, politician 정치인	We have different ____ points of view. 우리는 정치적 견해가 다르다.
006	spouse [spaus]	배우자 a good spouse 좋은 배우자	spousal 배우자의	____ should support each other to achieve a happy marriage. 배우자들은 행복한 결혼을 이루기 위해 서로 격려해야 한다.
007	constitution [kὰnstətjúːʃən]	구성, 조직	constitute 구성하다 / structure	It isn't easy to study the genetic ____ of cells. 세포의 유전자 조직을 연구하는 것은 어렵다.
008	interrelated [ìntərriléitid]	서로 관계가 있는 interrelated subjects 서로 연관된 과목들	interrelation 상호관계	If you study more, you will find that those two subjects are ____. 더 공부하면 그 두 과목이 서로 연관되어 있다는 것을 발견할 것이다.
009	stimulate [stímjulèit]	자극하다 stimulate competition 경쟁심을 자극하다	inspire	The hole in the wall ____ people's curiosity. 벽에 나 있는 구멍이 사람들의 호기심을 자극했다.
010	convey [kənvéi]	나르다, 전달하다 convey a meaning 의미를 전달하다	carry	Air ____ sound. 공기는 소리를 전달한다.
011	cope [koup]	대처하다 cope with a task 일을 처리하다	manage	I was amazed at her ability to ____ with the difficult situation. 나는 어려운 상황에 대처하는 그녀의 능력에 놀랐다.
012	correspondence [kɔ̀ːrəspάndəns]	일치, 조화 the correspondence of one's words with one's actions 언행 일치	correspond 일치하다	There is a close ____ between sounds and letters in some languages. 몇몇 언어는 소리와 글자 간에 완벽한 일치를 보인다.
013	flaw [flɔː]	결점, 약점 fundamental flaws 근본적인 결점	defect	The report had many ____ that we had not seen before. 그 보고서는 우리가 전에 보지 못했던 많은 결점을 가지고 있었다.
014	liable [láiəbl]	책임 있는, 책임져야 할 a liable situation 책임져야 할 상황		The government is ____ for the loss of soldiers. 정부는 군인들의 사망에 대해 책임이 있다.
015	quiver [kwívər]	떨다 quiver with fear 공포에 떨다	tremble	She ____ with rage at the insult. 그녀는 모욕에 분노하며 떨었다.

10 절대어휘 5100 3 DAY 01 11

No.	Word	Meaning / Phrase	Related	Example
029	urge [əːrdʒ]	촉구하다, 재촉하다 urge someone to do something 누군가에게 무엇을 하길 재촉하다		I would ____ people not to send their kids abroad. 나는 사람들에게 자녀들을 외국에 보내지 말라고 촉구하고 싶다.
030	vacant [véikənt]	비어 있는 a vacant seat 공석	vacancy 빈자리 / empty	The ____ seat next to him was too small to sit in. 그의 옆에 비어 있는 자리는 너무 좁아서 앉을 수가 없다.

12 절대어휘 5100 3 DAY 01 13

❶ **30일 구성의 계획적인 어휘 학습** : 하루 30개씩 30일 구성으로 총 900 단어 학습
❷ **두 가지 버전의 QR코드 바로 듣기** : 남녀 원어민 음성으로 정확한 발음 연습
1) 표제어 듣기 2) 표제어, 어구, 예문 순서로 듣고 익히기
❸ **DAY별 학습 진도 체크하기** : 학습 날짜를 기록하여 효과적으로 반복 학습
❹ **단어 → 어구 → 문장 순서**로 자연스럽게 표제어 응용 학습
❺ **다양한 Collocation 학습**으로 어휘 자신감 높이기
❻ **유의어, 반의어, 파생어** 등으로 어휘력 확장

2 | 7가지 유형의 REVIEW TEST

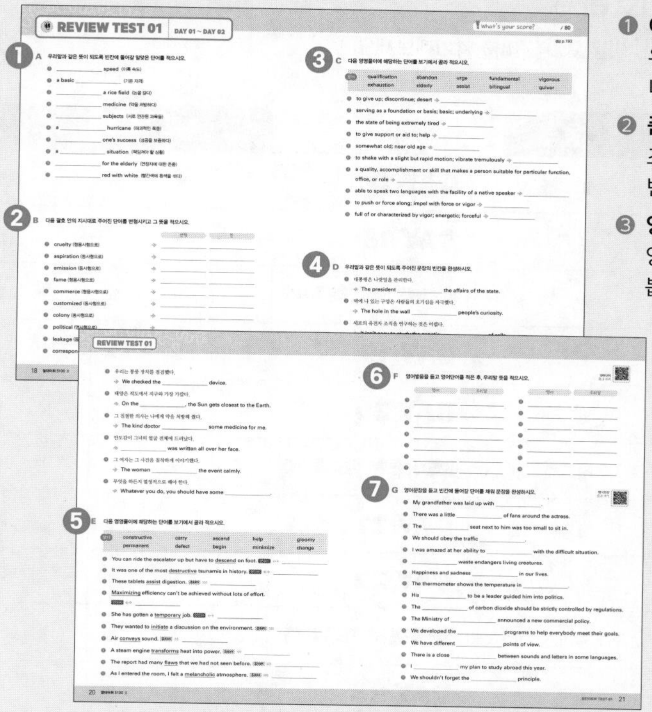

❶ **어구 빈칸 완성**
우리말과 일치하도록 어구의 빈칸을 완성합니다.

❷ **품사별 단어 변형**
조건에 따라 주어진 단어를 다양한 품사로 변형해 보고 우리말 뜻을 써 봅니다.

❸ **영영 풀이**
영영 풀이에 해당하는 단어를 보기에서 찾아 봅니다.

❹ **문장 빈칸 완성**
우리말과 일치하도록 문장의 빈칸을 완성합니다.

❺ **유의어 or 반의어**
문장 속 밑줄 친 어휘의 유의어 또는 반의어를 보기에서 찾아 써 봅니다.

❻ **단어 받아쓰기**
남녀 원어민의 음성을 듣고 영어와 우리말 뜻을 적어봅니다.

❼ **문장 듣고 받아쓰기**
남녀 원어민의 음성을 듣고 문장 속 빈칸을 완성합니다.

3 | WORKBOOK

쓰기 노트

STEP 1
영어의 우리말 의미를 생각하며 두 번씩 써 보기

일일테스트

STEP 2
DAY별로 학습한 단어로 최종 실력 점검하기

4 | 문제출제프로그램 voca.darakwon.co.kr

그 밖에 3종 이상의 다양한 테스트지를 원하는 범위에서 출제하고 출력해서 쓸 수 있는 문제출제프로그램을 제공합니다.

절대어휘 5100 학습 계획표

고등 내신 기본 900 단어 Master

30일 구성의 계획적인 어휘 학습으로 고등 내신 기본 900 단어를 암기해보세요.

	1회독		2회독	
DAY 01	월	일	월	일
DAY 02	월	일	월	일
REVIEW TEST 01	월	일	월	일
DAY 03	월	일	월	일
DAY 04	월	일	월	일
REVIEW TEST 02	월	일	월	일
DAY 05	월	일	월	일
DAY 06	월	일	월	일
REVIEW TEST 03	월	일	월	일
DAY 07	월	일	월	일
DAY 08	월	일	월	일
REVIEW TEST 04	월	일	월	일
DAY 09	월	일	월	일
DAY 10	월	일	월	일
REVIEW TEST 05	월	일	월	일
DAY 11	월	일	월	일
DAY 12	월	일	월	일
REVIEW TEST 06	월	일	월	일
DAY 13	월	일	월	일
DAY 14	월	일	월	일
REVIEW TEST 07	월	일	월	일
DAY 15	월	일	월	일
DAY 16	월	일	월	일
REVIEW TEST 08	월	일	월	일

	1회독		2회독	
DAY 17	월	일	월	일
DAY 18	월	일	월	일
REVIEW TEST 09	월	일	월	일
DAY 19	월	일	월	일
DAY 20	월	일	월	일
REVIEW TEST 10	월	일	월	일
DAY 21	월	일	월	일
DAY 22	월	일	월	일
REVIEW TEST 11	월	일	월	일
DAY 23	월	일	월	일
DAY 24	월	일	월	일
REVIEW TEST 12	월	일	월	일
DAY 25	월	일	월	일
DAY 26	월	일	월	일
REVIEW TEST 13	월	일	월	일
DAY 27	월	일	월	일
DAY 28	월	일	월	일
REVIEW TEST 14	월	일	월	일
DAY 29	월	일	월	일
DAY 30	월	일	월	일
REVIEW TEST 15	월	일	월	일

절대어휘 5100 권장 학습법

1 회독

❶ 하루에 30개의 표제어를 학습합니다. (30일 완성!)
❷ QR코드를 통해 표제어, 어구, 예문을 들으며 발음을 따라해 봅니다.
❸ 유의어, 반의어, 파생어 등을 살펴보며 어휘력을 확장합니다.
❹ REVIEW TEST로 2일 동안 학습한 단어들을 점검해 봅니다.
❺ 워크북을 활용하여 단어의 철자와 뜻을 한번 더 확인합니다.

2 회독

❶ 하루에 60개의 표제어를 학습합니다. (15일 완성!)
❷ QR코드를 통해 표제어를 들으며 발음을 따라해 봅니다.
❸ 표제어와 함께 유의어, 반의어, 파생어 등을 꼼꼼히 살펴봅니다.
❹ REVIEW TEST에서 자주 틀리거나 헷갈리는 단어들을 오답노트에 정리합니다.
❺ 단어테스트지와 문제출제프로그램을 통해 학습한 단어를 최종 점검합니다.

N 회독

❶ QR코드 또는 MP3를 반복해서 들어보세요.
❷ 반복 학습으로 고등 내신 기본 900 단어를 마스터해보세요.

■ 책 속의 책 Workbook 제공

3rd Edition

절대어휘 5100

3 고등 내신 기본 900

* DAY 01 ~ 30

책에 쓰인 여러 기호

동 동사	명 명사	대 대명사	형 형용사	부 부사
전 전치사	접 접속사	감 감탄사	유 유의어	반 반의어
참 참고어	단 단수형	복 복수형	pl. (~s)일 때의 뜻	

001	**abandon** [əbǽndən]	동 포기하다 abandon one's plan 계획을 포기하다	명 abandonment 포기 유 give up
002	**commerce** [kάmərs]	명 상업 Ministry of Commerce 상업부	형 commercial 상업상의 유 trade
003	**equator** [ikwéitər]	명 적도 on the equator 적도에서	
004	**inscribe** [inskráib]	동 새기다 inscribe a gravestone with a name 묘비에 이름을 새기다	명 inscription 비명, 명각
005	**political** [pəlítikəl]	형 정치적인 a political column (신문의) 정치 칼럼	명 politics 정치, politician 정치인
006	**spouse** [spaus]	명 배우자 a good spouse 좋은 배우자	형 spousal 배우자의
007	**constitution** [kὰnstətjúːʃən]	명 구성, 조직	동 constitute 구성하다 유 structure
008	**interrelated** [ìntərriléitid]	형 서로 관계가 있는 interrelated subjects 서로 연관된 과목들	명 interrelation 상호관계
009	**stimulate** [stímjulèit]	동 자극하다 stimulate competition 경쟁심을 자극하다	유 inspire
010	**convey** [kənvéi]	동 나르다, 전달하다 convey a meaning 의미를 전달하다	유 carry
011	**cope** [koup]	동 대처하다 cope with a task 일을 처리하다	유 manage
012	**correspondence** [kɔ̀ːrəspάndəns]	명 일치, 조화 the correspondence of one's words with one's actions 언행 일치	동 correspond 일치하다
013	**flaw** [flɔː]	명 결점, 약점 fundamental flaws 근본적인 결점	유 defect
014	**liable** [láiəbl]	형 책임 있는, 책임져야 할 a liable situation 책임져야 할 상황	
015	**quiver** [kwívər]	동 떨다 quiver with fear 공포에 떨다	유 tremble

✦ 주어진 우리말 문장에 맞도록 알맞은 단어를 넣어 문장을 완성하시오. 정답 p.193

I ______ my plan to study abroad this year.
나는 올해 유학 계획을 포기했다.

The Ministry of ______ announced a new commercial policy.
상업부는 새로운 상업 정책을 발표했다.

On the ______, the Sun gets closest to the Earth.
태양은 적도에서 지구와 가장 가깝다.

My father's words are ______ in my memory.
아버지께서 하신 말씀은 나의 기억에 각인되어 있다.

We have different ______ points of view.
우리는 정치적 견해가 다르다.

______ should support each other to achieve a happy marriage.
배우자들은 행복한 결혼을 이루기 위해 서로 격려해야 한다.

It isn't easy to study the genetic ______ of cells.
세포의 유전자 조직을 연구하는 것은 어렵다.

If you study more, you will find that those two subjects are ______.
더 공부하면 그 두 과목이 서로 연관되어 있다는 것을 발견할 것이다.

The hole in the wall ______ people's curiosity.
벽에 나 있는 구멍이 사람들의 호기심을 자극했다.

Air ______ sound.
공기는 소리를 전달한다.

I was amazed at her ability to ______ with the difficult situation.
나는 어려운 상황에 대처하는 그녀의 능력에 놀랐다.

There is a close ______ between sounds and letters in some languages.
몇몇 언어는 소리와 글자 간에 완벽한 일치를 보인다.

The report had many ______ that we had not seen before.
그 보고서는 우리가 전에 보지 못했던 많은 결점을 가지고 있었다.

The government is ______ for the loss of soldiers.
정부는 군인들의 사망에 대해 책임이 있다.

She ______ with rage at the insult.
그녀는 모욕에 분노하며 떨었다.

DAY 01

016	**temporary** [témpərèri]	형 일시적인, 임시의 a temporary employee 임시 직원	반 permanent 영구의
017	**assist** [əsíst]	동 돕다 assist a professor 교수를 돕다	명 assistance 조력 유 help
018	**customized** [kʌ́stəmàizd]	형 고객 맞춤화된 a customized program 고객 맞춤형 프로그램	명 customer 고객 동 customize 고객 맞춤화하다
019	**gadget** [gǽdʒit]	명 부품 a car gadget 자동차 부품	
020	**melancholic** [mélənkɑ̀lik]	형 우울한 a melancholic atmosphere 우울한 분위기	명 melancholy 우울 유 gloomy
021	**relief** [rilíːf]	명 안도, 경감 to one's relief 안도하여	동 relieve 안도하게 하다, 경감시키다
022	**transform** [trænsfɔ́ːrm]	동 변형시키다 transform energy into light 에너지를 빛으로 바꾸다	유 change
023	**blend** [blend]	동 섞다 blend red with white 빨간색에 흰색을 섞다	유 mix
024	**destructive** [distrʌ́ktiv]	형 파괴적인 a destructive hurricane 파괴적인 폭풍	동 destroy 파괴하다 반 constructive 건설적인
025	**guarantee** [gæ̀rəntíː]	동 보증하다 명 보증 guarantee one's success 성공을 보증하다	유 warranty
026	**narrate** [nǽreit]	동 이야기하다	명 narration 이야기하기, 서술
027	**revolver** [rivɑ́lvər]	명 연발 권총 be armed with a revolver 권총으로 무장하다	
028	**needy** [níːdi]	형 가난한 a needy family 가난한 가정	동 need 필요로 하다 유 poor
029	**urge** [əːrdʒ]	동 촉구하다, 재촉하다 urge someone to do something 누군가에게 무엇을 하길 재촉하다	
030	**vacant** [véikənt]	형 비어 있는 a vacant seat 공석	명 vacancy 빈자리 유 empty

✦ 주어진 우리말 문장에 맞도록 알맞은 단어를 넣어 문장을 완성하시오. 정답 p.193

She has gotten a ______ job.
그녀는 임시 직장을 얻었다.

These tablets ______ digestion.
이 알약들은 소화를 돕는다.

We developed the ______ programs to help everybody meet their goals.
우리는 모든 이가 자신의 목표를 달성할 수 있도록 도와주는 고객 맞춤형 프로그램을 개발했다.

To fix his car, he needs a new ______.
그의 차를 수리하려면 새로운 부품이 필요하다.

As I entered the room, I felt a ______ atmosphere.
방에 들어섰을 때 나는 우울한 분위기를 느꼈다.

______ was written all over her face.
안도감이 그녀의 얼굴 전체에 드러났다.

A steam engine ______ heat into power.
증기 기관은 열을 동력으로 바꾼다.

He ______ the butter and sugar together.
그는 버터와 설탕을 함께 섞었다.

It was one of the most ______ tsunamis in history.
그것은 역사상 가장 파괴적인 해일 중 하나였다.

Most parents believe that a good education will ______ their children's success.
대부분의 부모들은 훌륭한 교육이 자식의 성공을 보증하리라 믿는다.

The woman ______ the event calmly.
그 여자는 그 사건을 침착하게 이야기했다.

The robber was armed with a ______.
그 강도는 권총으로 무장했다.

They collected money to help ______ children.
그들은 가난한 아이들을 돕기 위해 모금했다.

I would ______ people not to send their kids abroad.
나는 사람들에게 자녀들을 외국에 보내지 말라고 촉구하고 싶다.

The ______ seat next to him was too small to sit in.
그의 옆에 비어 있는 자리는 너무 좁아서 앉을 수가 없다.

DAY 02

031 **ventilation** [vèntəléiʃən]
명 통풍
a ventilation device 통풍 장치

032 **vigorous** [vígərəs]
형 원기 왕성한
vigorous in body 신체적으로 건강한

033 **Celsius** [sélsiəs]
명 섭씨 형 섭씨의 　참 Fahrenheit 화씨
30 degrees Celsius 섭씨 30도

034 **elderly** [éldərli]
형 나이가 지긋한 　유 old 　참 the elderly 어르신들
respect for the elderly 연장자에 대한 존중

035 **emission** [imíʃən]
명 방출 　동 emit 방출하다 　유 discharge
emission control 배출가스 규제

036 **cluster** [klʌ́stər]
명 송이, 무리 　유 bunch
a cluster of bananas 바나나 한 송이

037 **simulate** [símjulèit]
동 흉내 내다, ~인 체하다 　명 simulation 흉내, 모의실험
simulate illness 꾀병을 부리다

038 **colony** [kάləni]
명 식민지 　동 colonize 식민지화하다
a colony settlement 식민지

039 **enthusiasm** [inθú:ziæ̀zm]
명 열광 　형 enthusiastic 열광적인

040 **initiate** [iníʃièit]
동 시작하다 　유 begin
initiate a reform 개혁을 일으키다

041 **plow** [plau]
명 쟁기 동 (밭을) 갈다
plow a rice field 논을 갈다

042 **spiral** [spáiərəl]
형 나선형의 　유 coiled
a spiral balance 나선형의 저울

043 **administer** [ædmínistər]
동 관리하다, 통치하다 　명 administration 관리 　유 manage
administer financial affairs 재무를 관리하다

044 **exhaustion** [igzɔ́:stʃən]
명 극도의 피로 　형 exhaustive 피로한 　유 fatigue
nervous exhaustion 신경 쇠약

045 **prescribe** [priskráib]
동 처방하다 　명 prescription 처방
prescribe medicine 약을 처방하다

✦ 주어진 우리말 문장에 맞도록 알맞은 단어를 넣어 문장을 완성하시오. 정답 p.193

We checked the ________ device.
우리는 그 통풍 장치를 점검했다.

A ________ person does things with great energy and enthusiasm.
원기왕성한 사람은 대단한 힘과 열정을 가지고 일을 한다.

The thermometer shows the temperature in ________.
온도계는 온도를 섭씨로 나타낸다.

Who will take care of the ________?
누가 어르신들을 돌볼 건가요?

The ________ of carbon dioxide should be strictly controlled by regulations.
이산화탄소의 방출은 법규에 의해 엄격하게 규제되어야 한다.

There was a little ________ of fans around the actress.
그 배우 주변에 적은 무리의 팬들이 몰려 있었다.

These insects can ________ dead leaves.
이 곤충들은 낙엽처럼 보일 수 있다.

The country was a ________ hundreds of years ago.
그 나라는 수백 년 전에 식민지였다.

Whatever you do, you should have some ________.
무엇을 하든지 열정적으로 해야 한다.

They wanted to ________ a discussion on the environment.
그들은 환경에 대한 토론을 시작하기를 원했다.

________ are still pulled by oxen in some countries.
어떤 나라에서는 여전히 소가 쟁기를 몬다.

There used to be a ________ staircase, but now it's gone.
저기에 나선형 계단이 있었는데 지금은 사라져버렸다.

The president ________ the affairs of the state.
대통령은 나랏일을 관리한다.

I am suffering from nervous ________ due to my problem.
나는 그 문제 때문에 신경 쇠약으로 고통받고 있다.

The kind doctor ________ some medicine for me.
그 친절한 의사는 나에게 약을 처방해 줬다.

DAY 02

046	**alternate** [ɔ́ːltərnèit]	동 교대시키다, 번갈아 하다 alternate A with B A와 B를 교대시키다	명 alternation 교대 유 replace
047	**fame** [feim]	명 명성 come to fame 유명해지다	형 famous 유명한 유 renown
048	**fatigue** [fətíːg]	명 피로 physical fatigue 육체의 피로	반 freshness 생생함, 상쾌함
049	**feminine** [fémənin]	형 여자의, 여자 같은 wear feminine clothes 여성스러운 옷을 입다	반 masculine 남성적인
050	**leakage** [líːkidʒ]	명 누출 a check for leakage 누출 점검	동 leak 새다
051	**qualification** [kwɑ̀ləfikéiʃən]	명 자격 a basic qualification 기본 자격	동 qualify 자격을 주다
052	**takeoff** [téikɔ̀(ː)f]	명 이륙, 출발 takeoff speed 이륙 속도	반 landing 착륙
053	**aspiration** [æ̀spəréiʃən]	명 열망, 포부 aspiration for fame 명예욕	동 aspire 열망하다 유 desire
054	**cruelty** [krú(ː)əlti]	명 잔혹 pl. 잔인한 행위 cruelty toward(s) animals 동물 학대	형 cruel 잔인한 유 brutality
055	**fundamental** [fʌ̀ndəméntl]	형 기본적인 fundamental colors 원색	명 fundamentalness 기본적인 것 유 central, key
056	**maximize** [mǽksəmàiz]	동 극대[최대]로 하다 maximize efficiency 효율성을 극대화하다	명 maximization 극대 반 minimize 최소화하다
057	**regulation** [règjuléiʃən]	명 규제 pl. 법규 traffic regulations 교통 법규	동 regulate 규제하다 유 law
058	**toxic** [tɑ́ksik]	형 독성의 toxic smoke 독가스	유 poisonous
059	**bilingual** [bailíŋgwəl]	형 2개 국어를 할 수 있는 a bilingual translator 2개 국어를 하는 번역가	
060	**descend** [disénd]	동 내려가다 descend from father to son 아버지로부터 아들에게 전해지다	명 descent 하강 반 ascend 오르다

✦ 주어진 우리말 문장에 맞도록 알맞은 단어를 넣어 문장을 완성하시오. 정답 p.193

Happiness and sadness ______ in our lives.
행복과 슬픔은 우리 인생에 번갈아 온다.

The film earned him international ______.
그 영화는 그에게 국제적인 명성을 안겨 주었다.

My grandfather was laid up with ______.
할아버지가 피로로 누워계셨다.

Her voice was gentle and ______.
그녀의 목소리는 부드럽고 여성스러웠다.

You should check the bottle for ______ before using it.
그것을 사용하기 전에 그 병이 새는지 점검해야 한다.

She has excellent ______.
그녀는 뛰어난 자격들을 갖추고 있다.

The plane zoomed down the runway for ______.
비행기는 이륙을 위해 활주로를 빠르게 달렸다.

His ______ to be a leader guided him into politics.
지도자가 되고자 하는 열망이 그를 정치계로 인도했다.

We'll never forget the ______ of the invaders.
우리는 침략자들의 잔인한 행위를 잊지 않을 것이다.

We shouldn't forget the ______ principle.
우리는 기본원칙을 잊어서는 안 된다.

______ efficiency can't be achieved without lots of effort.
효율성을 극대화하는 것은 많은 노력 없이는 달성될 수 없다.

We should obey the traffic ______.
우리는 교통 법규를 따라야 한다.

______ waste endangers living creatures.
유독성 폐기물은 살아 있는 생물을 위태롭게 한다.

He is ______ so he can speak Korean and English.
그는 한국어와 영어를 둘 다 말할 수 있다.

You can ride the escalator up but have to ______ on foot.
에스컬레이터를 타고 올라갈 수는 있지만 걸어서 내려와야 한다.

REVIEW TEST 01 DAY 01 ~ DAY 02

A 우리말과 같은 뜻이 되도록 빈칸에 들어갈 알맞은 단어를 적으시오.

1. ______________ speed (이륙 속도)
2. a basic ______________ (기본 자격)
3. ______________ a rice field (논을 갈다)
4. ______________ medicine (약을 처방하다)
5. ______________ subjects (서로 연관된 과목들)
6. a ______________ hurricane (파괴적인 폭풍)
7. ______________ one's success (성공을 보증하다)
8. a ______________ situation (책임져야 할 상황)
9. ______________ for the elderly (연장자에 대한 존중)
10. ______________ red with white (빨간색에 흰색을 섞다)

B 다음 괄호 안의 지시대로 주어진 단어를 변형시키고 그 뜻을 적으시오.

		변형	뜻
1	cruelty (형용사형으로) →	______________	______________
2	aspiration (동사형으로) →	______________	______________
3	emission (동사형으로) →	______________	______________
4	fame (형용사형으로) →	______________	______________
5	commerce (형용사형으로) →	______________	______________
6	customized (동사형으로) →	______________	______________
7	colony (동사형으로) →	______________	______________
8	political (명사형으로) →	______________	______________
9	leakage (동사형으로) →	______________	______________
10	correspondence (동사형으로) →	______________	______________

정답 p.193

C 다음 영영풀이에 해당하는 단어를 보기에서 골라 적으시오.

보기				
qualification	abandon	urge	fundamental	vigorous
exhaustion	elderly	assist	bilingual	quiver

❶ to give up; discontinue; desert → ______________

❷ serving as a foundation or basis; basic; underlying → ______________

❸ the state of being extremely tired → ______________

❹ to give support or aid to; help → ______________

❺ somewhat old; near old age → ______________

❻ to shake with a slight but rapid motion; vibrate tremulously → ______________

❼ a quality, accomplishment or skill that makes a person suitable for particular function, office, or role → ______________

❽ able to speak two languages with the facility of a native speaker → ______________

❾ to push or force along; impel with force or vigor → ______________

❿ full of or characterized by vigor; energetic; forceful → ______________

D 우리말과 같은 뜻이 되도록 주어진 문장의 빈칸을 완성하시오.

❶ 대통령은 나랏일을 관리한다.

→ The president ______________ the affairs of the state.

❷ 벽에 나 있는 구멍은 사람들의 호기심을 자극했다.

→ The hole in the wall ______________ people's curiosity.

❸ 세포의 유전자 조직을 연구하는 것은 어렵다.

→ It isn't easy to study the genetic ______________ of cells.

❹ 그의 차를 수리하려면 새로운 부품이 필요하다.

→ To fix his car, he needs a new ______________.

⑤ 우리는 통풍 장치를 점검했다.

→ We checked the ________________ device.

⑥ 태양은 적도에서 지구와 가장 가깝다.

→ On the ________________, the Sun gets closest to the Earth.

⑦ 그 친절한 의사는 나에게 약을 처방해 줬다.

→ The kind doctor ________________ some medicine for me.

⑧ 안도감이 그녀의 얼굴 전체에 드러났다.

→ ________________ was written all over her face.

⑨ 그 여자는 그 사건을 침착하게 이야기했다.

→ The woman ________________ the event calmly.

⑩ 무엇을 하든지 열정적으로 해야 한다.

→ Whatever you do, you should have some ________________.

E 다음 영영풀이에 해당하는 단어를 보기에서 골라 적으시오.

보기				
constructive	carry	ascend	help	gloomy
permanent	defect	begin	minimize	change

① You can ride the escalator up but have to descend on foot. 반의어 ↔ ________________

② It was one of the most destructive tsunamis in history. 반의어 ↔ ________________

③ These tablets assist digestion. 유의어 = ________________

④ Maximizing efficiency can't be achieved without lots of effort.
반의어 ↔ ________________

⑤ She has gotten a temporary job. 반의어 ↔ ________________

⑥ They wanted to initiate a discussion on the environment. 유의어 = ________________

⑦ Air conveys sound. 유의어 = ________________

⑧ A steam engine transforms heat into power. 유의어 = ________________

⑨ The report had many flaws that we had not seen before. 유의어 = ________________

⑩ As I entered the room, I felt a melancholic atmosphere. 유의어 = ________________

F 영어발음을 듣고 영어단어를 적은 후, 우리말 뜻을 적으시오.

영어단어
듣고 쓰기

	영어	우리말		영어	우리말
❶			❽		
❷			❾		
❸			❿		
❹			⓫		
❺			⓬		
❻			⓭		
❼			⓮		

G 영어문장을 듣고 빈칸에 들어갈 단어를 채워 문장을 완성하시오.

영어문장
듣고 쓰기

❶ My grandfather was laid up with ________________.

❷ There was a little ________________ of fans around the actress.

❸ The ________________ seat next to him was too small to sit in.

❹ We should obey the traffic ________________.

❺ I was amazed at her ability to ________________ with the difficult situation.

❻ ________________ waste endangers living creatures.

❼ Happiness and sadness ________________ in our lives.

❽ The thermometer shows the temperature in ________________.

❾ His ________________ to be a leader guided him into politics.

❿ The ________________ of carbon dioxide should be strictly controlled by regulations.

⓫ The Ministry of ________________ announced a new commercial policy.

⓬ We developed the ________________ programs to help everybody meet their goals.

⓭ We have different ________________ points of view.

⓮ There is a close ________________ between sounds and letters in some languages.

⓯ I ________________ my plan to study abroad this year.

⓰ We shouldn't forget the ________________ principle.

DAY 03

061 **gradual** [grǽdʒuəl]
형 점진적인 유 steady
a gradual improvement 점진적인 발전

062 **mourn** [mɔːrn]
동 애도하다, 슬퍼하다 형 mournful 슬퍼하는 유 grieve
mourn for ~을 슬퍼하다

063 **reunification** [rìːjuːnəfikéiʃən]
명 재통일 동 reunify 재통일시키다
the reunification of a country 나라의 통일

064 **union** [júːnjən]
명 결합, 조합
a labor union 노동조합

065 **roar** [rɔːr]
동 으르렁거리다, 고함치다 명 포효
the roar of a tiger 호랑이의 포효

066 **calculation** [kæ̀lkjəléiʃən]
명 계산 동 calculate 계산하다 유 computation
make a calculation 계산하다

067 **capitalism** [kǽpətəlìzm]
명 자본주의 반 communism 사회주의
financial capitalism 금융 자본주의

068 **carve** [kaːrv]
동 새기다, 조각하다 유 engrave
carve A for B A를 새겨서 B를 만들다

069 **caterpillar** [kǽtərpìlər]
명 애벌레

070 **efficiency** [ifíʃənsi]
명 효율성 형 efficient 효율적인 반 inefficiency 비효율성
energy efficiency 에너지 효율성

071 **impressed** [imprést]
형 감명 깊은 동 impress 감동시키다
be impressed by ~에 감동하다

072 **emphasis** [émfəsis]
명 강조 동 emphasize 강조하다 유 stress
put an emphasis on ~을 강조하다

073 **collaborate** [kəlǽbərèit]
동 협력하다, 공동으로 일하다 명 collaboration 협력 유 cooperate
collaborate with ~와 협력하다

074 **sin** [sin]
명 (종교·도덕상의) 죄 유 crime (법률상의) 죄
a social sin 사회적 관습에 대한 위반

075 **enlarge** [inláːrdʒ]
동 확대[증대]시키다 명 enlargement 증대 유 increase
enlarge a house 집을 증축하다

✦ 주어진 우리말 문장에 맞도록 알맞은 단어를 넣어 문장을 완성하시오. 정답 p.194

There has been a ______ increase in the number of customers.
고객 수가 점진적으로 증가해왔다.

He ______ his misfortune of losing all his money.
그는 모든 돈을 잃어버린 자신의 불행을 슬퍼했다.

The ______ of our country doesn't look easy.
우리나라의 통일은 쉽지 않아 보인다.

The labor ______ negotiated for the workers' wages.
노동조합은 근로자들의 임금 협상을 했다.

He ______ with anger.
그는 화가 나서 고함쳤다.

Did I make any errors in my ______?
제가 잘못 계산했나요?

What are the important characteristics of Korean-style ______?
한국식 자본주의의 중요한 특징은 무엇이죠?

The artist ______ the stone for the statue.
그 예술가는 돌을 새겨서 그 조각상을 만들었다.

______ change into butterflies.
애벌레는 나방으로 변신한다.

Since the price of oil has soared, it's necessary to consider energy ______.
석유값이 폭등했으므로 에너지 효율성을 고려할 필요가 있다.

We were ______ with their skill.
우리는 그들의 솜씨에 감탄했다.

Too much ______ on the fact caused him to exaggerate.
그 사실에 대한 너무 많은 강조가 그를 과장하게 했다.

The two nations agreed to ______.
두 나라는 협력하기로 동의했다.

The Vatican teaches that abortion is a ______.
로마 교황청은 낙태가 죄라고 가르친다.

Reading lots of storybooks will ______ your English vocabulary.
이야기책을 많이 읽으면 영어 어휘력이 증가할 것이다.

DAY 03

076	**ingenious** [indʒíːnjəs]	형 교묘한, 기발한 an ingenious excuse 교묘한 핑계	명 ingenuity 기발함 유 clever
077	**physicist** [fízəsist]	명 물리학자 a theoretical physicist 이론적 물리학자	명 physics 물리학
078	**span** [spæn]	명 한 뼘, 기간 a life span 수명	유 period 기간
079	**acupuncture** [ǽkjupʌ̀ŋktʃər]	명 침술 get acupuncture 침을 맞다	명 acupuncturist 침술사
080	**conscience** [kɑ́nʃəns]	명 양심 a man of conscience 양심 있는 사람	참 conscious 의식이 있는
081	**intention** [inténʃən]	명 의도 by intention 고의로	동 intend 의도하다 유 plan
082	**steep** [stiːp]	형 가파른 a steep valley 경사가 가파른 계곡	
083	**continual** [kəntínjuəl]	형 계속적인 a continual event 계속되는 이벤트	명 continuance 연속
084	**irreversible** [ìrivə́ːrsəbl]	형 되돌릴 수 없는, 취소할 수 없는 irreversible damage 되돌릴 수 없는 피해	반 reversible 취소할 수 있는
085	**ivory** [áivəri]	명 상아 an ivory tower 상아탑	
086	**landlord** [lǽndlɔ̀ːrd]	명 집주인 complain to the landlord 집주인에게 불평하다	반 tenant 세 들어 사는 사람
087	**psychological** [sàikəlɑ́dʒikəl]	형 심리적인, 심리학의 a psychological effect 심리적 효과	명 psychology 심리학
088	**swift** [swift]	형 빠른 a swift reaction 빠른 반응	부 swiftly 빠르게 반 slow 느린
089	**aroma** [əróumə]	명 향기 the aroma of soap 비누의 향기	유 fragrance
090	**crisis** [kráisis]	명 위기 come to a crisis 위기에 직면하다	복 crises

1회독 월 일
2회독 월 일

✦ 주어진 우리말 문장에 맞도록 알맞은 단어를 넣어 문장을 완성하시오. 정답 p.194

Don't give me any ______ excuses.
나에게 어떤 교묘한 핑계도 대지 마라.

Einstein was one of the world's most famous ______.
아인슈타인은 세계에서 가장 유명한 물리학자 중 한 사람이었다.

I worked with him over a ______ of six years.
나는 그와 6년이란 기간 동안 함께 일했다.

______ originated in China more than 2000 years ago.
침술은 2000년 이상 전에 중국에서 유래되었다.

He is tormented by a guilty ______.
그는 양심의 가책으로 괴로워 한다.

It wasn't my ______ to hit my brother.
난 내 남동생을 때릴 의도는 없었다.

The bird lived in a ______ valley.
그 새는 경사가 가파른 계곡에서 살았다.

Her ______ complaints annoyed me.
그녀의 계속적인 불평은 나를 짜증나게 했다.

Water pollution causes ______ damage to the sea.
수질오염은 바다에 되돌릴 수 없는 피해를 야기한다.

He is collecting articles made of ______.
그는 상아로 만든 제품들을 수집하고 있다.

Not many ______ let their tenants keep dogs in their houses.
많지 않은 집주인들만이 집에서 개를 키우는 것을 세입자들에게 허용한다.

She is suffering from ______ problems these days.
그녀는 요즈음 심리적인 문제로 고통스러워 하고 있다.

Cats have ______ reactions.
고양이는 반응이 빠르다.

The ______ of the soap smells like coffee.
비누에서 커피향이 난다.

If nothing is done, there will be an economic ______.
아무런 조치가 취해지지 않으면 경제위기가 올 것이다.

DAY 04

091 **frustration** [frʌstréiʃən]
명 좌절, 실패 | 동 frustrate 좌절시키다
lead to frustration 좌절을 초래하다

092 **maneuver** [mənúːvər]
명 조작, 책략 pl. 군사 훈련 | 명 maneuverer 책략가
sudden maneuvers 갑작스러운 군사 훈련

093 **refine** [rifáin]
동 정제하다, 불순물을 없애다 | 명 refinement 정제
refine petroleum 석유를 정제하다

094 **tighten** [táitn]
동 팽팽하게 치다 | 형 tight 팽팽한
tighten a rope 밧줄을 팽팽하게 치다

095 **barely** [bɛ́ərli]
부 간신히
barely finish one's work 간신히 일을 끝내다

096 **departure** [dipáːrtʃər]
명 출발 | 동 depart 출발하다 반 arrival 도착
take one's departure 출발하다

097 **glimmering** [glímәriŋ]
명 희미한 빛, 기색 | 동 glimmer 희미하게 빛나다
the glimmerings of twilight 황혼의 희미한 빛

098 **mortal** [mɔ́ːrtl]
형 치명적인, 죽을 운명의 | 유 fatal

099 **restless** [réstlis]
형 잠 못 이루는, 불안한 | 명 restlessness 휴식 없음 유 uneasy
a restless child 침착하지 못한 아이

100 **unearth** [ʌnə́ːrθ]
동 발굴하다 | 유 discover
unearth fossils 화석을 발굴하다

101 **brutal** [brúːtl]
형 잔인한 | 명 brutality 잔인함 유 cruel
a brutal action 잔인한 행동

102 **unload** [ʌnlóud]
동 짐을 내리다 | 유 unburden
unload cargo from a ship 배의 짐을 내리다

103 **distasteful** [distéistfəl]
형 불쾌한 | 유 unpleasant
distasteful food 맛없는 음식

104 **disturbance** [distə́ːrbəns]
명 방해, 소동 | 동 disturb 방해하다 유 interfere
cause a disturbance 소동을 일으키다

105 **donation** [dounéiʃən]
명 기부 | 동 donate 기부하다 유 endowment
make a donation of ~을 기부하다

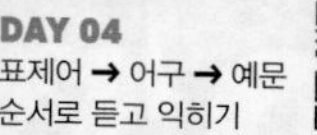

✦ 주어진 우리말 문장에 맞도록 알맞은 단어를 넣어 문장을 완성하시오. 정답 p.194

I asked out of anger and ______.
나는 분노와 좌절감에 질문했다.

You have to practice for sudden ______.
갑작스러운 군사 훈련을 위해 연습해야 한다.

It's fun for children to watch the process of ______ sugar.
아이들이 설탕을 정제하는 과정을 보는 것은 재미있다.

Before you pull the rope, you must ______ it.
밧줄을 당기기 전에 밧줄을 팽팽하게 쳐야 한다.

She ______ finished her work today.
그녀는 오늘 간신히 일을 끝냈다.

When is the ______ time from Busan?
부산에서의 출발시간이 언제입니까?

We began to see the ______ of a solution to the problem.
우리는 문제 해결의 실마리를 발견하기 시작했다.

He heard the news that the man is suffering from a ______ disease.
그는 그 남자가 죽을 병에 고통스러워한다는 소식을 들었다.

My father will have a ______ night because of his work.
아빠는 일 때문에 잠을 못 이루실 것이다.

The scientists ______ the area to find fossils.
과학자들이 화석을 찾기 위해 그 구역을 발굴했다.

The ______ actions of the terrorists shocked the entire nation.
테러리스트들의 잔인한 행동이 나라 전체에 충격을 주었다.

They are ______ the ship.
그들은 배에서 짐을 내리고 있다.

His behavior was ______ to everyone.
그의 행동 때문에 모든 사람들이 불쾌했다.

There shouldn't be any ______. He should get some rest.
어떤 방해도 있어서는 안 돼요. 그는 휴식을 취해야 해요.

Our church made a large ______ to the charity.
우리 교회는 자선단체에 많은 기부를 했다.

DAY 04

106	**drill** [dril]	동 구멍을 뚫다 drill a hole in a wall 벽에 구멍을 뚫다	
107	**impair** [impέər]	동 손상시키다, 약화시키다 impair one's health 건강을 해치다	유 hurt
108	**outlook** [áutlùk]	명 전망, 시야 a man with a broad outlook 시야가 넓은 사람	
109	**inaugural** [inɔ́:gjurəl]	형 취임의 명 취임식 an inaugural address 취임 연설	
110	**collaborative** [kəlǽbərèitiv]	형 협조적인 a collaborative attitude 협조적인 태도	명 collaboration 협조 유 supportive
111	**sincerity** [sinsérəti]	명 성실, 진실성	형 sincere 성실한, 진실한
112	**inflate** [infléit]	동 팽창시키다 inflate a balloon 풍선을 불다	명 inflation 팽창 유 expand
113	**perform** [pərfɔ́:rm]	동 이행하다, 공연하다	명 performance 수행, 공연
114	**snuggle** [snʌ́gl]	동 바싹 당기다, 끌어안다 snuggle up 꼭 끌어안다	유 cuddle
115	**accurately** [ǽkjurətli]	부 정확하게 quickly and accurately 신속 정확하게	명 accuracy 정확(도) 반 inaccurately 부정확하게
116	**concerning** [kənsə́:rniŋ]	전 ~에 관하여 concerning the past 과거에 관하여	동 concern 관계하다 유 regarding
117	**exceptional** [iksépʃənl]	형 예외적인, 특별한 an exceptional case 예외적인 경우	명 exception 예외
118	**precise** [prisáis]	형 정확한, 정밀한 a precise statement 정확한 설명	명 precision 정확, 정밀 유 correct
119	**affirmative** [əfə́:rmətiv]	형 긍정적인 명 긍정 an affirmative answer 긍정적인 답	반 negative 부정적인
120	**fade** [feid]	동 사라지다 fade away 사라지다	유 vanish

✦ 주어진 우리말 문장에 맞도록 알맞은 단어를 넣어 문장을 완성하시오. 정답 p.194

Do not ______ a hole in the wall until I say so.
내가 그렇게 하라고 할 때까지는 벽에 구멍을 뚫지 마라.

Alcohol can ______ your driving ability.
알코올은 당신의 운전 능력을 약화시킬 수 있다.

The room has a pleasant ______.
그 방은 전망이 좋다.

Everyone was moved by the president's ______ address.
모든 사람들은 대통령의 취임 연설에 감동 받았다.

A ______ attitude will lead you to success.
협조적인 태도가 당신을 성공으로 이끌 것이다.

My father expressed deep gratitude for his ______.
우리 아버지는 그의 성실함에 깊은 감사를 표했다.

You need to ______ your life jacket to survive.
살아남으려면 구명조끼를 부풀려야 한다.

The doctor ______ surgery for 2 hours.
그 의사는 두 시간 동안 수술을 했다.

She ______ up with her baby.
그녀는 아기를 꼭 끌어안았다.

The new navigation system will ______ guide you.
새로운 운항 시스템이 정확하게 여러분을 안내할 것입니다.

We read stories ______ visitors from outer space.
우리는 외계에서 온 방문자들에 대한 이야기를 읽었다.

His promotion was considered to be ______ in the company.
회사에서 그의 승진은 예외적인 것으로 간주되었다.

We like our teacher because he gives us ______ explanations all the time.
선생님께서는 항상 정확한 설명을 해 주셔서 우리는 그를 좋아한다.

He always gives me an ______ response.
그는 항상 나에게 긍정적인 답변을 해 준다.

The unidentified object ______ away into the fog.
그 미확인 물체는 안개 속으로 사라졌다.

REVIEW TEST 02 DAY 03 ~ DAY 04

A 우리말과 같은 뜻이 되도록 빈칸에 들어갈 알맞은 단어를 적으시오.

1. by ________________ (고의로)
2. a life ________________ (수명)
3. make a ________________ (계산하다)
4. take one's ________________ (출발하다)
5. energy ________________ (에너지 효율성)
6. make a ________________ of (~을 기부하다)
7. put an ________________ on (~을 강조하다)
8. a ________________ effect (심리적인 효과)
9. ________________ A for B (A를 새겨서 B를 만들다)
10. complain to the ________________ (집주인에게 불평하다)

B 다음 괄호 안의 지시대로 주어진 단어를 변형시키고 그 뜻을 적으시오.

		변형	뜻
1. mourn (형용사형으로)	→	________	________
2. reunification (동사형으로)	→	________	________
3. efficiency (형용사형으로)	→	________	________
4. enlarge (명사형으로)	→	________	________
5. ingenious (명사형으로)	→	________	________
6. intention (동사형으로)	→	________	________
7. continual (명사형으로)	→	________	________
8. brutal (명사형으로)	→	________	________
9. disturbance (동사형으로)	→	________	________
10. precise (명사형으로)	→	________	________

정답 p.194

C 다음 영영풀이에 해당하는 단어를 보기에서 골라 적으시오.

보기				
exceptional	unload	crisis	physicist	drill
outlook	steep	refine	distasteful	carve

1. to form from a solid material by cutting → ______________
2. a scientist who specializes in physics → ______________
3. having an almost vertical slope or pitch, or a relatively high gradient as a hill, an ascent, stairs, etc. → ______________
4. a condition of instability or danger, as in social, economic, political, or international affairs, leading to a decisive change → ______________
5. to bring to a fine or pure state → ______________
6. to take the load from; remove the cargo or freight from → ______________
7. unpleasant, offensive, or causing dislike → ______________
8. the view or prospect from a particular place → ______________
9. unusually excellent; superior → ______________
10. to pierce or bore a hole in something → ______________

D 우리말과 같은 뜻이 되도록 주어진 문장의 빈칸을 완성하시오.

1. 로마 교황청은 낙태가 죄라고 가르친다.
   → The Vatican teaches that abortion is a ______________.
2. 그는 상아로 만든 제품들을 수집하고 있다.
   → He is collecting articles made of ______________.
3. 고양이는 반응이 빠르다.
   → Cats have ______________ reactions.
4. 비누에서 커피향이 난다.
   → The ______________ of the soap smells like coffee.

5. 나는 분노와 좌절감에 질문했다.
   → I asked out of anger and ________________.

6. 그녀는 오늘 간신히 일을 끝냈다.
   → She ________________ finished her work today.

7. 알코올은 당신의 운전 능력을 약화시킬 수 있다.
   → Alcohol can ________________ your driving ability.

8. 협조적인 태도가 당신을 성공으로 이끌 것이다.
   → A ________________ attitude will lead you to success.

9. 살아남으려면 구명조끼를 부풀려야 한다.
   → You need to ________________ your life jacket to survive.

10. 그 의사는 두 시간 동안 수술을 했다.
   → The doctor ________________ surgery for 2 hours.

E 다음 영영풀이에 해당하는 단어를 보기에서 골라 적으시오.

보기				
cooperate	regarding	uneasy	reversible	vanish
inaccurately	negative	arrival	endowment	fatal

1. The two nations agreed to collaborate. 유의어 = ________________
2. Water pollution causes irreversible damage to the sea. 반의어 ↔ ________________
3. When is the departure time from Busan? 반의어 ↔ ________________
4. He heard the news that the man is suffering from a mortal disease.
   유의어 = ________________
5. My father will have a restless night because of his work. 유의어 = ________________
6. Our church made a large donation to the charity. 유의어 = ________________
7. The new navigation system will accurately guide you. 반의어 ↔ ________________
8. We read stories concerning visitors from outer space. 유의어 = ________________
9. He always gives me an affirmative response. 반의어 ↔ ________________
10. The unidentified object faded away into the fog. 유의어 = ________________

F 영어발음을 듣고 영어단어를 적은 후, 우리말 뜻을 적으시오.

영어단어 듣고 쓰기 

	영어	우리말		영어	우리말
1	______	______	8	______	______
2	______	______	9	______	______
3	______	______	10	______	______
4	______	______	11	______	______
5	______	______	12	______	______
6	______	______	13	______	______
7	______	______	14	______	______

G 영어문장을 듣고 빈칸에 들어갈 단어를 채워 문장을 완성하시오.

영어문장 듣고 쓰기

1. There has been a ______ increase in the number of customers.
2. The labor ______ negotiated for the workers' wages.
3. Did I make any errors in my ______?
4. What are the important characteristics of Korean-style ______?
5. I worked with him over a ______ of six years.
6. He is tormented by a guilty ______.
7. You have to practice for sudden ______.
8. He ______ his misfortune of losing all his money.
9. Since the price of oil has soared, it's necessary to consider energy ______.
10. Reading lots of storybooks will ______ your English vocabulary.
11. It wasn't my ______ to hit my brother.
12. The long, ______ event can reduce the influence on people.
13. There shouldn't be any ______. He should get some rest.
14. We like our teacher because he gives us ______ explanations all the time.
15. The doctor ______ surgery for 2 hours.
16. The artist ______ the stone for the statue.

121 **privacy** [práivəsi]
명 사생활, 개인적 자유 형 private 사적인 반 publicity 널리 알려짐
in privacy 몰래, 비밀리에

122 **profitable** [prɑ́fitəbl]
형 유익한, 이익이 되는 명 profit 이익 유 beneficial
a profitable deal 이익이 되는 거래

123 **promotion** [prəmóuʃən]
명 승진 동 promote 승진시키다
give a promotion to ~를 승진시키다

124 **superficial** [sù:pərfíʃəl]
형 피상적인, 얕은 부 superficially 피상적으로 반 profound 심오한
a superficial education 피상적인 교육

125 **archaeologist** [ɑ̀:rkiɑ́lədʒist]
명 고고학자
a well-known archaeologist 유명한 고고학자

126 **craze** [kreiz]
동 미치게 하다 명 열광 형 crazy 미친
be crazed about ~에 대해 미치다

127 **friendliness** [fréndlinis]
명 친절, 우정 유 amiability
with friendliness 호의적으로

128 **magnificent** [mægnífəsnt]
형 웅장한, 훌륭한 명 magnificence 웅장함 유 splendid
a magnificent sight 장관

129 **recovery** [rikʌ́vəri]
명 회복 동 recover 회복하다 유 healing
a full recovery 완전한 회복

130 **throb** [θrɑb]
동 맥박이 뛰다 명 맥박, 고동 유 beat
throb heavily 맥박이 몹시 뛰다

131 **awakening** [əwéikəniŋ]
형 깨닫게 하는 명 각성 동 awaken 깨닫게 하다
a vague awakening 희미한 각성

132 **degradable** [digréidəbl]
형 분해할 수 있는
a degradable element 분해할 수 있는 요소

133 **gladiator** [glǽdièitər]
명 검투사, 논객
a Roman gladiator 로마 검투사

134 **modest** [mɑ́dist]
형 겸손한, 적당한 명 modesty 겸손 유 moderate
in a modest way 겸손하게

135 **residence** [rézədəns]
명 주거 동 reside 살다, 거주하다 유 house
a temporary residence 임시 처소

✦ 주어진 우리말 문장에 맞도록 알맞은 단어를 넣어 문장을 완성하시오. 정답 p.195

The press always invades the ________ of celebrities.
신문은 언제나 유명인사의 사생활을 침해한다.

The farm is a highly ________ business.
농장은 매우 이익이 남는 사업이다.

I see a great chance of getting a ________ this time.
나는 이번에 승진할 가능성이 높다고 본다.

He criticized the book because of his ________ view.
그는 얕은 소견으로 그 책을 비판했다.

The ________ discovered several ancient tombs.
그 고고학자는 몇 개의 고대 무덤을 발견했다.

My daughter is ________ about the band.
내 딸은 그 밴드에 열광한다.

He took advantage of her ________.
그는 그녀의 친절을 이용했다.

We visited a ________ palace in the city.
우리는 도시의 웅장한 궁전을 방문했다.

A full ________ will take some time.
완전한 회복은 어느 정도의 시간이 걸릴 거에요.

Nervousness made my heart ________ heavily.
초조함으로 심장이 몹시 뛰었다.

The ________ of his interest in music made him happy.
음악에 대한 관심을 깨닫게 되어 그는 기뻤다.

Are there any ________ elements?
분해할 수 있는 요소들이 있습니까?

The Roman ________ were forced to fight to survive.
로마의 검투사들은 살기 위해 싸우도록 강요 당했다.

Despite her success, she remained ________.
그녀는 성공에도 불구하고 여전히 겸손했다.

That building over there is an official ________.
저기 있는 저 건물이 관저입니다.

DAY 05

136	**unbeaten** [ʌnbíːtn]	형 진 적이 없는, 무적의 반 beaten 패배한 an unbeaten record 무패 기록
137	**breeze** [briːz]	명 산들바람 동 산들바람이 불다 형 breezy 산들바람의 유 wind a strong breeze 강풍
138	**discrimination** [diskrìmənéiʃən]	명 차별 동 discriminate 차별하다 without discrimination 평등하게
139	**burp** [bəːrp]	동 트림하다 명 트림 유 belch a loud burp 소리가 큰 트림
140	**hospitality** [hɑ̀spətǽləti]	명 환대 형 hospitable 환대하는 유 welcome give warm hospitality 극진히 대접하다
141	**humid** [hjúːmid]	형 습한 명 humidness 습기, humidity 습도 hot and humid 덥고 습한
142	**identification** [aidèntəfikéiʃən]	명 (신원) 확인 동 identify 확인하다 유 recognition an identification card 주민등록증
143	**illusion** [ilúːʒən]	명 착각 형 illusory 착각의 유 fantasy
144	**organism** [ɔ́ːrgənìzm]	명 유기체 a living organism 살아 있는 유기체
145	**shabby** [ʃǽbi]	형 초라한, 누추한 look shabby 꼴이 초라하다
146	**incline** [inkláin]	동 마음을 내키게 하다 incline a person's mind to do ~하도록 남의 마음을 기울게 하다
147	**enchant** [intʃǽnt]	동 매혹하다 명 enchantment 매혹 유 attract be enchanted by ~에 매혹되다
148	**willingness** [wíliŋnis]	명 기꺼이 하는 마음 형 willing 기꺼이 하는 반 reluctance 마지못해 함 a willingness to do ~을 기꺼이 하려고 하는 마음
149	**peculiarity** [pikjùːliǽrəti]	명 특이한 성질, 특징 형 peculiar 특이한 유 feature a physical peculiarity 신체적 특징
150	**slope** [sloup]	명 비탈

✦ 주어진 우리말 문장에 맞도록 알맞은 단어를 넣어 문장을 완성하시오. 정답 p.195

The team has an __________ record in its last five games.
그 팀은 지난 다섯 번의 시합에서 무패 기록을 가지고 있다.

The strong __________ died down after several hours.
강풍은 몇 시간 후 차차 멎었다.

We must eliminate racial __________.
우리는 인종 차별을 없애야 한다.

He __________ after eating a large dinner.
그는 푸짐한 저녁을 먹은 후 트림을 했다.

Many thanks for the __________ you showed me.
당신이 보여 준 환대에 너무나 감사 드립니다.

The weather in summer is very hot and __________.
여름의 날씨는 매우 덥고 습하다.

The __________ of the dead body was a long and hard task.
사체의 신원 확인은 길고 힘든 작업이었다.

We have an __________ that we can fully control nature.
우리는 우리가 자연을 완전히 통제할 수 있다고 착각한다.

All __________ are able to reproduce.
모든 유기체는 생식이 가능하다.

An old man in __________ clothes came to the door.
초라한 옷을 입은 노인이 문으로 왔다.

Lack of money __________ many people towards crime.
자금 부족은 많은 사람으로 하여금 범죄를 마음먹게 한다.

The singer __________ many people with her beautiful voice.
그 가수는 아름다운 목소리로 많은 사람들을 매료시켰다.

His __________ to do his best led to his success.
기꺼이 최선을 다하려고 하는 마음이 그의 성공을 이끌었다.

He wants to know about many Korean cultural __________.
그는 한국의 다양한 문화적 특징들을 알고 싶어한다.

The longer the __________, the farther the ski jumpers can jump.
비탈이 길수록 스키점프가들이 더 멀리 점프할 수 있다.

DAY 06

151 **academic** [ækədémik]
형 학구적인 명 academy 학원 유 scholastic
an academic attitude 학구적인 태도

152 **composition** [kàmpəzíʃən]
명 구성, 작문
the composition of the atom 원자의 구조

153 **evoke** [ivóuk]
동 일깨우다 유 arouse
evoke sympathy 동정심을 자아내다

154 **integrity** [intégrəti]
명 고결, 청렴
a man of high integrity 청렴결백한 사람

155 **stale** [steil]
형 진부한 동 진부하게 하다 부 stalely 진부하게 유 outdated
a stale talk 진부한 이야기

156 **contemporary** [kəntémpərèri]
형 동시대의 명 같은 시대의 사람
be a contemporary of ~와 동시대 사람이다

157 **investigate** [invéstəgèit]
동 조사하다 명 investigation 조사 유 research
investigate a case 사건을 조사하다

158 **strain** [strein]
동 무리하게 사용하다 유 exert
strain oneself 무리하다

159 **subconscious** [sʌ̀bkánʃəs]
형 잠재의식의 명 잠재의식
the realm of the subconscious 잠재의식의 영역

160 **sufficient** [səfíʃənt]
형 충분한 반 insufficient 불충분한

161 **apprehend** [æprihénd]
동 체포하다 유 arrest
be apprehended 체포되다

162 **courteous** [kə́:rtiəs]
형 예의 바른, 공손한 명 courtesy 예의 바름 유 polite
a courteous young man 예의 바른 젊은이

163 **frank** [fræŋk]
형 솔직한 유 straightforward
to be frank with you 솔직하게 말하자면

164 **lottery** [látəri]
명 복권, 추첨
a lottery ticket 복권

165 **reap** [ri:p]
동 수확하다
reap what one has sown 뿌린 대로 거둔다

✦ 주어진 우리말 문장에 맞도록 알맞은 단어를 넣어 문장을 완성하시오. 정답 p.195

She has an ______ attitude.
그녀는 학구적인 태도를 가지고 있다.

Forests vary in ______ from one part of the country to another.
그 나라의 삼림은 곳곳마다 다양하게 구성되어 있다.

That old movie ______ memories of my childhood.
그 오래된 영화는 나의 유년시절의 기억을 일깨웠다.

The position requires honesty and ______.
그 자리는 정직함과 청렴함을 필요로 한다.

His ______ jokes don't make people laugh any more.
그의 진부한 농담은 더 이상 사람들을 웃기지 못한다.

The poet was a ______ of Beethoven.
그 시인은 베토벤과 같은 시대의 사람이었다.

The detective ______ the suspect.
형사는 그 용의자를 조사했다.

He is suffering from a ______ back muscle.
그는 무리하게 사용된 등의 근육 때문에 고통 받고 있다.

Her answer seemed to come from the ______.
그녀의 대답은 잠재의식에서 나온 것처럼 보였다.

Do you think that's ______ to feed all the people here?
그것으로 여기 사람들을 다 먹이는 게 충분하다고 생각하니?

The police ______ two people for starting the fire.
경찰은 방화 혐의로 두 명을 체포했다.

You should be ______ to her guests at the party.
너는 파티에서 그녀의 손님들에게 공손해야 한다.

To be ______ with you, I hardly ever study math.
솔직하게 말하자면 나는 수학을 거의 공부하지 않는다.

She bought a ______ ticket and won 3 billion won.
그녀는 복권을 사서 30억원에 당첨되었다.

The farmers were busy ______ the rice in the field.
농부들이 들판에서 쌀을 수확하느라 바빴다.

DAY 06

166 **thrash** [θræʃ]
동 때리다, 완패시키다
thrash an opponent 상대를 완패시키다

167 **attorney** [ətə́:rni]
명 변호사, 검사 유 lawyer, prosecutor
a district attorney 지방 검사

168 **defense** [diféns]
명 방어 동 defend 방어하다 반 offense 공격
a legal defense 정당방위

169 **geological** [dʒìːəlɑ́dʒikəl]
형 지질학의 명 geology 지질학
a geological way 지질학적인 방법

170 **mislead** [mislí:d]
동 잘못 인도하다 형 misleading 오해하기 쉬운
mislead A into B A를 B로 잘못 인도하다 *mislead-misled-misled*

171 **reproduce** [rì:prədjú:s]
동 재생하다, 복제하다 형 reproductive 생식의, 복제하는
reproduce a severed branch 잘려나간 가지를 재생하다

172 **tug** [tʌg]
동 당기다, 유인하다
tug a car out of the mire 진흙탕에서 차를 끌어당기다

173 **brainstorm** [bréinstɔ̀:rm]
동 브레인스토밍하다 참 outline 아웃라인을 잡다
brainstorm an idea 아이디어를 떠올리다

174 **dimple** [dímpl]
명 보조개 동 보조개를 짓다
a cute dimple 귀여운 보조개

175 **hearty** [hɑ́:rti]
형 마음에서 우러난 명 heart 마음
give a hearty welcome to ~을 진심으로 환영하다

176 **disrespectful** [dìsrispéktfəl]
형 무례한, 실례되는 반 respectful 예의 바른, 정중한
disrespectful manners 실례

177 **notable** [nóutəbl]
형 주목할 만한, 뛰어난 부 notably 현저하게 유 remarkable
a notable achievement 뛰어난 업적

178 **nutrient** [njú:triənt]
명 양분, 영양소 형 nutritious 영양소가 풍부한
rich in nutrients 영양소가 풍부한

179 **odor** [óudər]
명 냄새, 악취 형 odorous 냄새의
rank odors 악취

180 **onlooker** [ɑ́nlùkər]
명 방관자 유 bystander

1회독	월	일
2회독	월	일

✦ 주어진 우리말 문장에 맞도록 알맞은 단어를 넣어 문장을 완성하시오. 정답 p.195

He totally ______ the former champion.
그는 기존 챔피언을 완전하게 패배시켰다.

Our ______ will be making a presentation about the report.
우리 변호사가 그 보고서에 대해 발표할 것이다.

The immune system is our main ______ against disease.
면역체계는 질병에 대한 우리의 주요 방어책이다.

Think about the problem in a ______ way.
지질학적인 방법으로 그 문제에 대해 생각해봐라.

Some bad companions ______ him.
나쁜 친구들이 그를 잘못 꾀어냈다.

The cell is able to ______ itself.
그 세포는 자가복제가 가능하다.

If he helps us, maybe we can ______ the car out of here.
그가 도와준다면 아마도 우리는 여기서 차를 끌어낼 수 있을 거야.

______ your ideas before you write your essay.
글을 쓰기 전에 먼저 아이디어를 떠올려라.

The ______ on her face appears when she smiles.
그녀는 웃을 때 얼굴에 보조개가 보인다.

I give a ______ welcome to you.
나는 진심으로 너를 환영한다.

The mother apologized for her son's ______ behavior.
어머니는 아들의 무례한 행동에 대하여 사과했다.

There is a ______ difference between his earlier and later writings.
그의 초기와 후기 작품 사이에는 현저한 차이가 있다.

This bar contains all the ______ you need for a day.
이 바는 당신이 하루 동안 필요로 하는 모든 영양소를 포함하고 있다.

We can't breathe in this room because of the rank ______.
우리는 악취 때문에 이 방에서 숨을 쉴 수가 없다.

Don't just stand there like an ______.
방관자처럼 그곳에 그냥 서 있지 마라.

REVIEW TEST 03 DAY 05 ~ DAY 06

A 우리말과 같은 뜻이 되도록 빈칸에 들어갈 알맞은 단어를 적으시오.

1. a ________________ ticket (복권)
2. a legal ________________ (정당방위)
3. hot and ________________ (덥고 습한)
4. an ________________ card (주민등록증)
5. be ________________ by (~에 매혹되다)
6. in a ________________ way (겸손하게)
7. to be ________________ with you (솔직하게 말하자면)
8. a ________________ to do (~을 기꺼이 하려고 하는 마음)
9. ________________ A into B (A를 B로 잘못 인도하다)
10. ________________ what one has sown (뿌린 대로 거두다)

B 다음 괄호 안의 지시대로 주어진 단어를 변형시키고 그 뜻을 적으시오.

		변형	뜻
1	enchant (명사형으로)	→ ________________	________________
2	identification (동사형으로)	→ ________________	________________
3	investigate (명사형으로)	→ ________________	________________
4	hospitality (형용사형으로)	→ ________________	________________
5	breeze (형용사형으로)	→ ________________	________________
6	promotion (동사형으로)	→ ________________	________________
7	discrimination (동사형으로)	→ ________________	________________
8	mislead (형용사형으로)	→ ________________	________________
9	hearty (명사형으로)	→ ________________	________________
10	illusion (형용사형으로)	→ ________________	________________

정답 p.195

C 다음 영영풀이에 해당하는 단어를 보기에서 골라 적으시오.

보기				
courteous	craze	modest	awakening	apprehend
composition	evoke	contemporary	shabby	attorney

1. to take into custody; capture or arrest → ____________
2. having or showing a moderate or humble estimate of one's merits, importance, etc.
   → ____________
3. having or showing good manners; polite → ____________
4. a lawyer, especially one who represents someone in court → ____________
5. to derange or impair the mind of; make insane → ____________
6. rousing; quickening → ____________
7. impaired by wear, use, etc.; worn → ____________
8. the act of combining parts or elements to form a whole → ____________
9. existing, occurring, or living at the same time; of about the same age or date
   → ____________
10. to call up or produce memories, feelings, etc. → ____________

D 우리말과 같은 뜻이 되도록 주어진 문장의 빈칸을 완성하시오.

1. 저기 있는 저 건물이 관저입니다.
   → That building over there is an official ____________.
2. 그녀는 학구적인 태도를 가지고 있다.
   → She has an ____________ attitude.
3. 글을 쓰기 전에 먼저 아이디어를 떠올려라.
   → ____________ your ideas before you write your essay.
4. 그 자리는 정직함과 청렴함을 필요로 한다.
   → The position requires honesty and ____________.

⑤ 그녀의 대답은 잠재의식에서 나온 것처럼 보였다.

➜ Her answer seemed to come from the ______________.

⑥ 그는 기존 챔피언을 완전하게 패배시켰다.

➜ He totally ______________ the former champion.

⑦ 그 세포는 자가복제가 가능하다.

➜ The cell is able to ______________ itself.

⑧ 그녀는 웃을 때 얼굴에 보조개가 보인다.

➜ The ______________ on her face appears when she smiles.

⑨ 그의 초기와 후기 작품 사이에는 현저한 차이가 있다.

➜ There is a ______________ difference between his earlier and later writings.

⑩ 모든 유기체는 생식이 가능하다.

➜ All ______________ are able to reproduce.

E 문장의 밑줄 친 부분에 해당하는 유의어 혹은 반의어를 보기에서 골라 적으시오.

보기				
publicity	beneficial	insufficient	healing	bystander
feature	reluctance	respectful	offense	profound

① The mother apologized for her son's disrespectful behavior. 반의어 ↔ ______________

② He criticized the book because of his superficial view. 반의어 ↔ ______________

③ Do you think that's sufficient to feed all the people here? 반의어 ↔ ______________

④ The immune system is our main defense against disease. 반의어 ↔ ______________

⑤ The press always invades the privacy of celebrities. 반의어 ↔ ______________

⑥ The farm is a highly profitable business. 유의어 = ______________

⑦ Don't just stand there like an onlooker. 유의어 = ______________

⑧ He wants to know about many Korean cultural peculiarities. 유의어 = ______________

⑨ A full recovery will take some time. 유의어 = ______________

⑩ His willingness to do his best led to his success. 반의어 ↔ ______________

F 영어발음을 듣고 영어단어를 적은 후, 우리말 뜻을 적으시오.

	영어	우리말		영어	우리말
❶			❽		
❷			❾		
❸			❿		
❹			⓫		
❺			⓬		
❻			⓭		
❼			⓮		

G 영어문장을 듣고 빈칸에 들어갈 단어를 채워 문장을 완성하시오.

영어문장
듣고 쓰기

❶ His __________ jokes don't make people laugh any more.

❷ We visited a __________ palace in the city.

❸ To be __________ with you, I hardly ever study math.

❹ This bar contains all the __________ you need for a day.

❺ We can't breathe in this room because of the rank __________.

❻ The singer __________ many people with her beautiful voice.

❼ The detective __________ the suspect.

❽ Many thanks for the __________ you showed me.

❾ The strong __________ died down after several hours.

❿ I see a great chance of getting a __________ this time.

⓫ We must eliminate racial __________.

⓬ I give a __________ welcome to you.

⓭ We have an __________ that we can fully control nature.

⓮ The police __________ two people for starting the fire.

⓯ You should be __________ to her guests at the party.

⓰ Our __________ will be making a presentation about the report.

DAY 07

181 **sentiment** [séntəmənt]
명 감정, 정서　형 sentimental 감정적인 유 emotion
public sentiment 여론

182 **wag** [wæg]
동 (꼬리, 머리 등을) 흔들다
wag one's tail 꼬리를 흔들다

183 **inconvenience** [ìnkənví:njəns]
명 불편　형 inconvenient 불편한 유 trouble
feel inconvenience 불편을 느끼다

184 **enchanting** [intʃǽntiŋ]
형 매혹적인　동 enchant 매혹시키다 유 fascinating
an enchanting view 매혹적인 경치

185 **withhold** [wiθhóuld]
동 보류하다　유 hold back
withhold one's payment 지불을 보류하다

186 **skeleton** [skélətn]
명 골격, 해골　형 skeletal 골격의
the human skeleton 인간의 골격

187 **absent** 형 [ǽbsənt] 동 [æbsént]
형 결석한 동 결석하다　반 present 출석한
be absent from ~에 결석하다

188 **companion** [kəmpǽnjən]
명 동료　유 friend
a male companion 남자 동료

189 **eternally** [itə́:rnəli]
부 언제나, 영원히
eternally grateful 언제나 감사하는

190 **insulate** [ínsəlèit]
동 절연하다, 분리하다　유 isolate
insulate a patient 환자를 격리하다

191 **portion** [pɔ́:rʃən]
명 부분　명 portioner 받는 사람
a small portion of the population 인구 중 일부분

192 **adverse** [ædvə́:rs]
형 거스르는, 부정적인　부 adversely 반대로
an adverse wind 거스르는 바람 [역풍]

193 **extensive** [iksténsiv]
형 광범위한　부 extensively 광범위하게 유 wide
extensive reading 다독

194 **preventable** [privéntəbl]
형 막을 수 있는　명 prevention 예방
a preventable accident 막을 수 있는 사고

195 **amnesty** [ǽmnəsti]
명 사면
grant amnesty to ~에게 사면을 허락하다

✦ 주어진 우리말 문장에 맞도록 알맞은 단어를 넣어 문장을 완성하시오. 정답 p.196

Public ________ turned against the Japanese.
여론이 일본에 등을 돌렸다. (여론이 일본에 부정적으로 변했다.)

She ________ her head.
그녀는 고개를 흔들었다.

Not having a computer is an ________.
컴퓨터가 없으면 불편하다.

It was ________ to see the view from the tower.
타워에서 바라본 경치는 정말 매혹적이었다.

Consent was ________ for several reasons.
승낙은 여러 가지 이유에서 보류되었다.

They plan to display a dinosaur ________ in the museum.
그들은 박물관에 공룡의 뼈를 전시할 계획이다.

She was so sick that she was ________ from school.
그녀는 너무 아파서 학교에 결석했다.

If you are selfish, you won't have any ________.
이기적이면 어떤 친구도 사귈 수 없다.

She will ________ remember their kindness.
그녀는 그들의 친절을 영원히 기억할 것이다.

The room is ________ against noise.
그 방은 방음이 되어 있다.

Only a small ________ of people will benefit.
적은 부류의 사람들만이 혜택을 받을 것이다.

________ criticism in politics can sometimes be very helpful.
정치권에서의 혹평은 때때로 매우 유용하다.

The fire will cause ________ damage since the whole building is burning.
건물 전체가 타고 있으므로 그 화재는 광범위한 피해를 초래할 것이다.

If we had been more careful, the accident could have been ________.
우리가 조금만 더 주의했었다면 그 사고는 예방할 수 있었을 텐데.

The court granted ________ to the prisoner.
법원이 죄수에게 사면을 허락했다.

DAY 07

196	**antibiotic** [æ̀ntibaiɑ́tik]	형 항생물질의 명 항생물질 an antibiotic substance 항생물질	
197	**appliance** [əpláiəns]	명 기구, 전기제품 office appliances 사무용품	동 apply 사용하다, 적용하다
198	**counsel** [káunsəl]	명 상담, 조언 seek counsel from ~에게 조언을 구하다	참 counselor 상담사
199	**folklore** [fóuklɔ̀ːr]	명 민속, 민간 전승 Indian folklore 인디언 민속	
200	**loan** [loun]	명 대출 a public loan 공채	형 loanable 대출할 수 있는
201	**rash** [ræʃ]	형 분별없는, 경솔한 a rash act 분별없는 행동	부 rashly 분별없이 반 cautious 신중한
202	**testify** [téstəfài]	동 증명하다, 증언하다 testify against a person ~에게 불리한 증언을 하다	명 testification 증언
203	**atlas** [ǽtləs]	명 지도책 new atlas of Seoul 서울의 새 지도책	참 Atlas 아틀라스(그리스 신화 인물)
204	**decayed** [dikéid]	형 썩은 a decayed tooth 충치	동 decay 부식하다, 부패하다 유 rot
205	**generosity** [dʒènərɑ́səti]	명 관용, 너그러움 the virtue of generosity 관용의 미덕	형 generous 관대한 유 kindness
206	**mighty** [máiti]	형 강력한, 위력적인 mighty tides 강력한 파도	명 might 힘 유 strong
207	**repetitive** [ripétətiv]	형 반복적인 a repetitive heartbeat 반복적인 심장 박동	명 repetition 반복 유 monotonous
208	**tribute** [tríbjuːt]	명 찬사, 감사의 표시, 공물 pay tribute 공물을 바치다	형 tributary 공물을 바치는, 속국의
209	**boredom** [bɔ́ːrdəm]	명 지루함 without a sense of boredom 지루한 줄 모르게	형 bored 지루한 유 tedium
210	**digest** [didʒést ǀ dɑi-]	동 소화하다, 잘 이해하다 digest one's learning 학문을 제대로 이해하다	명 digestion 소화

✦ 주어진 우리말 문장에 맞도록 알맞은 단어를 넣어 문장을 완성하시오. 정답 p.196

________ substances prevent bodily infections.
항생물질은 육체의 감염을 막아 준다.

The kitchen is equipped with modern ________.
주방이 현대 기구들로 갖춰져 있다.

You should not forget that you have to listen to your parents' ________.
부모님의 조언에 귀 기울여야 한다는 것을 잊어서는 안 된다.

The story about a brave boy became a part of Indian ________.
한 용감한 소년에 관한 이야기는 인디언 민담 중 하나가 되었다.

Sometimes, we need ________ to buy things.
때때로 우리는 물건을 사기 위해 대출이 필요하다.

He regrets his ________ decision.
그는 자신의 분별없는 결정을 후회한다.

Her deep sighs ________ her sadness.
그녀의 깊은 한숨은 그녀의 슬픔을 증명했다.

This ________ has gone out of date.
이 지도책은 구식이 되었다.

Should the ________ tooth be removed?
그 충치를 빼야 하나요?

They were so happy that they were treated with ________ by him.
그들은 그에게서 후한 대접을 받아서 매우 기뻤다.

The ________ lord conquered the entire land.
그 강력한 군주는 모든 영토를 점령했다.

He was tired of ________ jobs.
그는 반복적인 일에 진저리가 났다.

We pay ________ to his courage.
우리는 그의 용기에 찬사를 보낸다.

I'm dying of ________!
지루해 죽겠다!

I like vegetables more than meat because they are easy to ________.
나는 고기보다 채소가 소화가 잘돼서 더 좋다.

DAY 08

211 **haul** [hɔːl]
동 (세게) 끌어당기다 명 잡아당기기 유 draw
haul in a net 그물을 끌어당기다

212 **natural** [nǽtʃərəl]
형 자연의, 자연 그대로의 명 naturalness 자연스러움
a natural product 천연 제품

213 **hobble** [hábl]
동 절뚝거리며 걷다
hobble on a cane 지팡이를 짚고 절뚝거리며 걷다

214 **scar** [skɑːr]
명 흉터 동 상처를 내다
scar one's face 얼굴에 상처를 남기다

215 **scoop** [skuːp]
명 국자, 한 숟가락(의 양) 유 ladle
a scoop of ice cream 아이스크림 한 숟가락

216 **seasoning** [síːzəniŋ]
명 조미료 동 season 양념을 치다 유 spices
various seasonings 다양한 조미료

217 **selfishness** [sélfiʃnis]
명 이기적임, 이기심 형 selfish 이기적인
hate selfishness 이기적인 것을 싫어하다

218 **vivid** [vívid]
형 생생한 부 vividly 생생히
a vivid description 생생한 묘사

219 **chilly** [tʃíli]
형 추운, 냉담한 명 chill 냉기, 차가움 유 shivery
feel chilly 으스스하다

220 **incurable** [inkjúərəbl]
형 불치의
an incurable disease 불치병

221 **enclose** [inklóuz]
동 둘러싸다, 동봉하다 명 enclosure 둘러쌈, 동봉 유 surround
enclose with an iron fence 철책을 두르다

222 **workforce** [wə́ːrkfɔ̀ːrs]
명 (모든) 노동자, 노동 인구
ten percent of the workforce 노동 인구의 10%

223 **abide** [əbáid]
동 머물다, 체류하다 유 stay
abide in a little village 작은 마을에 머무르다

224 **commit** [kəmít]
동 저지르다, 범하다 명 commitment 범행 유 do
commit a crime 죄를 범하다

225 **equivalent** [ikwívələnt]
형 동등한 명 equivalence 동등 유 equal

✦ 주어진 우리말 문장에 맞도록 알맞은 단어를 넣어 문장을 완성하시오. 정답 p.196

The horse effortlessly ________ a big wagon.
그 말은 큰 마차를 쉽게 끌었다.

I like their ________ products.
나는 그들이 만든 천연 제품을 좋아한다.

He got up slowly and ________ to the table.
그는 천천히 일어나서 탁자로 절뚝거리며 걸어갔다.

The wound left a ________.
그 상처는 흉터를 남겼다.

Can I get a ________ of chocolate ice cream?
초콜릿 아이스크림 한 숟가락만 줄래요?

________ such as salt and pepper can make food more delicious.
소금, 후추와 같은 조미료들은 음식을 더 맛있게 해준다.

The ________ inside him made other people stay away from him.
그 사람의 이기심이 다른 사람들이 그를 멀리하게끔 만들었다.

Koreans in their seventies have ________ memories of the Korean War.
70대의 한국인들은 한국전쟁에 대한 생생한 기억을 가지고 있다.

It was too ________ for swimming in March.
3월은 수영하기에는 너무 추웠다.

He is suffering from an ________ disease.
그는 불치병을 앓고 있다.

The palace is ________ by a high wall.
그 궁전은 높은 담으로 둘러싸여 있다.

The whole ________ is on strike.
노동자 전체가 파업 중이다.

He is not a person who can ________ in a small village.
그는 작은 마을에 머물 수 있는 사람이 아니다.

We should educate young men since they ________ the most crimes these days.
요즘 대부분의 범죄를 젊은이들이 저지르기 때문에 우리는 그들을 교육시켜야 한다.

One kilometer is ________ to 1,000 meters.
1킬로미터는 1,000미터와 같다.

DAY 08

226 **insight** [ínsàit]
명 통찰력
a man of insight 통찰력 있는 사람

227 **pollen** [pálən]
명 꽃가루
a pollen sac 꽃가루 주머니

228 **squeeze** [skwi:z]
동 쥐어 짜다 참 grip 쥐다, grasp 잡다
squeeze the water out 물을 짜내다

229 **construct** [kənstrʌ́kt]
동 건설하다 명 construction 건설 반 destruct
construct a bridge 다리를 건설하다

230 **interruption** [ìntərʌ́pʃən]
명 방해, 훼방 동 interrupt 방해하다 유 intervention
without interruption 간섭 없이

231 **stimulation** [stìmjuléiʃən]
명 자극 동 stimulate 자극하다
a strong stimulation 강한 자극

232 **convict** [kənvíkt]
동 유죄를 선고하다 명 conviction 유죄 판결 유 sentence
convict a person of robbery ~에게 절도죄를 선고하다

233 **core** [kɔːr]
명 중심, 핵심
to the core 속속들이, 철두철미하게

234 **corridor** [kɔ́:ridər]
명 복도
wipe the corridor with a mop 복도를 대걸레로 닦다

235 **flexibility** [flèksəbíləti]
명 융통성, 유연성 형 flexible 유연한 유 elasticity
a flexibility exercise 유연성 운동

236 **likewise** [láikwàiz]
부 마찬가지로 전 like ~ 같은 유 similarly
do likewise 마찬가지로 하다

237 **quotient** [kwóuʃənt]
명 지수, 몫
intelligence quotient 지능 지수

238 **tendency** [téndənsi]
명 경향, 풍조 동 tend ~하는 경향이 있다 유 inclination
a tendency to+동사원형 ~하는 경향

239 **assistance** [əsístəns]
명 원조, 도움 동 assist 원조하다 유 help
give assistance to ~에게 도움을 주다

240 **damp** [dæmp]
형 축축한 명 습기 동 축축하게 하다, (기를) 꺾다 유 moist
damp spirits 사기를 저하시키다

1회독 월 일
2회독 월 일

✦ 주어진 우리말 문장에 맞도록 알맞은 단어를 넣어 문장을 완성하시오. 정답 p.196

This book is full of profound ________.
이 책은 심오한 통찰력으로 가득 찼다.

She is allergic to ________.
그녀는 꽃가루 알레르기가 있다.

Drink freshly ________ juice every morning.
신선하게 짠 주스를 매일 아침 마셔라.

The same company ________ the bridge in my town.
똑같은 회사가 우리 마을에 다리를 건설했다.

She could study for three hours without ________.
그녀는 간섭 없이 3시간 동안 공부할 수 있었다.

Too much ________ can cause side effects.
너무 많은 자극은 부작용을 일으킬 수 있다.

The court ________ the young man of robbery.
법원은 그 젊은 사람에게 절도죄를 선고했다.

The Earth's ________ is not solid.
지구의 중심은 고체가 아니다.

The ________ echoed from the footsteps.
복도에 발소리가 울려 퍼졌다.

Leaders must show leadership, self-confidence, and ________.
지도자는 리더십, 자신감, 융통성을 보여줘야 한다.

He doesn't play computer games any more, and he expects his friends to do ________.
그는 더 이상 컴퓨터 게임을 하지 않으며 자신의 친구들도 마찬가지로 그렇게 해 주길 바란다.

Did you know that IQ stands for intelligence ________?
너는 IQ가 지능 지수를 뜻한다는 것을 알았니?

He has a ________ to cross his arms when listening.
그는 경청할 때 팔짱을 끼는 경향이 있다.

I could successfully finish the ceremony with his ________.
나는 그의 도움으로 예식을 성공적으로 마칠 수 있었다.

It's still ________ in this room.
이 방은 여전히 축축하다.

REVIEW TEST 04 DAY 07 ~ DAY 08

A 우리말과 같은 뜻이 되도록 빈칸에 들어갈 알맞은 단어를 적으시오.

1. a ______________ tooth (충치)
2. do ______________ (마찬가지로 하다)
3. ______________ a crime (죄를 범하다)
4. Indian ______________ (인디언 민속)
5. ______________ one's tail (꼬리를 흔들다)
6. a ______________ exercise (유연성 운동)
7. the virtue of ______________ (관용의 미덕)
8. a ______________ accident (막을 수 있는 사고)
9. ______________ one's face (얼굴에 상처를 남기다)
10. ______________ in a little village (작은 마을에 머무르다)

B 다음 괄호 안의 지시대로 주어진 단어를 변형시키고 그 뜻을 적으시오.

		변형	뜻
1	likewise (전치사형으로) →	______	______
2	flexibility (형용사형으로) →	______	______
3	sentiment (형용사형으로) →	______	______
4	repetitive (명사형으로) →	______	______
5	convict (명사형으로) →	______	______
6	mighty (명사형으로) →	______	______
7	adverse (부사형으로) →	______	______
8	generosity (형용사형으로) →	______	______
9	skeleton (형용사형으로) →	______	______
10	preventable (명사형으로) →	______	______

정답 p.196

C 다음 영영풀이에 해당하는 단어를 보기에서 골라 적으시오.

보기				
core	testify	stimulation	extensive	insight
haul	withhold	inconvenience	corridor	companion

❶ to pull or draw with force; move by drawing; drag → ______________

❷ to hold back; to refrain from giving or granting → ______________

❸ the quality or state of being inconvenient → ______________

❹ of great extent; wide; broad → ______________

❺ to bear witness; give or afford evidence → ______________

❻ an instance of apprehending the true nature of a thing, especially through intuitive understanding → ______________

❼ the act of rousing someone to action or effort, as by encouragement or pressure → ______________

❽ the central, innermost, or most essential part of anything → ______________

❾ a gallery or passage connecting parts of a building; hallway → ______________

❿ a person who is frequently in the company of, associates with, or accompanies another → ______________

D 우리말과 같은 뜻이 되도록 주어진 문장의 빈칸을 완성하시오.

❶ 그 궁전은 높은 담으로 둘러싸여 있다.

→ The palace is ______________ by a high wall.

❷ 지구의 중심은 고체가 아니다.

→ The Earth's ______________ is not solid.

❸ 신선하게 짠 주스를 매일 아침 마셔라.

→ Drink freshly ______________ juice every morning.

❹ 항생물질은 육체의 감염을 막아 준다.

→ ______________ substances prevent bodily infections.

⑤ 우리는 그의 용기에 찬사를 보낸다.

→ We pay ______________ to his courage.

⑥ 나는 그들이 만든 천연 제품을 좋아한다.

→ I like their ______________ products.

⑦ 노동자 전체가 파업 중이다.

→ The whole ______________ is on strike.

⑧ 그녀는 꽃가루 알레르기가 있다.

→ She is allergic to ______________.

⑨ 너는 IQ가 지능 지수를 뜻한다는 것을 알았니?

→ Did you know that IQ stands for intelligence ______________?

⑩ 소금, 후추와 같은 조미료들은 음식을 더 맛있게 해준다.

→ ______________ such as salt and pepper can make food more delicious.

E 문장의 밑줄 친 부분에 해당하는 유의어 혹은 반의어를 보기에서 골라 적으시오.

보기				
fascinating	inclination	present	cautious	moist
tedium	destruct	equal	help	shivery

① He regrets his rash decision. 반의어 ↔ ______________

② The same company constructed the bridge in my town. 반의어 ↔ ______________

③ She was so sick that she was absent from school. 반의어 ↔ ______________

④ One kilometer is equivalent to 1,000 meters. 유의어 = ______________

⑤ It was enchanting to see the view from the tower. 유의어 = ______________

⑥ He has a tendency to cross his arms when listening. 유의어 = ______________

⑦ It's still damp in this room. 유의어 = ______________

⑧ I could successfully finish the ceremony with his assistance.
유의어 = ______________

⑨ It was too chilly for swimming in March. 유의어 = ______________

⑩ I'm dying of boredom! 유의어 = ______________

F 영어발음을 듣고 영어단어를 적은 후, 우리말 뜻을 적으시오.

영어단어 듣고 쓰기 

	영어	우리말		영어	우리말
❶	________	________	❽	________	________
❷	________	________	❾	________	________
❸	________	________	❿	________	________
❹	________	________	⓫	________	________
❺	________	________	⓬	________	________
❻	________	________	⓭	________	________
❼	________	________	⓮	________	________

G 영어문장을 듣고 빈칸에 들어갈 단어를 채워 문장을 완성하시오.

영어문장 듣고 쓰기

❶ He doesn't play computer games any more, and he expects his friends to do ________.

❷ Leaders must show leadership, self-confidence, and ________.

❸ Public ________ turned against the Japanese.

❹ The court ________ the young man of robbery.

❺ The ________ lord conquered the entire land.

❻ ________ criticism in politics can sometimes be very helpful.

❼ They plan to display a dinosaur ________ in the museum.

❽ If we had been more careful, the accident could have been ________.

❾ She could study for three hours without ________.

❿ Can I get a ________ of chocolate ice cream?

⓫ She ________ her head.

⓬ The court granted ________ to the prisoner.

⓭ Koreans in their seventies have ________ memories of the Korean War.

⓮ He is suffering from an ________ disease.

⓯ The horse is effortlessly ________ a big wagon.

⓰ Not having a computer is an ________.

DAY 09

241	**gambling** [gǽmbliŋ]	명 도박 prevalent gambling 성행 중인 도박	동 gamble 도박을 하다 유 betting
242	**melody** [mélədi]	명 선율 old Irish melodies 옛 아일랜드 선율	형 melodious 선율적인
243	**religious** [rilídʒəs]	형 신앙심이 깊은 a religious person 신앙심이 깊은 사람	명 religion 종교
244	**transparency** [trænspέərənsi]	명 투명성	유 clarity
245	**bless** [bles]	동 신의 은총을 빌다, 축복하다 bless oneself 신의 축복을 빌다	명 bliss 더없는 기쁨
246	**detective** [ditéktiv]	명 탐정, 형사 형 탐정의 a private detective 사립 탐정	동 detect 탐색하다
247	**guard** [gɑːrd]	명 보호자, 감시인 a security guard 경비	
248	**narration** [næréiʃən]	명 이야기하기, 서술 the manner of narration 화법	동 narrate 이야기하다 유 account
249	**rhyme** [raim]	명 (시의) 운 pl. 운문, 시 nursery rhymes 동요, 자장가	
250	**negative** [négətiv]	형 부정적인 a negative answer 부정적인 대답	반 positive 긍정적인
251	**utensil** [juːténsəl]	명 기구 kitchen utensils 주방기구	
252	**variation** [vὲəriéiʃən]	명 변화 be subject to variation 변화의 대상이다	동 vary 변하다 유 change
253	**vertical** [vəːrtikəl]	형 수직의, 세로의 a vertical line 수직선	명 verticality 수직 반 horizontal 수평의
254	**violate** [váiəlèit]	동 어기다, 위반하다 violate the law 법을 어기다	명 violation 위반
255	**certify** [səːrtəfài]	동 증명하다 be certified as ~로 증명되다	명 certification 증명 유 prove

✦ 주어진 우리말 문장에 맞도록 알맞은 단어를 넣어 문장을 완성하시오. 정답 p.197

________ is prohibited in the city.
그 도시에서 도박은 금지되었다.

When I was young, I used to play the ________ I am listening to now.
나는 어릴 때 지금 듣고 있는 선율을 연주하곤 했다.

My parents are very ________.
우리 부모님은 신앙심이 매우 깊으시다.

The president promised to promote government ________.
대통령은 정부의 투명성을 높이겠다고 약속했다.

May God always ________ you!
언제나 신의 은총이 있기를!

I like ________ stories.
나는 탐정 소설을 좋아한다.

He argued that the security ________ was responsible for it.
그는 경비가 이 일에 책임이 있다고 주장했다.

Her ________ with a strong accent irritated many people.
그녀는 강한 억양으로 이야기를 해서 많은 사람들을 짜증나게 했다.

I always sing my favorite nursery ________ when I'm sad.
나는 슬플 때 항상 내가 가장 좋아하는 동요를 부른다.

His reaction gave them a ________ impression of him.
그의 반응은 그들에게 그에 대한 부정적인 인상을 주었다.

This store sells cooking ________.
이 가게는 조리기구들을 판다.

You can see many ________ of this style.
당신은 이 스타일의 다양한 변화들을 볼 수 있어요.

This fish is odd because it has ________ fins.
이 물고기는 세로로 된 지느러미를 가지고 있어서 특이하다.

We must not ________ the law.
우리는 법을 어기지 말아야 한다.

Her reports were ________ as true.
그녀의 보고서들은 사실로 증명되었다.

DAY 09

	단어	뜻	관련어
256	**elevate** [éləvèit]	동 높이다, 들어올리다 elevate one's voice 목소리를 높이다	명 elevation 높이, 고도 유 raise
257	**industrial** [indʌ́striəl]	형 산업의 industrial workers 산업 근로자	명 industry 산업
258	**endurance** [indjúərəns]	명 인내(심) beyond endurance 참을 수 없을 정도로	동 endure 참다 유 patience
259	**yearn** [jəːrn]	동 갈망하다 yearn for ~을 갈망하다	유 long
260	**column** [kάləm]	명 기둥 a column of water 물기둥	
261	**lull** [lʌl]	동 (어린아이를) 달래다, 어르다 lull a crying baby 우는 아이를 달래다	유 soothe, calm
262	**innocent** [ínəsnt]	형 순진한, 결백한 an innocent person 순진한 사람	명 innocence 결백
263	**poetic** [pouétik]	형 시의, 시적인 a poetic gift 시적 재능	명 poet 시인, poem 시
264	**spit** [spit]	동 (침을) 뱉다 spit on the pavement 길에 침을 뱉다	
265	**adolescent** [æ̀dəlésnt]	형 청년기의 명 청소년 adolescent psychology 청소년의 심리	명 adolescence 청소년기 유 juvenile
266	**expanse** [ikspǽns]	명 넓게 펼쳐진 공간 the blue expanse 파란 창공	동 expand 펼치다, 확장하다
267	**prescription** [priskrípʃən]	명 처방 medical prescriptions 처방약	동 prescribe 처방하다
268	**altogether** [ɔ̀ːltəgéðər]	부 완전히, 전적으로 stop altogether 완전히 그만두다	유 wholly, completely
269	**famine** [fǽmin]	명 기근 a severe famine 심각한 기근	동 famish 굶주리게 하다
270	**faucet** [fɔ́ːsit]	명 수도꼭지 faucet water 수돗물	유 tap

✦ 주어진 우리말 문장에 맞도록 알맞은 단어를 넣어 문장을 완성하시오. 정답 p.197

Stress can ____________ your blood pressure.
스트레스는 혈압을 높일 수 있다.

____________ workers are the core of industry.
산업 근로자들은 산업의 핵심이다.

The task definitely requires ____________.
그 일은 확실히 인내심을 요구한다.

She ____________ to be a movie actress.
그녀는 영화배우가 되기를 갈망했다.

Many massive ____________ are seen from here.
여기서부터 거대한 기둥들이 많이 보인다.

They couldn't ____________ a crying baby to sleep.
그들은 우는 아이를 달래어 재우지 못했다.

She is as ____________ as a child.
그녀는 어린아이만큼이나 순진하다.

Robert Browning was very gifted at ____________ monologues.
로버트 브라우닝은 시적 독백에 대단한 재능이 있었다.

____________ your gum out before you come into the classroom.
수업에 들어가기 전에 껌을 뱉어라.

Their youth program can help ____________ grow to reach their potential.
그들이 제공하는 청소년 프로그램은 청소년들이 자신의 가능성에 도달할 수 있도록 성장시켜 준다.

The boundless ____________ of water went into my eyes.
망망대해가 내 눈에 들어왔다.

The patients without a ____________ cannot buy any drugs.
처방전이 없는 환자는 약을 조금도 살 수 없다.

His parents aren't ____________ happy about his decision.
그의 부모님은 그의 결정에 전적으로 기뻐하진 않는다.

The African countries suffered a severe ____________ last year.
작년에 아프리카 국가들은 심각한 기근을 겪었다.

Turn off the ____________ when not using it.
사용하지 않을 때는 수도꼭지를 잠그세요.

DAY 10

DAY 10 표제어 듣기

271	**feverish** [fí:vəriʃ]	형 열이 있는 feel feverish 열이 나는 기분이 들다	명 fever 열
272	**leash** [li:ʃ]	명 사슬, 속박 slip a dog from the leash 개를 사슬에서 풀어 주다	참 lease 임대차 계약
273	**qualify** [kwάləfài]	동 자격을 부여하다 be qualified to+동사원형 ~할 자격이 있다	명 qualification 자격 유 entitle
274	**technical** [téknikəl]	형 기술의 a technical problem 기술적인 문제	명 technic 기술
275	**assemble** [əsémbl]	동 조립하다 assemble the parts 부품들을 조립하다	명 assembly 조립
276	**crumble** [krʌ́mbl]	동 빻다, 부수다 crumble into ruins 산산이 부서져 폐허가 되다	
277	**furious** [fjúəriəs]	형 격노한, 맹렬한 at a furious pace 고속력으로	명 fury 격노 유 angry
278	**meantime** [mí:ntàim]	명 그동안	유 meanwhile
279	**reject** [ridʒékt]	동 거절하다 reject a proposal 제안을 거절하다	명 rejection 거절 반 accept 수용하다
280	**trackless** [trǽklis]	형 자취를 남기지 않은 be trackless 흔적을 남기지 않다	
281	**bound** [baund]	형 ~행의, ~로 향하는 be bound for ~로 향하다	
282	**deserve** [dizə́:rv]	동 ~할 만하다, ~을 받을 자격이 있다 deserve well of ~로부터 칭찬받을 만하다	
283	**greasy** [grí:si]	형 기름이 묻은 greasy food 기름기가 많은 음식	명 grease 기름
284	**multilayered** [mʌ̀ltiléiərd]	형 다층의 a multilayered cake 다층의 케이크	명 multilayer 다층
285	**reveal** [riví:l]	동 드러내다, 폭로하다 reveal a secret 비밀을 폭로하다	명 revealment 폭로 유 disclose

✦ 주어진 우리말 문장에 맞도록 알맞은 단어를 넣어 문장을 완성하시오. 정답 p.197

He touched her ______ head.
그는 열이 있는 그녀의 머리를 만졌다.

My brother let his dog off the ______.
내 남동생은 자신의 개를 사슬에서 풀어 주었다.

You need to obtain a teacher's certificate to be ______ to teach.
가르치기 위한 자격을 갖추려면 교원 자격증을 취득해야 한다.

The spaceship is suffering from a ______ problem.
그 우주선은 기술적인 문제 때문에 골머리를 앓고 있다.

It is hard work to ______ a ship.
배를 조립하는 것은 어려운 일이다.

Roughly ______ the cheese into a bowl.
치즈를 대충 부수어 그릇에 넣으세요.

The boss will be ______ with us if we're late.
우리가 늦으면 사장이 매우 화를 낼 것이다.

In the ______, what are you going to do?
그동안 너는 뭐하고 있을 거야?

He was very disappointed when his proposal was ______.
그는 자신의 제안이 거절되었을 때 매우 실망했다.

Planes are ______. We can't find traces of them in the air.
비행기는 자취를 남기지 않는다. 우리는 하늘에서 비행기가 지나간 흔적을 찾을 수 없다.

This plane is ______ for Seoul.
이 비행기는 서울행이다.

He ______ help.
그는 도움을 받을 자격이 있었다.

Too much ______ food isn't good for you.
너무 기름기가 많은 음식은 너에게 해롭다.

Having a ______ cake was the girl's dream.
층이 많은 케이크를 먹는 것이 그 소녀의 꿈이었다.

It will be ______ that she doesn't tell the truth.
그녀가 사실을 말하고 있지 않음이 드러날 것이다.

DAY 10

286	**unity** [jú:nəti]	명 통일	동 unite 통일시키다
287	**rubbish** [rʌ́biʃ]	명 쓰레기 a pile of rubbish 쓰레기 더미	유 litter
288	**calmly** [kɑ́:mli]	부 침착하게 wait calmly 침착하게 기다리다	명 calmness 침착, 평온 형 calm 고요한
289	**carbonate** [kɑ́:rbənèit]	동 탄산가스로 포화시키다 carbonated water 탄산수	
290	**casual** [kǽʒuəl]	명 평상복 형 평상복의 casual wear 평상복	참 suit 정장
291	**cathedral** [kəθí:drəl]	명 대성당 St. Paul's Cathedral 성 폴 성당	
292	**efficient** [ifíʃənt]	형 효율적인 an efficient system 효율적인 체계	명 efficiency 능률 반 inefficient 비효율적인
293	**impulse** [ímpʌls]	명 충동 on impulse 충동적으로	
294	**overact** [òuvərǽkt]	동 과장하여 행하다 overact excessively 지나치게 과장해서 행동하다	명 overaction 과장 유 exaggerate
295	**enhance** [inhǽns]	동 높이다 enhance the quality 품질을 높이다	명 enhancement 상승
296	**youthful** [jú:θfəl]	형 젊은	명 youthfulness 젊음 유 young
297	**enlist** [inlíst]	동 입대하다 enlist in the army 육군에 입대하다	
298	**ingredient** [ingrí:diənt]	명 성분, 재료 a basic ingredient 기본 재료	
299	**pilgrim** [pílgrim]	명 순례자	
300	**specialist** [spéʃəlist]	명 전문가 a computer specialist 컴퓨터 전문가	유 expert

1회독 월 일
2회독 월 일

✦ 주어진 우리말 문장에 맞도록 알맞은 단어를 넣어 문장을 완성하시오. 정답 p.197

His words lack ______.
그의 말은 통일성이 없다.

Visitors to the national park should not leave their ______ behind.
국립공원 방문객들은 쓰레기를 버려두고 가면 안 됩니다.

He ______ addressed them.
그는 침착하게 그들에게 말을 걸었다.

Soda water is a ______ drink.
소다수는 탄산음료이다.

This is too ______. I want something special for the party.
이것은 너무 평상복이에요. 나는 파티를 위한 뭔가 특별한 것을 원해요.

The huge ______ in the center of the town attracts many tourists.
그 마을 중심에 있는 큰 성당은 많은 관광객들을 불러모은다.

The results of the ______ system were much better than we had expected.
그 효율적인 체계의 결과는 우리가 예상했던 것보다 훨씬 더 좋았다.

______ buying causes regret later.
충동구매는 나중에 후회를 낳는다.

Every time he meets her, he always ______.
그는 그녀를 만날 때마다 항상 과장해서 행동한다.

The company is struggling to ______ the quality of its product.
그 회사는 자신들의 제품의 질을 높이기 위해 고군분투하고 있다.

He is a ______ father.
그는 나이 어린 가장이다.

He will ______ in the army at the end of this month.
그는 이달 말 군에 입대할 것이다.

I use a cream that contains natural ______ for my face.
나는 천연 성분들이 함유된 크림을 얼굴에 사용한다.

Hundreds of ______ gathered in Jerusalem.
수백 명의 순례자들이 예루살렘에 모였다.

Doctors are ______ in medicine.
의사는 의학 전문가들이다.

REVIEW TEST 05 DAY 09 ~ DAY 10

A 우리말과 같은 뜻이 되도록 빈칸에 들어갈 알맞은 단어를 적으시오.

1. ________ wear (평상복)
2. on ________ (충동적으로)
3. a ________ of water (물기둥)
4. a private ________ (사립 탐정)
5. be ________ for (~로 향하다)
6. ________ a secret (비밀을 폭로하다)
7. wait ________ (침착하게 기다리다)
8. ________ the quality (품질을 높이다)
9. ________ a proposal (제안을 거절하다)
10. a severe ________ (심각한 기근)

B 다음 괄호 안의 지시대로 주어진 단어를 변형시키고 그 뜻을 적으시오.

		변형	뜻
1 melody (형용사형으로)	→	________	________
2 religious (명사형으로)	→	________	________
3 detective (동사형으로)	→	________	________
4 industrial (명사형으로)	→	________	________
5 innocent (명사형으로)	→	________	________
6 technical (명사형으로)	→	________	________
7 greasy (명사형으로)	→	________	________
8 multilayered (명사형으로)	→	________	________
9 calmness (형용사형으로)	→	________	________
10 overact (명사형으로)	→	________	________

정답 p.197

C 다음 영영풀이에 해당하는 단어를 보기에서 골라 적으시오.

보기				
prescription	yearn	gambling	certify	specialist
trackless	qualify	transparency	unity	endurance

1. the act of playing at any game of chance for money → ____________
2. the quality or state of being transparent → ____________
3. to attest as certain; give reliable information of; confirm → ____________
4. the fact or power of enduring or bearing pain, hardships, etc. → ____________
5. to have an earnest or strong desire; long → ____________
6. a direction, usually written, by the physician to the pharmacist for the preparation and use of a medicine or remedy → ____________
7. not making or leaving a track → ____________
8. the state of being one; oneness → ____________
9. to provide with proper or necessary skills, knowledge, credentials, etc.; make someone competent → ____________
10. a person who devotes himself or herself to one subject or to one particular branch of a subject or pursuit → ____________

D 우리말과 같은 뜻이 되도록 주어진 문장의 빈칸을 완성하시오.

1. 그녀는 캐나다에 가는 것에 대해 열광적이었다.
   → She was ____________ about going to Canada.
2. 언제나 신의 은총이 있기를!
   → May God always ____________ you!
3. 당신은 이 스타일의 다양한 변화들을 볼 수 있어요.
   → You can see many ____________ of this style.
4. 우리는 법을 어기지 말아야 한다.
   → We must not ____________ the law.

⑤ 스트레스는 혈압을 높일 수 있다. ➔ Stress can ________________ your blood pressure.

⑥ 망망대해가 내 눈에 들어왔다.

➔ The boundless ________________ of water went into my eyes.

⑦ 배를 조립하는 것은 어려운 일이다. ➔ It is hard work to ________________ a ship.

⑧ 그녀가 사실을 말하고 있지 않음이 드러날 것이다.

➔ It will be ________________ that she doesn't tell the truth.

⑨ 충동구매는 나중에 후회를 낳는다. ➔ ________________ buying causes regret later.

⑩ 그 회사는 자신들의 제품의 질을 높이기 위해 고군분투하고 있다.

➔ The company is struggling to ________________ the quality of its product.

E 문장의 밑줄 친 부분에 해당하는 유의어 혹은 반의어를 보기에서 골라 적으시오.

보기				
horizontal	juvenile	inefficient	tap	proved
account	positive	angry	accepted	litter

① Her narration with a strong accent irritated many people. 유의어 = ________________

② His reaction gave them a negative impression of him. 반의어 ↔ ________________

③ This fish is odd because it has vertical fins. 반의어 ↔ ________________

④ Their youth program can help adolescents grow to reach their potential.

유의어 = ________________

⑤ Turn off the faucet when not using it. 유의어 = ________________

⑥ The boss will be furious with us if we're late. 유의어 = ________________

⑦ He was disappointed when his proposal was rejected. 반의어 ↔ ________________

⑧ Visitors to the national park should not leave their rubbish behind.

유의어 = ________________

⑨ The results of the efficient system were much better than we had expected.

반의어 ↔ ________________

⑩ Her reports were certified as true. 유의어 = ________________

F 영어발음을 듣고 영어단어를 적은 후, 우리말 뜻을 적으시오.

영어단어 듣고 쓰기

	영어	우리말		영어	우리말
❶	______	______	❽	______	______
❷	______	______	❾	______	______
❸	______	______	❿	______	______
❹	______	______	⓫	______	______
❺	______	______	⓬	______	______
❻	______	______	⓭	______	______
❼	______	______	⓮	______	______

G 영어문장을 듣고 빈칸에 들어갈 단어를 채워 문장을 완성하시오.

영어문장 듣고 쓰기

❶ Many massive ______________ are seen from here.

❷ The African countries suffered a severe ______________ last year.

❸ My brother let his dog off the ______________.

❹ In the ______________, what are you going to do?

❺ Soda water is a ______________ drink.

❻ This is too ______________. I want something special for the party.

❼ Hundreds of ______________ gathered in Jerusalem.

❽ His parents aren't ______________ happy about his decision.

❾ When I was young, I used to play the ______________ I am listening to now.

❿ I like ______________ stories.

⓫ ______________ workers are the core of industry.

⓬ She is as ______________ as a child.

⓭ Having a ______________ cake was the girl's dream.

⓮ He ______________ addressed them.

⓯ Every time he meets her, he always ______________.

⓰ Robert Browning was very gifted at ______________ monologues.

301 **adapt** [ədǽpt]
동 적응하다 명 adaptation 적응, 각색 유 adjust
adapt to new circumstances 새로운 상황에 적응하다

302 **conservation** [kὰnsərvéiʃən]
명 보존 동 conserve 보존하다 유 preservation
energy conservation 에너지 보존

303 **interact** [ìntərǽkt]
동 상호작용하다 명 interaction 상호작용
an ability to interact 상호작용하는 능력

304 **steer** [stiːər]
동 조종하다, 몰다 유 navigate
steer a ship 배를 몰다

305 **continuous** [kəntínjuəs]
형 계속적인 동 continue 계속하다 유 continual
a continuous development 부단한 발전

306 **irrigate** [írəgèit]
동 물을 대다 명 irrigation 관개 유 water
irrigate a dry land 마른 땅에 물을 대다

307 **kidney** [kídni]
명 신장
kidney disease 신장병

308 **launch** [lɔːntʃ]
동 (새 배를) 진수시키다, 발사하다
launch a rocket 로켓을 발사하다

309 **pupil** [pjúːpil]
명 학생 유 student
a docile pupil 유순한 학생

310 **symbolic** [simbάlik]
형 상징적인 명 symbol 상징
be symbolic of ~을 상징하다

311 **arrest** [ərést]
동 체포하다 명 체포 유 seize
arrest A for B A를 B 혐의로 체포하다

312 **criticize** [krítəsàiz]
동 비판하다 명 critic 비평가 반 praise 칭찬하다

313 **fulfill** [fulfíl]
동 이행하다 명 fulfillment 이행
fulfill a promise 약속을 지키다

314 **mansion** [mǽnʃən]
명 대저택
a roomy mansion 넓은 저택

315 **reform** [rifɔ́ːrm]
동 개혁하다 참 form 형성하다
reform a system 제도를 개혁하다

✦ 주어진 우리말 문장에 맞도록 알맞은 단어를 넣어 문장을 완성하시오. 정답 p.198

Newcomers in a country have trouble ________.
어떤 나라에 새로 온 사람들은 적응하는 데 어려움을 겪는다.

Water ________ is of great importance in desert areas.
사막지대에서 물을 보존하는 것은 굉장히 중요하다.

________ with customers is one of my duties.
고객들과 상호작용하는 것이 내 임무 중 하나이다.

The sailor is carefully ________ the ship into the harbor.
그 선원은 조심스럽게 항구 쪽으로 배를 몰고 있다.

The rain has been ________ since I woke up this morning.
그 비는 내가 오늘 아침 일어난 후부터 계속 내렸다.

People ________ the dry land all day.
사람들은 종일 마른 땅에 물을 댔다.

Drinking a lot of water helps the ________ do their jobs.
물을 많이 마시는 것은 신장이 제 기능을 할 수 있도록 돕는다.

The new ship was ________ today.
새 배가 오늘 진수되었다(처음으로 물에 띄워졌다).

You should treat all the ________ fairly.
당신은 모든 학생을 공평하게 다뤄야 한다.

Most people know the dove is ________ of peace.
대부분의 사람들은 비둘기가 평화를 상징한다는 것을 안다.

The police ________ him for murdering his friend.
경찰은 그를 그의 친구를 살해한 혐의로 체포했다.

The director ________ the film.
감독은 그 영화를 비판했다.

The workers complained that the company did not ________ its promise.
근로자들은 회사가 약속을 이행하지 않았다고 불평했다.

I spent two nights in the ________.
나는 대저택에서 이틀밤을 묵었다.

________ the system will be the first priority for the president.
제도를 개혁하는 것이 대통령에게 최우선 사항이 될 것이다.

No.	Word	Meaning	Related	Example
316	**tiresome** [táiərsəm]	형 지루한, 싫증나는	동 tire 싫증나게 하다 유 tedious	a tiresome sermon 지루한 설교
317	**baron** [bǽrən]	명 거물, ~왕	유 tycoon	a steel baron 강철왕
318	**dependable** [dipéndəbl]	형 의지할 수 있는	명 dependance 의존 유 reliant	a dependable person 의지할 수 있는 사람
319	**glimpse** [glimps]	명 흘깃 봄 동 흘깃 보다	유 glance	in glimpses 흘깃흘깃
320	**moth** [mɔ(:)θ]	명 나방		catch a moth 나방을 잡다
321	**retail** [rí:teil]	명 소매	반 wholesale 도매	by retail 소매로
322	**unethical** [ʌ̀néθikəl]	형 비도덕적인	반 ethical 도덕적인	unethical behavior 비도덕적 행위
323	**bulk** [bʌlk]	명 크기, 덩치	유 size	be of great bulk 매우 크다
324	**unnoticeable** [ʌ̀nnóutisəbl]	형 중요하지 않은, 눈에 안 띄는		an unnoticeable man 중요하지 않은 인물
325	**distinct** [distíŋkt]	형 뚜렷한, 명백한	반 vague 애매모호한	be distinct from ~와는 다르다
326	**diversion** [divə́:rʒən]	명 전환	동 divert 전환하다	be good for diversion 기분 전환에 좋다
327	**doom** [du:m]	명 운명, 파멸	유 fate	the day of doom 파멸의 날
328	**drip** [drip]	동 뚝뚝 떨어지다 명 물방울	유 drop	drip rain 빗방울이 뚝뚝 떨어지다
329	**imperialism** [impíəriəlìzm]	명 제국주의	형 imperial 제국의	
330	**overall** [óuvərɔ̀:l]	형 종합적인, 전체의 부 종합적으로		an overall effect 전반적인 효과

✦ 주어진 우리말 문장에 맞도록 알맞은 단어를 넣어 문장을 완성하시오. 정답 p.198

Children can be ______ after a long drive.
아이들은 오랫동안 차를 타고나면 지루해 할 수 있다.

An oil ______ has so much money that he can buy an island.
한 석유왕은 돈이 너무나 많아서 섬 하나를 살 수 있다.

It's good to have a ______ person near you.
당신 근처에 의지할 수 있는 사람이 있는 것은 좋다.

People shouted and pushed to catch ______ of the star players.
사람들은 인기 있는 운동 선수들을 흘깃 보기 위해 소리치며 밀었다.

Is that a butterfly or a ______?
그것은 나비인가요, 아니면 나방인가요?

We don't sell them by ______.
우리는 그것들을 소매로 팔지 않아요.

______ behavior is hard to forgive.
비도덕적인 행위는 용서받기 어렵다.

In spite of its ______, the animal is extremely fast.
큰 몸집에도 불구하고 그 동물은 굉장히 빠르다.

There is an ______ cigarette burn on the carpet.
양탄자 위에 눈에 띄지 않는 담뱃불 자국이 있다.

After Tony went away, there was a ______ change in her attitude.
토니가 가버리고 난 후 그녀의 태도에 뚜렷한 변화가 있었다.

Soccer is good for ______ when I am depressed.
우울할 때 축구가 기분전환으로 좋다.

She could not resist her ______.
그녀는 자신의 운명을 피할 수 없었다.

When it rains, water ______ down the walls in my house.
비가 오면 물이 우리 집 벽 아래로 뚝뚝 떨어진다.

The First World War broke out because of ______.
제1차 세계대전은 제국주의 때문에 일어났다.

Cut down your ______ spending on clothes.
옷에 드는 총지출을 줄여라.

331 **overhead** [òuvərhéd]
형 머리 위의 부 머리 위에
an overhead walkway 육교

332 **industrious** [indʌ́striəs]
형 부지런한 명 industry 근면, 산업 유 diligent
an industrious student 근면한 학생

333 **influenza** [ìnfluénzə]
명 독감, 유행성 감기
have influenza 유행성 감기에 걸리다

334 **periodic** [pìəriάdik]
형 주기적인, 정기적인 명 period 주기
a periodic wind 계절풍

335 **socialize** [sóuʃəlàiz]
동 사교적으로 만들다, 교제하다 명 society 사회
socialize with friends 친구들과 교제하다

336 **acid** [ǽsid]
명 산성 형 산성의 부 acidly 까다롭게
acid rain 산성비

337 **conference** [kάnfərəns]
명 회담 동 confer 의논하다 유 convention
hold a conference 회담을 열다

338 **exclamation** [èkskləméiʃən]
명 외침, 감탄 동 exclaim 외치다
an exclamation mark 감탄 부호

339 **precision** [prisíʒən]
명 정확 형 정밀한 형 precise 정확한 유 exactness
a precision tool 정밀 공구

340 **agenda** [ədʒéndə]
명 의제, 안건
the next item on the agenda 그 의제의 다음 항목

341 **faithfully** [féiθfəli]
부 충실하게, 굳게 형 faithful 충실한 반 unfaithfully 불성실하게
deal faithfully with ~을 충실하게 다루다

342 **procedure** [prəsí:dʒər]
명 절차 동 proceed 나아가다 유 process
start a procedure 절차를 시작하다

343 **progressive** [prəgrésiv]
형 진보적인, 점진적인 명 progress 진보, 전진 반 traditional 전통적인
make progressive advances 점진적으로 나아가다

344 **propel** [prəpél]
동 추진하다 유 push
propelling power 추진력

345 **suppress** [səprés]
동 진압하다 명 suppression 진압 반 encourage 고무하다
suppress one's laughter 웃음을 억누르다

✦ 주어진 우리말 문장에 맞도록 알맞은 단어를 넣어 문장을 완성하시오. 정답 p.198

Take out the suitcase from the ________ bin.
머리 위 짐칸에서 짐을 꺼내세요.

Eventually an ________ person will be successful.
결국 부지런한 사람이 성공할 것이다.

According to the news, people are getting ________ all over the country.
뉴스에 따르면 전국에 독감이 유행 중이다.

________ checks are required to make sure that they are all right.
그들이 괜찮은지 확실히 하기 위해 정기적인 점검이 요구된다.

I like to ________ with other people.
나는 다른 사람들과 어울리는 것을 좋아한다.

Try not to get wet when the ________ rain falls.
산성비가 내릴 때 젖지 않도록 해라.

He is going to attend a ________ tonight.
그는 오늘 저녁 회담에 참석할 예정이다.

They embraced him with ________ of joy.
그들은 기쁨의 환호성을 지르며 그를 안았다.

There has been ________ bombing in Iraq.
이라크에 정밀 폭격이 있었다.

What's next on the ________?
다음 회의 안건이 뭐죠?

My friend ________ promised not to tell anyone my secret.
내 친구는 어떤 이에게도 내 비밀을 말하지 않겠다고 굳게 약속했다.

Can you explain the ________ to us?
그 절차를 우리에게 설명해 줄 수 있니?

The new president supports ________ education.
새 대통령은 진보적인 교육을 지지한다.

He is a person ________ by ambition.
그는 야망에 의해 일을 추진하는 사람이다.

The uprising cannot be ________ unless more policemen are brought in.
더 많은 경찰력이 출동하지 않는 한 폭동은 진압될 수 없다.

DAY 12

No.	Word	Pronunciation	Meaning	Related	Example
346	**validity**	[vəlídəti]	명 유효성, 타당성	형 valid 유효한 유 legality	the term of validity 유효 기간
347	**creativity**	[krìːeitívəti]	명 창조성	형 creative 창조적인 유 originality	writing with creativity 독창적인 글
348	**frown**	[fraun]	동 눈살을 찌푸리다	명 frowner 눈살을 찌푸리는 사람	frown at someone 누군가에게 눈살을 찌푸리다
349	**maintenance**	[méintənəns]	명 유지, 정비		a maintenance shop 정비 공장
350	**rectangle**	[réktæ̀ŋgl]	명 직사각형		four corners of a rectangle 직사각형의 네 모서리
351	**throng**	[θrɔ(ː)ŋ]	명 군중		a throng of beggars 거지 무리
352	**bail**	[beil]	명 보석(금)		accept bail 보석을 허가하다
353	**democracy**	[dimákrəsi]	명 민주주의	형 democratic 민주주의의	a liberal democracy 자유민주주의
354	**glamorous**	[glǽmərəs]	형 매혹적인, 매력적인	명 glamour 매력	a glamorous job 매력적인 직업
355	**mold**	[mould]	명 틀, 거푸집		a mold of jelly 젤리를 만드는 틀
356	**respectable**	[rispéktəbl]	형 존경할 만한, 훌륭한	명 respectability 존경할 만함 동 respect 존경하다 유 honorable 반 disrespectable 존경할 가치가 없는	a respectable person 존경할 만한 인물
357	**uncared**	[ʌnkɛ́ərd]	형 손질하지 않는		an uncared for hairstyle 손질되지 않은 헤어스타일
358	**bribe**	[braib]	명 뇌물	참 bride 신부	accept a bribe 뇌물을 받다
359	**dishonest**	[disánist]	형 부정직한	명 dishonesty 부정직 반 honest 정직한	a dishonest friend 부정직한 친구
360	**bush**	[buʃ]	명 관목, 덤불		

✦ 주어진 우리말 문장에 맞도록 알맞은 단어를 넣어 문장을 완성하시오. 정답 p.198

You can't use your credit card because the term of ______ has expired.
유효기간이 만료되어 귀하의 신용 카드를 사용하실 수 없습니다.

Being a good designer requires a lot of ______.
훌륭한 디자이너가 되는 것은 많은 창조성을 필요로 한다.

She ______ at me for not doing the work.
그녀는 그 일을 하지 않은 것 때문에 나에게 눈살을 찌푸렸다.

She did none of the ______ on her car.
그녀는 자신의 차를 전혀 정비하지 않았다.

Father folded his newspaper into a ______.
아버지는 신문을 직사각형으로 접으셨다.

A ______ of people have gathered together on the street. Is something going on?
사람이 떼로 거리에 모여 있어. 무슨 일이 있는 거지?

I am sure he will be released on ______.
나는 그가 보석으로 풀려날 것이라 확신한다.

People should obey the principles of ______.
사람들은 민주주의 원칙을 준수해야 한다.

I think you have a ______ job.
나는 네가 매력적인 직업을 가지고 있다고 생각해.

Pour the mixture carefully into the ______.
혼합물을 틀에 조심스럽게 부어라.

It is not ______ to spit on the sidewalk.
인도에 침을 뱉는 것은 올바르지 않은 행동이다.

He is the one with the somewhat ______ for hair.
그는 다소 정돈되지 않은 헤어스타일을 가진 사람이다.

The politician asked me for a ______.
그 정치가는 나에게 뇌물을 요구했다.

If I pretend to dislike him, it will be ______ of me.
만약 내가 그를 좋아하지 않는 척 하면 그것은 정직하지 못한 행동일 것이다.

The snake went into the ______.
그 뱀은 덤불 속으로 들어갔다.

REVIEW TEST 06 DAY 11 ~ DAY 12

A 우리말과 같은 뜻이 되도록 빈칸에 들어갈 알맞은 단어를 적으시오.

1. by ______________ (소매로)
2. a steel ______________ (강철왕)
3. an ______________ walkway (육교)
4. the term of ______________ (유효기간)
5. catch a ______________ (나방을 잡다)
6. an ______________ effect (전반적인 효과)
7. accept a ______________ (뇌물을 받다)
8. ______________ a dry land (마른 땅에 물을 대다)
9. ______________ A for B (A를 B 혐의로 체포하다)
10. deal ______________ with (~을 충실하게 다루다)

B 다음 괄호 안의 지시대로 주어진 단어를 변형시키고 그 뜻을 적으시오.

		변형	뜻
1. tiresome (동사형으로)	→	______________	______________
2. imperialism (형용사형으로)	→	______________	______________
3. periodic (명사형으로)	→	______________	______________
4. acid (부사형으로)	→	______________	______________
5. exclamation (동사형으로)	→	______________	______________
6. faithfully (형용사형으로)	→	______________	______________
7. frown (명사형으로)	→	______________	______________
8. democracy (형용사형으로)	→	______________	______________
9. respectable (동사형으로)	→	______________	______________
10. dishonest (명사형으로)	→	______________	______________

정답 p.198

C 다음 영영풀이에 해당하는 단어를 보기에서 골라 적으시오.

보기				
conservation	reform	irrigate	conference	adapt
influenza	diversion	suppress	arrest	procedure

1. to adjust to different conditions → ______________
2. to seize a person by legal authority or warrant → ______________
3. to form again → ______________
4. the act of diverting from a specified course → ______________
5. a meeting for consultation or discussion → ______________
6. an act or a manner of proceeding in any action or process → ______________
7. to put an end to the activities of a person, body of persons, etc. → ______________
8. the act of conserving; prevention of injury, decay, waste, or loss; preservation → ______________
9. to supply land with water by artificial means, as by diverting streams, flooding, or spraying → ______________
10. an acute, contagious, infectious disease, occurring in several forms, caused by numerous rapidly mutating viral strains → ______________

D 우리말과 같은 뜻이 되도록 주어진 문장의 빈칸을 완성하시오.

1. 그 선원은 조심스럽게 항구 쪽으로 배를 몰고 있다.
   → The sailor is carefully ______________ the ship into the harbor.
2. 물을 많이 마시는 것은 신장이 제 기능을 할 수 있도록 돕는다.
   → Drinking a lot of water helps the ______________ do their jobs.
3. 새 배가 오늘 진수되었다(처음으로 물에 띄어졌다).
   → The new ship was ______________ today.
4. 대부분의 사람들은 비둘기가 평화를 상징한다는 것을 안다.
   → Most people know the dove is ______________ of peace.

5 나는 대저택에서 이틀밤을 묵었다.

→ I spent two nights in the ______________.

6 양탄자 위에 눈에 띄지 않는 담뱃불 자국이 있다.

→ There is an ______________ cigarette burn on the carpet.

7 새 대통령은 진보적 교육을 지지한다.

→ The new president supports ______________ education.

8 그녀는 자신의 차를 전혀 정비하지 않았다.

→ She did none of the ______________ on her car.

9 나는 그가 보석으로 풀려날 것이라 확신한다.

→ I am sure he will be released on ______________.

10 그는 다소 정돈되지 않은 헤어스타일을 가진 사람이다.

→ He is the one with the somewhat ______________ for hair.

E 문장의 밑줄 친 부분에 해당하는 유의어 혹은 반의어를 보기에서 골라 적으시오.

보기				
exactness	diligent	student	continual	praise
ethical	originality	reliant	pushed	fate

1 The rain has been continuous since I woke up this morning.
유의어 = ______________

2 You should treat all the pupils fairly. 유의어 = ______________

3 The director criticized the film. 반의어 ↔ ______________

4 It's good to have a dependable person near you. 유의어 = ______________

5 Unethical behavior is hard to forgive. 반의어 ↔ ______________

6 She could not resist her doom. 유의어 = ______________

7 Eventually an industrious person will be successful. 유의어 = ______________

8 There has been precision bombing in Iraq. 유의어 = ______________

9 He is a person propelled by ambition. 유의어 = ______________

10 Being a good designer requires a lot of creativity. 유의어 = ______________

F 영어발음을 듣고 영어단어를 적은 후, 우리말 뜻을 적으시오.

영어단어
듣고 쓰기

	영어	우리말		영어	우리말
1			8		
2			9		
3			10		
4			11		
5			12		
6			13		
7			14		

G 영어문장을 듣고 빈칸에 들어갈 단어를 채워 문장을 완성하시오.

영어문장
듣고 쓰기

1. An oil ______________ has so much money that he can buy an island.
2. We don't sell them by ______________.
3. When it rains, water ______________ down the walls in my house.
4. Take out the suitcase from the ______________ bin.
5. Father folded his newspaper into a ______________.
6. A ______________ of people have gathered together on the street. Is something going on?
7. Pour the mixture carefully into the ______________.
8. The snake went into the ______________.
9. Children can be ______________ after a long drive.
10. ______________ checks are required to make sure that they are all right.
11. Try not to get wet when the ______________ rain falls.
12. They embraced him with ______________ of joy.
13. She ______________ at me for not doing the work.
14. People should obey the principles of ______________.
15. It is not ______________ to spit on the sidewalk.
16. ______________ with customers is one of my duties.

361	**hound** [haund]	명 사냥개 breed hounds 사냥개를 키우다
362	**hunchback** [hʌ́ntʃbæ̀k]	명 등이 굽은 사람 *The Hunchback of Notre Dame* 노틀담의 꼽추
363	**idle** [áidl]	형 한가한, 놀고 있는 유 unemployed idle workers 일 없는 노동자들
364	**imagination** [imæ̀dʒənéiʃən]	명 상상(력) 동 imagine 상상하다 a rich imagination 풍부한 상상력
365	**originality** [ərìdʒənǽləti]	명 독창성 형 original 독창적인 rich in originality 독창성이 풍부한
366	**shallow** [ʃǽlou]	형 얕은 반 deep a shallow stream 얕은 냇물
367	**overload** 동 [òuvərlóud] 명 [óuvərlòud]	동 (짐을) 너무 많이 싣다 명 과부하 an overloaded bus 사람이 너무 많은 버스
368	**inevitable** [inévətəbl]	형 피할 수 없는, 당연한 명 inevitableness 불가피함 반 avoidable an inevitable conclusion 당연한 결론
369	**perceive** [pərsí:v]	동 알아차리다, 인지하다 명 perception 인식 유 notice perceive by one's face 누군가의 얼굴에서 알아차리다
370	**slot** [slɑt]	명 길쭉한 구멍 동 구멍을 내다 a huge slot 큰 구멍
371	**acceptable** [ækséptəbl]	형 수락할 수 있는 명 acceptability 수락할 수 있음 acceptable behavior 받아들여지는 행동 반 unacceptable 수락할 수 없는
372	**comprehend** [kɑ̀mprihénd]	동 이해하다 명 comprehension 이해 유 understand comprehend other people 다른 사람들을 이해하다
373	**evolution** [èvəlú:ʃən]	명 발전, 진화 the theory of evolution 진화론
374	**intellectual** [ìntəléktʃuəl]	형 지적인 명 intellect 지력 intellectual power 지능
375	**stance** [stæns]	명 자세 take a positive stance 긍정적인 자세를 취하다

✦ 주어진 우리말 문장에 맞도록 알맞은 단어를 넣어 문장을 완성하시오. 정답 p.199

The fox was surrounded by a pack of ＿＿＿＿＿＿＿.
그 여우는 한 무리의 사냥개들에 둘러싸였다.

Children made fun of the ＿＿＿＿＿＿＿, so he was angry.
아이들이 그 등이 굽은 사람을 놀려서 그는 화가 났다.

An old machine remains ＿＿＿＿＿＿＿ in the room.
방 안에 있는 낡은 기계는 여전히 놀고 있다.

You should use your ＿＿＿＿＿＿＿ to come up with a good idea.
좋은 아이디어를 생각해내려면 당신의 상상력을 이용해야 해요.

My sister is rich in ＿＿＿＿＿＿＿.
내 여동생은 독창성이 풍부하다.

Put the milk in a ＿＿＿＿＿＿＿ dish so that the kitten can drink it.
새끼 고양이가 마실 수 있도록 얕은 접시에 우유를 놓아 주세요.

Don't ＿＿＿＿＿＿＿ the electrical system by using too many machines.
너무 많은 기계들을 사용해서 전기 시스템에 과부하를 걸리게 해서는 안 된다.

Is an economic downturn really ＿＿＿＿＿＿＿?
불경기는 정말 피할 수 없는 것인가요?

I ＿＿＿＿＿＿＿ by her face that she had refused his proposal.
나는 표정에서 그녀가 그의 제안을 거절했음을 알아차렸다.

We should put some coins in the ＿＿＿＿＿＿＿ in the vending machine to buy a snack.
스낵을 사려면 자판기에 있는 구멍에 동전을 좀 넣어야 한다.

Children should behave in a socially ＿＿＿＿＿＿＿ way.
아이들은 사회적으로 허용되는 방식으로 행동해야 한다.

It's not easy to ＿＿＿＿＿＿＿ others' minds.
다른 사람들의 마음을 이해하기란 어렵다.

Darwin suggested the theory of the biological ＿＿＿＿＿＿＿ of species.
다윈은 종의 생물학적인 진화론을 제창했다.

Chess is a highly ＿＿＿＿＿＿＿ game.
체스는 매우 지적인 게임이다.

Why don't you take a positive ＿＿＿＿＿＿＿ toward this?
이것에 대해 긍정적인 자세를 취해 보는 것이 어때?

376 **contend** [kənténd]
동 주장하다, 다투다 명 contention 싸움 유 argue

377 **investment** [invéstmənt]
명 투자 동 invest 투자하다
make an investment in ~에 투자하다

378 **striking** [stráikiŋ]
형 파업 중인 명 strike 파업
striking workers 파업 중인 근로자

379 **subsequent** [sʌ́bsikwənt]
형 그 후의 유 following
subsequent events 그 후의 사건들

380 **sufficiently** [səfíʃəntli]
부 충분히 형 sufficient 충분한
sufficiently qualified 충분히 자격이 있는

381 **approval** [əprúːvəl]
명 찬성, 승인 동 approve 찬성하다, 승인하다 유 consent
show one's approval 찬성을 나타내다

382 **arise** [əráiz]
동 일어나다 유 happen
arise from ~에서 기인하다, 발생하다 *arise-arose-arisen*

383 **fraud** [frɔːd]
명 사기 형 fraudulent 속이는 유 deceit 참 deceive 속이다
actual fraud 고의적 사기

384 **lotus** [lóutəs]
명 (식물) 연, 연꽃 무늬
a lotus blossom 연꽃

385 **recall** [rikɔ́ːl]
동 상기하다[시키다] 유 recollect
recall to one's mind ~을 생각해내다

386 **threaten** [θrétn]
동 협박하다, 위협하다 명 threat 협박 유 intimidate
threaten to kill 죽인다고 협박하다

387 **attraction** [ətrǽkʃən]
명 끌어당김, 매력 동 attract 끌다 유 appeal
the attraction of gravity 중력

388 **defensive** [difénsiv]
형 방어적인 동 defend 방어하다 반 offensive
a defensive weapon 방어용 무기

389 **geometry** [dʒiɑ́mətri]
명 기하학 형 geometric 기하학의
plane geometry 평면 기하학

390 **misty** [místi]
형 안개가 짙은 명 mist 안개 유 foggy
a misty land 안개가 자욱한 땅

✦ 주어진 우리말 문장에 맞도록 알맞은 단어를 넣어 문장을 완성하시오. 정답 p.199

He ______ that he is innocent.
그는 자신이 결백하다고 주장한다.

The ______ in education is very important in this country.
교육에 대한 투자는 이 나라에서 매우 중요하다.

The police arrested some ______ workers.
경찰은 몇몇 파업 중인 근로자를 체포했다.

The population increased in ______ years.
그 후에 수년간 인구가 늘어났다.

She is ______ fluent in English.
그녀는 충분히 유창한 영어를 구사한다.

We went to the party with our parents' ______.
우리는 부모님들의 승인 하에 파티에 갔다.

Many questions about him have ______.
그에 대한 많은 질문들이 떠올랐다.

They obtained a huge amount of money through ______.
그들은 사기로 많은 액수의 돈을 얻었다.

My sister likes ______.
내 여동생은 연꽃 무늬들을 좋아한다.

The incident ______ other memories of a bygone age.
그 사건은 지나간 시절의 다른 기억들을 상기시킨다.

He ______ to sue.
그는 고소하겠다고 협박했다.

The tides are caused by the ______ of the Moon to the Earth.
조류는 지구에 대한 달의 인력으로 발생한다.

Can you really say what we need now is to be ______ and not be offensive?
우리에게 지금 필요한 것은 공격적인 게 아니라 방어적인 거라고 확실히 말할 수 있나요?

My uncle is an expert in analytic ______.
나의 삼촌은 해석 기하학의 전문가이다.

The ______ land prevented us from having a clear view.
안개가 자욱한 그 땅은 우리로 하여금 잘 보지 못하게끔 했다.

391	**reptile** [réptil | -tail]	명 파충류 a cold-blooded reptile 냉혈 파충류	
392	**twinkle** [twíŋkl]	동 반짝반짝 빛나다 in a twinkle 눈 깜짝할 동안에	
393	**brass** [bræs]	명 놋쇠, 금관악기 형 금관악기의 as bold as brass 낯가죽이 두꺼운, 아주 뻔뻔스러운	동 braze 놋쇠로 만들다
394	**directive** [diréktiv]	명 지시 형 지시하는 thanks to a new directive 새로운 지시 덕분에	동 direct 지시하다 유 order
395	**hesitate** [hézətèit]	동 주저하다 hesitate to do ~하기를 주저하다	명 hesitation 주저 유 be reluctant
396	**dissatisfy** [dissǽtisfài]	동 불만을 느끼게 하다	명 dissatisfaction 불만족 형 dissatisfactory 불만족스러운
397	**notion** [nóuʃən]	명 개념, 생각 a common notion 통념	유 concept
398	**object** 동 [əbdʒékt] 명 [ábdʒikt | -dʒekt]	동 반대하다 명 물건, 대상, 목적 an object of study 연구 대상	형 objective 목적의, 객관적인
399	**offend** [əfénd]	동 기분을 상하게 하다 offend one's feelings 누군가의 기분을 상하게 하다	형 offensive 공격적인 반 please 기쁘게 하다
400	**orally** [ɔ́:rəli]	부 구두로 test orally 구두로 시험보다	형 oral 구두의
401	**sequence** [sí:kwəns]	명 연속 a sequence of events 일련의 사건들	형 sequent 연속적인 유 continuance
402	**walkabout** [wɔ́:kəbàut]	명 도보여행, (왕실·정치가의) 민정 시찰 go on a walkabout 도보여행을 가다	
403	**overuse** [òuvərjú:z]	동 남용하다 명 남용 overuse drugs 약물을 남용하다	유 abuse
404	**infant** [ínfənt]	명 유아 형 유아의, 초기의 an infant in one's arms 품 안의 아기	명 infancy 유년기, 초기 유 baby
405	**skull** [skʌl]	명 해골 have a thick skull 머리가 둔하다	유 skeleton

✦ 주어진 우리말 문장에 맞도록 알맞은 단어를 넣어 문장을 완성하시오. 정답 p.199

Scientists have long believed that dinosaurs were ______.
과학자들은 오랫동안 공룡이 파충류였다고 믿어왔다.

The stars ______ in the sky.
별들이 밤하늘에 빛났다.

The band has some excellent ______ players.
그 밴드에는 몇몇 실력 있는 금관악기 연주자들이 있다.

Thanks to his ______, the overall profits of the company have increased.
그의 지시 덕분에 회사의 전체 이득이 증가했다.

I ______ to believe what I had heard for a moment.
나는 잠시 동안 내가 들었던 것을 믿는 것을 망설였다.

The test result ______ me.
나에게 그 시험 결과는 불만족스러웠다.

The ______ of native English speakers is quite confusing these days.
요즘 원어민들의 개념은 꽤 이해하기 힘들다.

No one ______ to the plan.
아무도 그 계획에 반대하지 않았다.

My mom was deeply ______ by her coworker.
엄마는 직장 동료 때문에 기분이 매우 상했다.

Taking a test ______ is much harder than taking a written test.
구두로 시험을 보는 것이 필기 시험보다 훨씬 더 어렵다.

The ______ of events was a mystery to everyone.
그 일련의 사건들은 모든 사람들에게 미스터리였다.

The prime minister encountered a group of protesters during his ______ in the suburb. 국무총리는 민정 시찰 중 교외에서 시위자들과 마주쳤다.

Antibiotics are ______ these days.
최근에 항생제가 남용되고 있다.

Tourism was then still in its ______ stage.
관광사업은 그 당시 여전히 초기단계였다.

Isn't it the ______ that I am looking at?
내가 보고 있는 것이 해골 아니지?

DAY 14

406	**absorption** [æbsɔ́ːrpʃən ǀ əb-]	명 흡수, 흡수작용 shock absorption 충격 흡수	동 absorb 흡수하다 유 soaking up
407	**comparison** [kəmpǽrəsn]	명 비교 make a comparison 비교하다	동 compare 비교하다 유 contrast
408	**eternity** [itə́ːrnəti]	명 영원 pursue eternity 영원을 추구하다	형 eternal 영원한 유 immortality
409	**insulation** [ìnsəléiʃən]	명 차단, 절연 insulation material 차단 물질	
410	**pose** [pouz]	명 자세 동 자세를 취하다 pose for a photograph 사진을 찍기 위해 자세를 취하다	유 posture
411	**advertisement** [æ̀dvərtáizmənt]	명 광고	동 advertise 광고하다 유 ad
412	**extinguish** [ikstíŋgwiʃ]	동 진화하다 extinguish a candle 촛불을 끄다	유 put out 참 (fire) extinguisher 소화기
413	**prevention** [privénʃən]	명 예방, 방지 the prevention of juvenile crimes 청소년 범죄 예방	동 prevent 막다
414	**analogy** [ənǽlədʒi]	명 유사, 비슷함 by the analogy with ~와의 유사점에 의해	형 analogous 유사한 유 likeness
415	**anxiety** [æŋzáiəti]	명 걱정	형 anxious 걱정하는 유 concern
416	**applicable** [ǽplikəbl ǀ əplík-]	형 적용할 수 있는, 적절한 an applicable theory 적용할 수 있는 이론	동 apply 적용하다 반 inapplicable 적용할 수 없는
417	**counteract** [kàuntərǽkt]	동 방해하다, 중화하다 counteract a person's plan 어떤 사람의 계획을 훼방놓다	명 counteraction 방해, 중화
418	**craft** [kræft ǀ krɑːft]	명 기술, 재주 the craft of writings 글쓰는 재주	유 skill
419	**location** [loukéiʃən]	명 위치 an exact location 정확한 위치	동 locate 위치시키다, 장소를 알아내다
420	**ratio** [réiʃou ǀ -ʃiòu]	명 비율 a ratio of 2 to 3 2대 3의 비율	

✦ 주어진 우리말 문장에 맞도록 알맞은 단어를 넣어 문장을 완성하시오. 정답 p.199

They are the shoes with greater ______.
그것들은 더 나은 흡수력을 가진 신발이다.

It is hard to make a ______ between him and his brother.
그와 그의 형을 비교하는 것은 어렵다.

Men pursue ______.
사람은 영원을 추구한다.

Birds' feathers work as a form of heat ______.
새의 깃털은 단열 기능을 한다.

"Hold that ______," said the photographer.
"그 자세를 유지하세요."라고 사진사가 말했다.

The wall was covered with ______.
벽이 광고들로 덮여 있었다.

The fire was not ______ soon.
화재는 빨리 진압되지 않았다.

______ is better than a cure.
예방은 치료보다 낫다.

There are many ______ between me and my best friend.
나와 내 친구 사이에는 비슷한 점이 많다.

My mother has a lot of ______.
우리 엄마는 걱정이 굉장히 많으시다.

Discounts are not ______ to new products.
신상품에는 할인이 적용되지 않는다.

Alkalis ______ acids.
알칼리는 산을 중화한다.

There is a close relation between one's linguistic skills and writing ______.
언어 능력과 글쓰기 기술에는 밀접한 관련이 있다.

Tell me the exact ______ of the nearest library, please.
가장 가까이에 있는 도서관의 정확한 위치를 말해 주세요.

The ______ of casualties to survivors was 2 to 3.
사망자와 생존자의 비율은 2대 3이었다.

REVIEW TEST 07 DAY 13 ~ DAY 14

A 우리말과 같은 뜻이 되도록 빈칸에 들어갈 알맞은 단어를 적으시오.

1. a common ______________ (통념)
2. a rich ______________ (풍부한 상상력)
3. in a ______________ (눈 깜짝할 동안에)
4. an ______________ of study (연구 대상)
5. show one's ______________ (찬성을 나타내다)
6. a ______________ of events (연속적인 사건들)
7. an ______________ theory (적용할 수 있는 이론)
8. ______________ from (~에서 기인하다, 발생하다)
9. ______________ other people (다른 사람들을 이해하다)
10. ______________ for a photograph (사진을 찍기 위해 자세를 취하다)

B 다음 괄호 안의 지시대로 주어진 단어를 변형시키고 그 뜻을 적으시오.

		변형	뜻
1	inevitable (명사형으로)	→ ______________	______________
2	comprehend (명사형으로)	→ ______________	______________
3	contend (명사형으로)	→ ______________	______________
4	approval (동사형으로)	→ ______________	______________
5	fraud (형용사형으로)	→ ______________	______________
6	attraction (동사형으로)	→ ______________	______________
7	geometry (형용사형으로)	→ ______________	______________
8	eternity (형용사형으로)	→ ______________	______________
9	analogy (형용사형으로)	→ ______________	______________
10	counteract (명사형으로)	→ ______________	______________

정답 p.199

C 다음 영영풀이에 해당하는 단어를 보기에서 골라 적으시오.

보기				
directive	recall	advertisement	perceive	evolution
location	investment	absorption	overuse	pose

❶ to become aware of, know, or identify by means of the senses → ______________

❷ any process of formation or growth; development → ______________

❸ the act of investing of money to gain profitable returns → ______________

❹ to bring back from memory; recollect; remember → ______________

❺ an authoritative instruction or direction; specific order → ______________

❻ to use too much or too often → ______________

❼ the act of absorbing; the state or process of being absorbed → ______________

❽ to put a particular attitude or stance → ______________

❾ a paid announcement as of goods for sale, in newspapers or magazines, on radio or television, etc. → ______________

❿ a place of settlement, activity, or residence → ______________

D 우리말과 같은 뜻이 되도록 주어진 문장의 빈칸을 완성하시오.

❶ 그 여우는 한 무리의 사냥개들에게 둘러싸였다.
→ The fox was surrounded by a pack of ______________ .

❷ 체스는 매우 지적인 게임이다.
→ Chess is a highly ______________ game.

❸ 경찰은 몇몇 파업 중인 근로자를 체포했다.
→ The police arrested some ______________ workers.

❹ 그녀는 충분히 유창한 영어를 구사한다.
→ She is ______________ fluent in English.

❺ 별들이 밤하늘에 빛났다. → The stars ______________ in the sky.

⑥ 나는 잠시 동안 내가 들었던 것을 믿는 것을 망설였다.

→ I ________________ to believe what I had heard for a moment.

⑦ 구두로 시험을 보는 것이 필기 시험보다 훨씬 더 어렵다.

→ Taking a test ________________ is much harder than taking a written test.

⑧ 내가 보고 있는 것이 해골 아니지?

→ Isn't it the ________________ that I am looking at?

⑨ 우리 엄마는 걱정이 굉장히 많으시다.

→ My mother has a lot of ________________.

⑩ 사망자와 생존자의 비율은 2대 3이었다.

→ The ________________ of casualties to survivors was 2 to 3.

E 문장의 밑줄 친 부분에 해당하는 유의어 혹은 반의어를 보기에서 골라 적으시오.

보기				
following	satisfy	unemployed	contrast	intimidate
put out	deep	upset	baby	foggy

① An old machine remains idle in the room. 유의어 = ________________

② Put the milk in a shallow dish so that the kitten can drink it.
반의어 ↔ ________________

③ The population increased in subsequent years. 유의어 = ________________

④ He threatened to sue. 유의어 = ________________

⑤ The misty land prevented us from having a clear view. 유의어 = ________________

⑥ The test result dissatisfied me. 반의어 ↔ ________________

⑦ My mom was deeply offended by her coworker. 유의어 = ________________

⑧ Tourism was then still in its infant stage. 유의어 = ________________

⑨ It is hard to make a comparison between him and his brother.
유의어 = ________________

⑩ The fire was not extinguished soon. 유의어 = ________________

F 영어발음을 듣고 영어단어를 적은 후, 우리말 뜻을 적으시오.

영어단어
듣고 쓰기

	영어	우리말		영어	우리말
❶	______	______	❽	______	______
❷	______	______	❾	______	______
❸	______	______	❿	______	______
❹	______	______	⓫	______	______
❺	______	______	⓬	______	______
❻	______	______	⓭	______	______
❼	______	______	⓮	______	______

G 영어문장을 듣고 빈칸에 들어갈 단어를 채워 문장을 완성하시오.

영어문장
듣고 쓰기

❶ Children made fun of the ______, so he was angry.

❷ Don't ______ the electrical system by using too many machines.

❸ My sister likes ______.

❹ Scientists have long believed that dinosaurs were ______.

❺ The ______ of events was a mystery to everyone.

❻ The prime minister encountered a group of protesters during his ______ in the suburb.

❼ Birds' feathers work as a form of heat ______.

❽ Is an economic downturn really ______?

❾ He ______ that he is innocent.

❿ We went to the party with our parents' ______.

⓫ They obtained a huge amount of money through ______.

⓬ The tides are caused by the ______ of the Moon to the Earth.

⓭ My uncle is an expert in analytic ______.

⓮ There are many ______ between me and my best friend.

⓯ Alkalis ______ acids.

⓰ You should use your ______ to come up with a good idea.

DAY 15

DAY 15 표제어 듣기

421 **thermometer** [θərmámətər]
명 온도계
a centigrade thermometer 섭씨 온도계

422 **atomic** [ətámik]
형 원자의 명 atom 원자
an atomic bomb 원자폭탄

423 **decibel** [désəbèl | -bəl]
명 데시벨
reach 70 decibels 70 데시벨에 이르다

424 **genre** [ʒɑ́:nrə]
명 장르 유 type
a favorite genre 가장 좋아하는 장르

425 **migrate** [máigreit]
동 이주하다 명 migration 이주 유 move
migrate from A to B A에서 B로 이주하다

426 **reportedly** [ripɔ́:rtidli]
부 보도에 의하면 명 report 보고

427 **triumph** [tráiəmf]
명 승리 형 triumphant 성공한, 의기양양한 유 victory
a shout of triumph 승리의 함성

428 **bounce** [bauns]
동 튀다 명 튀어오름 유 bound
bounce back 다시 회복하다

429 **dignity** [dígnəti]
명 존엄 동 dignify 위엄 있게 하다
a man of dignity 위엄 있는 사람

430 **hardship** [hɑ́:rdʃip]
명 고충, 곤란 형 hard 어려운, 힘든
live through various hardships 갖은 고충을 겪고 살다

431 **navigation** [nævəgéiʃən]
명 항해, 항공 형 navigational 항해의
aerial navigation 항공술

432 **hoe** [hou]
명 괭이

433 **scarce** [skεərs]
형 부족한, 드문 부 scarcely 거의 ~ 아니다 유 rare
scarce natural resources 부족한 천연자원

434 **scrap** [skræp]
명 조각
scrap paper 메모 용지

435 **secure** [sikjúər]
형 안전한 명 security 안전 유 safe
be secure against ~에 대해 안전하다

✦ 주어진 우리말 문장에 맞도록 알맞은 단어를 넣어 문장을 완성하시오. 정답 p.200

A ______ is a device that measures temperature.
온도계는 온도를 재는 장치이다.

Japan surrendered after the dropping of the ______ bombs.
일본은 원자폭탄 투하 후 항복했다.

Some snores reached 75 ______.
어떤 코골이 소리는 75 데시벨까지 이르렀다.

What is your favorite ______?
가장 좋아하는 장르가 뭐예요?

Birds ______ south to look for food in the winter.
새들은 겨울에 먹이를 찾아 남쪽으로 이동한다.

She has ______ agreed to release the hostage.
보도에 의하면 그녀는 인질을 풀어 주기로 합의했다.

The successful operation was a ______ of modern medicine.
그 성공적인 수술은 근대 의학의 승리였다.

He ______ the ball back to me.
그는 나에게 공을 다시 튀어 보냈다.

Although she is very poor, she has not lost her ______.
그녀는 가난하지만 위엄을 잃지는 않았다.

She had to undergo many ______ in her life.
그녀는 삶에서 많은 고충을 겪어야만 했다.

The company will hire an expert in ______ this week.
그 회사는 이번 주에 항해 전문가를 고용할 것이다.

The farmer forgot to bring a ______ with him.
그 농부는 괭이를 가지고 와야 하는 것을 잊어버렸다.

______ water resources are shared among countries in Africa.
아프리카의 여러 나라가 부족한 물 자원을 공유한다.

Put the ______ of paper in the wastebasket.
종이조각들을 쓰레기통에 넣어라.

Staying here, we will be ______ against the animals.
우리가 여기 머무르면 동물들로부터는 안전할 거에요.

DAY 15

436	**semiconductor** [sèmikəndʌ́ktər]	명 반도체 an electronic semiconductor 전자 반도체	
437	**vocalist** [vóukəlist]	명 보컬리스트, 가수	형 vocal 목소리의 유 singer
438	**chunk** [tʃʌŋk]	명 상당한 양	
439	**painful** [péinfəl]	형 아픈, 힘드는 a painful result 아픈 결과	명 pain 고통
440	**infection** [infékʃən]	명 감염 by infection 감염에 의해	유 contamination
441	**abolish** [əbáliʃ]	동 폐지하다 abolish slavery 노예제도를 없애다	반 establish 설립하다
442	**commitment** [kəmítmənt]	명 헌신 make a commitment 헌신하다	동 commit 전념하다, 헌신하다 유 dedication
443	**erect** [irékt]	동 세우다 형 똑바로 선 erect a monument 기념비를 세우다	명 erection 건립 유 build
444	**inspection** [inspékʃən]	명 정밀검사 a medical inspection 건강진단	동 inspect 점검하다 유 examination
445	**pollution** [pəlú:ʃən]	명 오염 air pollution 대기오염	동 pollute 오염시키다 유 contamination
446	**squid** [skwid]	명 오징어 dried squid 마른 오징어	
447	**constructive** [kənstrʌ́ktiv]	형 건설적인, 구조적인 constructive criticism 건설적 비판	동 construct 건설하다 반 destructive 파괴적인
448	**interval** [íntərvəl]	명 간격, 중간 휴식 시간 after a long interval 오랜 휴식 뒤에	
449	**stimulus** [stímjuləs]	명 자극 under the stimulus of ~의 자극을 받아	동 stimulate 자극하다 유 stimulant
450	**conviction** [kənvíkʃən]	명 유죄 판결 a summary conviction 즉결 재판	동 convict 유죄를 입증하다 유 sentence

1회독 월 일
2회독 월 일

✦ 주어진 우리말 문장에 맞도록 알맞은 단어를 넣어 문장을 완성하시오. 정답 p.200

Devices containing ______ are used in the factory.
반도체를 포함한 장비들이 그 공장에 사용된다.

The band's ______ retired.
그 밴드의 보컬리스트가 은퇴했다.

A large ______ of information has been saved on his computer.
상당한 양의 정보가 그의 컴퓨터 안에 저장되었다.

The shocking result was very ______ to all of us.
그 충격적인 결과는 우리 모두에게 매우 힘든 것이었다.

Antibiotics should be used to prevent ______.
감염을 막기 위해 항생물질을 사용해야 한다.

Lincoln ______ slavery because he thought it was wrong.
링컨은 노예제도가 잘못된 것이라고 생각했기 때문에 그것을 폐지했다.

I know it is a lifetime ______.
나는 그것이 평생 헌신해야 하는 일임을 알고 있다.

The church was ______ in 1689 and was destroyed last year.
그 교회는 1689년에 세워졌고 작년에 무너졌다.

Undergo regular medical ______ to make sure you are healthy.
건강한지 확인하려면 정기적으로 건강진단을 받아라.

The air ______ in big cities is exceeding acceptable levels.
대도시에서의 대기오염은 허용범위를 넘어서고 있다.

Today, I want to eat some sliced fried ______.
오늘은 얇게 썬 오징어포가 먹고 싶다.

He put forward a ______ suggestion.
그는 건설적인 안을 제안했다.

We'll have a ten-minute ______.
십 분간 휴식을 하도록 하겠습니다.

The teacher's sermon provided the students with a ______ to study hard.
그 선생님의 설교는 학생들에게 열심히 공부하도록 자극을 주었다.

They have two previous ______ for robbery.
그들은 강도를 저지른 두 번의 전과가 있다.

DAY 16

DAY 16 표제어 듣기

451 **corporate** [kɔ́ːrpərət]
형 법인의 명 corporation 법인
corporate property 법인 재산

452 **corruption** [kərʌ́pʃən]
명 부패, 타락 형 corrupt 부패한
political corruption 정치적 부패

453 **flourish** [flə́ːriʃ]
동 번창하다 유 thrive
a flourishing business 잘나가는 사업

454 **foremost** [fɔ́ːrmòust]
형 맨 앞의, 첫 번째의 유 leading, primary
first and foremost 맨 먼저

455 **rage** [reidʒ]
명 분노 동 격노하다 유 anger
with rage 격노하여

456 **tender** [téndər]
형 부드러운 명 tenderness 부드러움 유 soft
tender meat 부드러운 고기

457 **association** [əsòusiéiʃən]
명 단체, 협회 동 associate 관련시키다 유 group
a soccer association 축구협회

458 **dare** [dεər]
동 감히 ~ 하다
I dare say (that)+절 감히 말하건대 ~일 것이다

459 **gaze** [geiz]
동 응시하다 유 stare
gaze in the face 얼굴을 응시하다

460 **mentally** [méntəli]
부 정신적으로 형 mental 정신적인
be mentally strong 정신적으로 강하다

461 **remark** [rimáːrk]
동 말하다 명 논평 형 remarkable 주목할 만한 유 comment
remark on ~에 대해 논평하다

462 **transplant** [trænsplǽnt]
동 이식하다 명 transplantation 이식
transplant organs 기관들을 이식하다

463 **blister** [blístər]
명 물집 형 blistery 물집이 있는
get a blister 물집이 생기다

464 **détente** [deitɑ́ːnt | détɑnt]
명 국제간 긴장 완화, 데탕트
a policy of détente 긴장 완화 정책

465 **guilty** [gílti]
형 유죄의 명 guilt 유죄 반 innocent 결백한
be found guilty 유죄로 판결되다

✦ 주어진 우리말 문장에 맞도록 알맞은 단어를 넣어 문장을 완성하시오. 정답 p.200

This land was once ______ property.
이 땅은 한때 법인 재산이었다.

He was charged with ______.
그는 부정부패 혐의로 기소되었다.

This type of plants ______ in hot countries.
이런 종류의 식물은 열대 지역에서 잘 자란다.

Miss Park is the ______ expert in this field.
박씨는 이 분야에서 첫째가는 전문가이다.

My father yelled at my brother with ______.
아빠는 화가 나서 형에게 소리질렀다.

Some people are fond of ______ meat.
어떤 사람들은 부드러운 고기를 좋아한다.

He is a member of the ______.
그는 그 단체의 회원이다.

They didn't ______ to look at each other.
그들은 감히 서로를 마주보지 않았다.

The child ______ at the toys in the shop window.
아이는 가게 창문 너머의 장난감들을 뚫어지게 보았다.

His daughter is a ______ strong child.
그의 딸은 정신적으로 강한 아이이다.

Most people ______ on the movie in a negative way.
대부분의 사람들은 부정적으로 그 영화에 대해 논평했다.

The doctor ______ some organs.
의사는 몇 개의 장기들을 이식했다.

I got a ______ on my finger.
손가락에 물집이 생겼다.

The president pursued a policy of ______.
대통령은 국제간의 긴장 완화 정책을 추구했다.

He confessed that he was ______.
그는 스스로 유죄임을 자백했다.

DAY 16

466 **narrative** [nǽrətiv]
명 이야기 | 명 narration 서술, 담화
a personal narrative 개인적 이야기

467 **ridge** [ridʒ]
명 융기, 마루 | 형 ridgy 융기한
the ridge of the nose 콧등

468 **neighborhood** [néibərhùd]
명 이웃, 동네 형 근처의 | 유 neighbor

469 **utter** [ʌ́tər]
형 전적의, 완전한 | 부 utterly 완전히 유 absolute
an utter stranger 생판 모르는 남

470 **varnish** [vɑ́ːrniʃ]
동 니스를 칠하다 명 니스
varnish a table 테이블에 니스를 칠하다

471 **veteran** [vétərən]
형 노련한 명 베테랑, 전문가 | 반 novice 초심자
a veteran skater 노련한 스케이트 선수

472 **virtue** [vә́ːrtʃuː]
명 덕, 미덕 | 형 virtuous 미덕의 반 vice 악
the virtue of humility 겸양의 미덕

473 **chamber** [tʃéimbər]
명 방, 회의실 | 유 room
an audience chamber 접견실

474 **elevation** [èləvéiʃən]
명 높이 | 동 elevate 올리다 유 altitude
to an elevation of ~의 높이까지

475 **sheriff** [ʃérif]
명 보안관
a strict sheriff 엄격한 보안관

476 **inferior** [infíəriər]
형 하위의, 열등한 | 명 inferiority 열등 반 superior 우위의
inferior to ~보다 열등한

477 **combat** 동 [kəmbǽt] 명 [kɑ́mbæt]
동 싸우다 명 전투 | 명 combatant 전투원 유 fight
combat for freedom 자유를 얻기 위해 싸우다

478 **envelope** [énvəlòup]
명 봉투
The envelope was sealed. 봉투는 봉해져 있었다.

479 **innovate** [ínəvèit]
동 혁신하다 | 형 innovative 혁신적인
innovate new ideas 생각을 새롭게 바꿔 하다

480 **poetry** [póuitri]
명 시집 | 형 poetic 시적인

✦ 주어진 우리말 문장에 맞도록 알맞은 단어를 넣어 문장을 완성하시오. 정답 p.200

I like the ______ of the book.
나는 그 책의 이야기를 좋아한다.

The high ______ of a wave stopped people from swimming.
파도의 높은 물마루는 사람들이 수영을 못하게 했다.

This is a friendly ______.
이곳은 친절한 동네이다.

This is ______ nonsense.
이건 완전히 말도 안돼.

I sanded the desk and ______ it.
나는 책상을 사포로 닦고 니스 칠을 했다.

Minsu's father is a ______ golfer.
민수의 아버지는 노련한 골프 선수이다.

Patience is a ______ that she wants to have.
인내심은 그녀가 갖고 싶어하는 미덕이다.

They hid in a vast underground ______ to run away from the owner.
그들은 주인으로부터 도망치기 위해 큰 지하 방에 숨었다.

The smoke went up to the same ______ as the mountaintop.
연기가 산꼭대기 높이까지 올라갔다.

He was elected ______ of the town last month.
그는 지난달 그 마을의 보안관으로 선출되었다.

The functions of this machine are ______ to those of that one.
이 기계의 기능들은 저 기계의 기능들보다 떨어진다.

______ between good and evil will continue forever.
선과 악의 전쟁은 영원히 계속될 것이다.

After she opened the ______, she began to laugh.
봉투를 열어본 후, 그녀는 웃기 시작했다.

The student are not afraid to ______.
그 학생들은 혁신하는 것을 두려워하지 않는다.

I bought a book of ______ at a bookstore.
나는 서점에서 시집을 샀다.

REVIEW TEST 08 DAY 15 ~ DAY 16

A 우리말과 같은 뜻이 되도록 빈칸에 들어갈 알맞은 단어를 적으시오.

❶ air ________________ (대기오염)

❷ dried ________________ (마른 오징어)

❸ make a ________________ (헌신하다)

❹ get a ________________ (물집이 생기다)

❺ ________________ criticism (건설적인 비판)

❻ be ________________ against (~로부터 안전하다)

❼ a ________________ skater (노련한 스케이트 선수)

❽ an electronic ________________ (전자 반도체)

❾ ________________ from A to B (A에서 B로 이주하다)

❿ ________________ natural resources (부족한 천연자원)

B 다음 괄호 안의 지시대로 주어진 단어를 변형시키고 그 뜻을 적으시오.

		변형	뜻
❶ migrate (명사형으로)	➔		
❷ reportedly (명사형으로)	➔		
❸ hardship (형용사형으로)	➔		
❹ scarce (부사형으로)	➔		
❺ pollution (동사형으로)	➔		
❻ stimulus (동사형으로)	➔		
❼ conviction (동사형으로)	➔		
❽ transplant (명사형으로)	➔		
❾ elevation (동사형으로)	➔		
❿ innovate (형용사형으로)	➔		

정답 p.200

C 다음 영영풀이에 해당하는 단어를 보기에서 골라 적으시오.

보기					
	narrative	infection	secure	envelope	inspection
	navigation	neighborhood	foremost	dignity	association

1. the act or process of navigating; sailing → ______________
2. first in place, order, rank, etc. → ______________
3. nobility or elevation of character; worthiness → ______________
4. free from or not exposed to danger or harm; safe → ______________
5. the act or process of infection; state of being infected → ______________
6. the act of inspecting or viewing, especially carefully or critically → ______________
7. the area or region around or near some place or thing; vicinity → ______________
8. a flat paper container, as for a letter or thin package, usually having a gummed flap or other means of closure → ______________
9. an organization of people with a common purpose and having a formal structure → ______________
10. a story or account of events, experiences, or the like, whether true or fictitious → ______________

D 우리말과 같은 뜻이 되도록 주어진 문장의 빈칸을 완성하시오.

1. 가장 좋아하는 장르가 뭐예요?
   → What is your favorite ______________?
2. 그 밴드의 보컬리스트가 은퇴했다.
   → The band's ______________ retired.
3. 링컨은 노예제도가 잘못된 것이라고 생각했기 때문에 그것을 폐지했다.
   → Lincoln ______________ slavery because he thought it was wrong.
4. 십 분간 휴식을 하도록 하겠습니다.
   → We'll have a ten-minute ______________.

5. 이 땅은 한때 법인 재산이었다. ➔ This land was once ______________ property.

6. 그의 딸은 정신적으로 강한 아이다. ➔ His daughter is a ______________ strong child.

7. 대통령은 국제간의 긴장 완화 정책을 추구했다.
➔ The president pursued a policy of ______________.

8. 나는 책상을 사포로 닦고 니스 칠을 했다. ➔ I sanded the desk and ______________ it.

9. 그들은 주인으로부터 도망치기 위해 큰 지하 방에 숨었다.
➔ They hid in a vast underground ______________ to run away from the owner.

10. 나는 서점에서 시집을 샀다. ➔ I bought a book of ______________ at a bookstore.

E 문장의 밑줄 친 부분에 해당하는 유의어 혹은 반의어를 보기에서 골라 적으시오.

보기				
superior	soft	stare	thrive	victory
destructive	innocent	absolute	dedication	built

1. The successful operation was a triumph of modern medicine.
유의어 = ______________

2. I know it is a lifetime commitment. 유의어 = ______________

3. The church was erected in 1689 and was destroyed last year.
유의어 = ______________

4. He put forward a constructive suggestion. 반의어 ↔ ______________

5. This type of plants flourishes in hot countries. 유의어 = ______________

6. Some people are fond of tender meat. 유의어 = ______________

7. The child gazed at the toys in the shop window. 유의어 = ______________

8. He confessed that he was guilty. 반의어 ↔ ______________

9. This is utter nonsense. 유의어 = ______________

10. The functions of this machine are inferior to those of that one.
반의어 ↔ ______________

F 영어발음을 듣고 영어단어를 적은 후, 우리말 뜻을 적으시오.

	영어	우리말		영어	우리말
❶			❽		
❷			❾		
❸			❿		
❹			⓫		
❺			⓬		
❻			⓭		
❼			⓮		

G 영어문장을 듣고 빈칸에 들어갈 단어를 채워 문장을 완성하시오.

영어문장
듣고 쓰기

❶ A ______________ is a device that measures temperature.

❷ The farmer forgot to bring a ______________ with him.

❸ Devices containing ______________ are used in the factory.

❹ A large ______________ of information has been saved on his computer.

❺ Today, I want to eat some sliced fried ______________.

❻ The high ______________ of a wave stopped people from swimming.

❼ He was elected ______________ of the town last month.

❽ Birds ______________ south to look for food in the winter.

❾ She had to undergo many ______________ in her life.

❿ ______________ water resources are shared among countries in Africa.

⓫ The air ______________ in big cities is exceeding acceptable levels.

⓬ The teacher's sermon provided the students with a ______________ to study hard.

⓭ They have two previous ______________ for robbery.

⓮ The doctor ______________ some organs.

⓯ The student made an ______________ design, so he was rewarded.

⓰ He ______________ the ball back to me.

DAY 17

DAY 17 표제어 듣기

481 **splinter** [splíntər]
명 부서진 조각 유 fragment
smashed into splinters 산산조각이 난

482 **adoration** [ædəréiʃən]
명 동경, 찬양 동 adore 동경하다, 찬양하다 유 praise
in adoration 몹시 좋아하며, 예찬하여

483 **expose** [ikspóuz]
동 드러내다, 폭로하다 명 exposure 폭로, exposition 박람회 유 uncover
expose a secret 비밀을 폭로하다

484 **presence** [prézns]
명 존재, 출석 반 absence
Your presence is requested. 귀하의 출석이 요구됩니다.

485 **amber** [ǽmbər]
명 황갈색, 호박색
an amber button 호박색의 버튼

486 **fare** [fɛər]
명 요금 유 price
a single fare 편도 운임

487 **feast** [fí:st]
명 축하연 형 festal 축제의
a wedding feast 결혼 피로연

488 **finite** [fáinait]
형 한정된 반 infinite 무한한
finite resources 한정된 자원

489 **legal** [lí:gəl]
형 법률의 반 illegal 불법의
a legal defense 정당방위

490 **lineup** [láinʌ̀p]
명 정렬, 사람의 줄
a long lineup of people 길게 늘어선 사람의 줄

491 **technological** [tèknəlɑ́dʒikəl]
형 기술적인 명 technology 과학 기술
a technological innovation 기술 혁신

492 **assessment** [əsésmənt]
명 평가 동 assess 평가하다 유 evaluation
a detailed assessment 자세한 평가

493 **curator** [kjuəréitər]
명 전시 책임자

494 **fusion** [fjú:ʒən]
명 융합, 용해 동 fuse 융합하다 유 dissolve
nuclear fusion 핵 융합

495 **medication** [mèdəkéiʃən]
명 약물 (치료) 유 medicine
be on medication 약물 치료를 받고 있다

✦ 주어진 우리말 문장에 맞도록 알맞은 단어를 넣어 문장을 완성하시오. 정답 p.201

He avoided the ______ of glass.
그는 유리조각들을 피했다.

He read Browning's poems in ______.
그는 브라우닝의 시를 예찬하며 읽었다.

Don't ______ the film to light.
필름을 빛에 노출시키지 마라.

Do you believe in the ______ of spirits?
유령의 존재를 믿나요?

______ is used when we describe something which is yellowish-brown.
호박색은 우리가 황갈색의 무언가를 묘사할 때 쓰인다.

Children can enter the museum to see the paintings at half ______.
아이들은 반 값에 그림을 보러 박물관에 입장할 수 있다.

The wedding ______ was held after the ceremony.
결혼식 후에 결혼 피로연이 열렸다.

The physical universe is ______ in time and space.
물리적 우주는 시공간적으로 한정적이다.

When you drive, you must not exceed the ______ limit.
운전할 때는 법정제한 속도를 넘어서는 안 된다.

There is a long ______ of people in the store.
가게에 사람들이 길게 줄을 서 있다.

The company has hired many experts to achieve its ______ innovations.
그 회사는 기술 혁신을 달성하기 위해 많은 전문가들을 고용해 왔다.

The ______ of the situation should be accurate.
그 상황에 대한 평가는 정확해야 한다.

The ______ patrols the museum every day.
그 전시 책임자는 박물관을 매일 순찰한다.

His ______ of jazz and hip-hop was very successful.
그가 한 재즈와 힙합의 융합은 매우 성공적이었다.

It is better to sleep naturally without taking any ______.
어떤 약도 먹지 않고 그냥 자는 것이 더 낫다.

496	**relaxation** [rìːlækséiʃən]	명 휴식, 이완 watch TV for relaxation 휴식을 위해 TV를 보다	동 relax 쉬다 유 leisure, entertainment
497	**tragedy** [trǽdʒədi]	명 비극 a tragedy of war 전쟁의 비극	형 tragic 비극적인 반 fortune 행운
498	**biological** [bàiəládʒikəl]	형 생물학적인 a biological child 친자	명 biology 생물학
499	**despair** [dispɛ́ər]	명 절망 live in despair 절망하며 살다	형 desperate 절망적인 반 hope 희망
500	**grief** [griːf]	명 슬픔 come to grief 불행에 빠지다	동 grieve 슬프게 하다 유 sorrow
501	**nag** [næg]	동 잔소리하다 nag one's husband to death 바가지를 긁어 남편을 못살게 굴다	형 nagging 잔소리가 심한
502	**revolutionary** [rèvəlúːʃənèri]	형 혁명의 a revolutionary discovery 혁명적 발견	명 revolution 혁명
503	**universal** [jùːnəvə́ːrsəl]	형 보편적인 universal superstitions 널리 퍼져 있는 미신	부 universally 보편적으로 유 general
504	**sacred** [séikrid]	형 신성한 a sacred place 신성한 장소	명 sacredness 신성함 유 holy
505	**capable** [kéipəbl]	형 유능한 a capable salesperson 유능한 판매원	명 capability 능력 유 able
506	**cardiac** [káːrdiæ̀k]	형 심장의 cardiac surgery 심장외과	
507	**catalog(ue)** [kǽtəlɔ̀ːg]	명 목록 a library catalogue 도서 목록	유 list
508	**caution** [kɔ́ːʃən]	명 조심 use caution 조심하다	유 care
509	**effortlessly** [éfərtlisli]	부 쉽게 do effortlessly 쉽게 하다	형 effortless 쉬운
510	**inactivity** [ìnæktívəti]	명 비활동, 부진 be inactive 활동하지 않다	형 inactive 활동하지 않는 반 activity 활동

✦ 주어진 우리말 문장에 맞도록 알맞은 단어를 넣어 문장을 완성하시오. 정답 p.201

Let's just do something for ________.
휴식을 위해 무언가 하자.

It's a ________ that her mother died in a car accident.
비극적이게도 그녀의 어머니는 자동차 사고로 돌아가셨다.

Orphans don't know their ________ parents.
고아들은 그들의 친부모를 모른다.

The man who lost his family lived in ________.
가족을 잃은 그 남자는 절망하며 살았다.

Her voice was husky with ________.
슬픔에 젖어 그녀는 목이 쉬었다.

She ________ at him all day long.
그녀는 온종일 그에게 잔소리를 했다.

The creation of the Internet has brought us many ________ changes.
인터넷의 발명은 우리에게 많은 혁명적 변화를 가져다 주었다.

Those symptoms are ________ features of a cold.
그 증상은 감기의 보편적인 특징들이다.

They consider the temple to be a ________ place.
그들은 그 사원을 신성한 장소로 여긴다.

The company needs a ________ salesperson.
그 회사는 유능한 판매원을 필요로 한다.

He was a ________ surgeon.
그는 심장외과 의사였다.

Can you show us your ________?
우리에게 목록을 좀 보여 주실 수 있나요?

When crossing the street, you should use ________.
길을 건널 땐 조심해야 해요.

It seems that he plays the guitar ________.
그는 기타를 쉽게 연주하는 것 같다.

The ________ of the government was unacceptable.
정부의 부진함은 받아들이기 어렵다.

DAY 18

511 **shift** [ʃift]
동 위치를 바꾸다, 이동하다 유 move
shift from one place to another 장소를 이리저리 옮기다

512 **spend** [spend]
동 (돈을) 쓰다, 소비하다
spend money on ~에 돈을 쓰다

513 **enormous** [inɔ́ːrməs]
형 거대한 유 huge
an enormous expense 막대한 비용

514 **inhabitant** [inhǽbətənt]
명 주민 유 occupant
the inhabitants of the village 마을 주민

515 **pitiful** [pítifəl]
형 불쌍한, 측은한 부 pitifully 불쌍하게
look pitiful 안쓰러워 보이다

516 **specialize** [spéʃəlàiz]
동 전공하다, 전문으로 하다 형 special 특별한 유 major
specialize in a field 어떤 분야를 전공하다

517 **adequate** [ǽdikwət]
형 알맞은 명 adequacy 적절 유 suitable

518 **considerate** [kənsídərət]
형 인정 많은, 사려 깊은 참 considerable 중요한, 꽤 많은
a considerate person 인정 많은 사람

519 **intermediate** [ìntərmíːdiət]
형 중간의 동 중재하다 유 middle
an intermediate level 중급

520 **sticky** [stíki]
형 끈적거리는 동 stick 붙다 참 stick 막대기
The paper is sticky. 그 종이는 끈적거린다.

521 **contract** 동 [kəntrǽkt] 명 [kántrækt]
동 계약하다 명 계약(서) 유 agreement
a verbal contract 구두 계약

522 **irritate** [írətèit]
동 짜증나게 하다 형 irritating 짜증나게 하는, irritated 짜증이 난 유 ann
be irritated by ~ 때문에 화나다

523 **knit** [nit]
동 뜨다, 짜다
knit ~ together ~을 접합시키다 *knit-knit[knitted]-knit[knitted]*

524 **laundry** [lɔ́ːndri]
명 빨래
a laundry basket 빨래 바구니

525 **purify** [pjúərəfài]
동 정화하다, 정제하다 명 purification 정화 형 pure 순수한
purify the air 공기를 정화하다

✦ 주어진 우리말 문장에 맞도록 알맞은 단어를 넣어 문장을 완성하시오. 정답 p.201

She ______ about for many years.
그녀는 여러 해 동안 여기저기 옮겨 다녔다.

I ______ $500 on buying new computer games.
나는 새 컴퓨터 게임을 사는 데 500달러를 썼다.

This fire caused ______ damage.
이번 화재는 막대한 피해를 일으켰다.

All the ______ of the village are occupied with agriculture.
그 마을의 모든 주민들은 농업에 종사하고 있다.

The injured bird looked ______ with its broken wing.
다친 새는 부러진 날개로 인해 안쓰러워 보였다.

She ______ in a field of science.
그녀는 과학 분야를 전공한다.

This food is ______ for those patients.
이 음식은 저 환자들에게 적합하다.

Please be ______ to others.
다른 사람들을 생각해 주시기 바랍니다.

I'm taking an ______ level English course.
나는 중급 영어 수업을 듣고 있다.

First, make this paper very ______.
먼저 이 종이를 매우 끈적거리게 만들어라.

We will exchange some gifts after we sign the ______.
우리는 계약서에 사인하고 나서 약간의 선물을 교환할 거예요.

He was really ______ by his younger brother.
그는 자신의 남동생 때문에 정말 화가 났다.

My mother ______ the two torn parts together.
우리 엄마는 찢어진 두 부분을 접합시켰다.

I sorted the ______.
나는 빨래를 분류했다.

This salt has been ______ for use in medicine.
이 소금은 약으로 사용하기 위해 정제되었다.

DAY 18

526	**queasy** [kwí:zi]	형 메스꺼운, 역겨운 feel queasy 메스꺼워지다	명 queasiness 멀미, 메스꺼움
527	**arrogant** [ǽrəgənt]	형 거만한 too arrogant 너무 거만한	명 arrogance 거만함
528	**crook** [kruk]	동 구부리다 명 굽은 것 crook one's neck 목을 굽히다	유 bend
529	**functional** [fʌ́ŋkʃənl]	형 기능의 functional characteristics 기능적 특징	명 function 기능
530	**massive** [mǽsiv]	형 육중한, 엄청난 a massive pillar 육중한 기둥	유 enormous
531	**refresh** [rifréʃ]	동 상쾌하게 하다 refresh oneself 기분 전환을 하다	명 refreshment 원기 회복
532	**tolerable** [tálərəbl]	형 참을 수 있는 be no longer tolerable 더 이상 참을 수 없다	동 tolerate 참아내다 유 bearable
533	**behalf** [bihǽf]	명 편, 측, 이익 on behalf of ~을 대신하여	
534	**dependent** [dipéndənt]	형 의존하고 있는 dependent on ~에 의존하는	동 depend 의존하다 반 independent 독립의
535	**glow** [glou]	동 빛나다 glow in the dark 어둠 속에서 빛나다	
536	**motivation** [mòutəvéiʃən]	명 동기부여, 자극 personal motivation 개인적 동기	동 motivate 자극하다 유 incentive
537	**retain** [ritéin]	동 계속 유지하다, 간직하다 retain an old custom 옛 관습을 존속시키다	유 maintain
538	**uneven** [ʌní:vən]	형 고르지 않는 an uneven surface 고르지 않은 표면	반 even 고른
539	**bundle** [bʌ́ndl]	명 묶음 sell things in a bundle 묶음 단위로 팔다	유 bunch
540	**untimely** [ʌntáimli]	형 때 아닌, 시기적으로 부적절한	

✦ 주어진 우리말 문장에 맞도록 알맞은 단어를 넣어 문장을 완성하시오. 정답 p.201

I get ________ very easily.
나는 매우 쉽게 메스꺼움을 느낀다.

I don't like people who are ________ and self-involved.
나는 거만하고 자신밖에 모르는 사람이 싫다.

She ________ her little finger whenever she drinks tea.
그녀는 차를 마실 때마다 새끼손가락을 구부린다.

The presenter explained the ________ characteristics of the product.
그 발표자는 그 제품의 기능적 특징들에 대해서 설명했다.

The cows were grazing around a ________ tree.
소들이 육중한 나무 주변에서 풀을 뜯고 있었다.

This glass of iced tea will ________ you.
이 아이스티 한 잔이 기분을 상쾌하게 해줄 것이다.

The pain was not ________ at all.
그 고통은 절대 참기 힘들었다.

She will get the prize on ________ of her husband.
그녀는 자신의 남편을 대신하여 상을 받을 것이다.

Children are very ________ on their parents before they become adults.
아이들은 어른이 되기 전까지 그들의 부모에게 매우 의존한다.

Her face ________ in the dark.
그녀의 얼굴이 어둠 속에서 빛났다.

His poor grades are because of his lack of ________.
그의 형편없는 점수는 동기부여의 결여 때문이다.

She ________ a clear memory of her school days.
그녀는 학창시절에 대한 선명한 기억을 간직하고 있었다.

The surface of the wall is ________.
벽의 표면이 고르지 않아요.

I saw a ________ of letters on the floor.
난 방바닥에서 편지 뭉치를 보았다.

It was an ________ visit this time.
이번 방문은 시기적절하지 않았다.

REVIEW TEST 09 DAY 17 ~ DAY 18

A 우리말과 같은 뜻이 되도록 빈칸에 들어갈 알맞은 단어를 적으시오.

1. use ________________ (조심하다)
2. a ________________ place (신성한 장소)
3. on ________________ of (~을 대신하여)
4. a single ________________ (편도 운임)
5. a ________________ basket (빨래 바구니)
6. a ________________ person (사려 깊은 사람)
7. ________________ in the dark (어둠 속에서 빛나다)
8. the ________________ of the village (마을 주민들)
9. sell things in a ________________ (묶음 단위로 팔다)
10. ________________ money on (~에 돈을 쓰다)

B 다음 괄호 안의 지시대로 주어진 단어를 변형시키고 그 뜻을 적으시오.

		변형	뜻
1. feast (형용사형으로)	→	________	________
2. technological (명사형으로)	→	________	________
3. tragedy (형용사형으로)	→	________	________
4. biological (명사형으로)	→	________	________
5. revolutionary (명사형으로)	→	________	________
6. capable (명사형으로)	→	________	________
7. specialize (형용사형으로)	→	________	________
8. sticky (동사형으로)	→	________	________
9. irritate (형용사형으로)	→	________	________
10. purify (명사형으로)	→	________	________

정답 p.201

C 다음 영영풀이에 해당하는 단어를 보기에서 골라 적으시오.

보기				
assessment	universal	arrogant	uneven	fusion
queasy	motivation	curator	contract	laundry

1. the act of assessing; appraisal; evaluation → ________________
2. the person in charge of a museum, art collection, etc. → ________________
3. the act or process of fusing; the state of being fused → ________________
4. pertaining to or characteristic of all or the whole → ________________
5. an agreement between two or more parties to do or refrain from doing something specified → ________________
6. articles of clothing, linens, etc., that have been or are to be washed → ________________
7. causing nausea, especially in the stomach → ________________
8. making claims or pretensions to superior importance or rights → ________________
9. the act or an instance of motivating → ________________
10. not level or flat; rough; rugged → ________________

D 우리말과 같은 뜻이 되도록 주어진 문장의 빈칸을 완성하시오.

1. 그는 브라우닝의 시를 예찬하며 읽었다.
   → He read Browning's poems in ________________.
2. 필름을 빛에 노출시키지 마라.
   → Don't ________________ the film to light.
3. 아이들은 반 값에 그림을 보러 박물관에 입장할 수 있다.
   → Children can enter the museum to see the paintings at half ________________.
4. 어떤 약도 먹지 않고 그냥 자는 것이 더 낫다.
   → It is better to sleep naturally without taking any ________________.

⑤ 휴식을 위해 무언가 하자.

➔ Let's just do something for ______________.

⑥ 그녀는 여러 해 동안 여기저기 옮겨 다녔다.

➔ She ______________ about for many years.

⑦ 다친 새는 부러진 날개로 인해 안쓰러워 보였다.

➔ The injured bird looked ______________ with its broken wing.

⑧ 나는 중급 영어 수업을 듣고 있다.

➔ I'm taking an ______________ level English course.

⑨ 그 발표자는 그 제품의 기능적 특징들에 대해서 설명했다.

➔ The presenter explained the ______________ characteristics of the product.

⑩ 이 아이스티 한 잔이 기분을 상쾌하게 해줄 것이다.

➔ This glass of iced tea will ______________ you.

E 문장의 밑줄 친 부분에 해당하는 유의어 혹은 반의어를 보기에서 골라 적으시오.

보기					
	huge	illegal	bearable	infinite	suitable
	fragment	sorrow	hope	independent	bend

① He avoided the splinters of glass. 유의어 = ______________

② The physical universe is finite in time and space. 반의어 ↔ ______________

③ When you drive, you must not exceed the legal limit. 반의어 ↔ ______________

④ The man who lost his family lived in despair. 반의어 ↔ ______________

⑤ Her voice was husky with grief. 유의어 = ______________

⑥ This fire caused enormous damage. 유의어 = ______________

⑦ This food is adequate for those patients. 유의어 = ______________

⑧ I am crooking my knees to take a picture with children. 유의어 = ______________

⑨ The pain was not tolerable at all. 유의어 = ______________

⑩ Children are very dependent on their parents before they become adults.

반의어 ↔ ______________

F 영어발음을 듣고 영어단어를 적은 후, 우리말 뜻을 적으시오.

영어단어 듣고 쓰기

	영어	우리말		영어	우리말
❶			❽		
❷			❾		
❸			❿		
❹			⓫		
❺			⓬		
❻			⓭		
❼			⓮		

G 영어문장을 듣고 빈칸에 들어갈 단어를 채워 문장을 완성하시오.

영어문장 듣고 쓰기

❶ He was a ______________ surgeon.

❷ Can you show us your ______________?

❸ It seems that he plays the guitar ______________.

❹ The ______________ of the government was unacceptable.

❺ My mother ______________ the two torn parts together.

❻ Her face ______________ in the dark.

❼ I saw a ______________ of letters on the floor.

❽ It was an ______________ visit this time.

❾ The wedding ______________ was held after the ceremony.

❿ The company has hired many experts to achieve its ______________ innovations.

⓫ Orphans don't know their ______________ parents.

⓬ The creation of the Internet has brought us many ______________ changes.

⓭ The company needs a ______________ salesperson.

⓮ First, make this paper very ______________.

⓯ He was really ______________ by his younger brother.

⓰ This salt has been ______________ for use in medicine.

541 **distort** [distɔ́ːrt]
동 왜곡하다 명 distortion 왜곡
distort history 역사를 왜곡하다

542 **diversity** [divə́ːrsəti | dai-]
명 다양성 형 diverse 다양한 유 variety
cultural diversity 문화적 다양성

543 **doubtless** [dáutlis]
형 의심 없는, 확실한 부 확실히 반 probably 아마
a doubtless fact 확실한 사실

544 **dwell** [dwel]
동 살다, 깃들다
dwell at home 국내에서 거주하다

545 **impersonal** [ìmpə́ːrsənl]
형 비인격적인, 객관적인 명 impersonality 비인간성, 비정함
an impersonal attitude 공평한 태도 반 biased 편견의

546 **overcome** [òuvərkʌ́m]
동 극복하다 유 conquer
overcome a difficult situation 어려운 상황을 극복하다

547 **shiver** [ʃívər]
동 떨다 명 떨림 형 shivery 오싹한 유 tremble
shiver from the cold 추워서 오슬오슬 떨다

548 **panic** [pǽnik]
명 공포 유 fear
in a panic 공포에 휩싸여

549 **inform** [infɔ́ːrm]
동 알리다 명 information 정보
inform the police 경찰에 알리다

550 **perish** [périʃ]
동 죽다 유 die
perish from a famine 굶어 죽다

551 **sophisticated** [səfístəkèitid]
형 세련된, 교양 있는 부 sophisticatedly 세련되게 유 elegant
a sophisticated woman 세련된 여성

552 **acknowledge** [æknálidʒ | ək-]
동 인정하다 명 acknowledgement 인정 유 admit
acknowlege a fact 사실을 인정하다

553 **confess** [kənfés]
동 고백하다 명 confession 고백
confess one's guilt 잘못을 고백하다

554 **executive** [igzékjutiv]
명 경영진 형 집행의
a chief executive officer 최고 경영자(CEO)

555 **preference** [préfərəns]
명 더 좋아함 동 prefer ~을 더 좋아하다
in preference to ~에 우선하여

✦ 주어진 우리말 문장에 맞도록 알맞은 단어를 넣어 문장을 완성하시오. 정답 p.202

Japan shouldn't ______ Korean history.
일본은 한국의 역사를 왜곡해서는 안 된다.

America is a country with cultural ______.
미국은 문화적 다양성을 가진 나라이다.

It was ______ his fault.
그것은 확실히 그의 잘못이다.

A sound mind ______ in a sound body.
건강한 정신은 건강한 신체에 깃든다.

When you criticize someone, you should be ______.
네가 누군가를 비판할 때 너는 객관적이어야 한다.

Everyone has to ______ difficult situations.
모든 사람들은 어려운 상황을 극복해야 한다.

She ______ as she walked into the cold room.
그녀는 차가운 방에 들어왔을 때 오슬오슬 떨었다.

He cried out in a ______.
그는 공포에 휩싸여 소리질렀다.

I ______ her parents of her safe arrival.
나는 그녀의 부모에게 그녀가 무사히 도착했음을 알렸다.

There are still many people who ______ from famines around the world.
아직도 전 세계에는 굶어 죽는 사람들이 많다.

Everyone considers her a ______ woman.
모두가 그녀를 세련된 여성으로 생각한다.

I didn't ______ that he could solve this problem.
나는 그가 이 문제를 해결할 수 있을 거라고 인정하지 않았다.

The child ______ that he hadn't done his homework.
아이가 숙제를 끝내지 않았다고 고백했다.

He is the chief ______ of the company.
그는 그 회사의 최고 경영자이다.

A window seat is my ______.
나는 창문 쪽 좌석이 더 좋다.

DAY 19

No.	Word	Meaning	Related
556	**aisle** [ail]	명 통로 an aisle seat 통로 측 좌석	유 passageway
557	**fake** [feik]	형 가짜의 명 가짜 fake nails 가짜 손톱	반 real 진짜의
558	**procession** [prəséʃən]	명 행진, 행렬, 진행 a funeral procession 장례 행렬	동 proceed 나아가다 유 parade
559	**prohibit** [prouhíbit]	동 금지하다 prohibit imports 수입을 금지하다	명 prohibition 금지 유 forbid
560	**proportion** [prəpɔ́ːrʃən]	명 비율, 비례 a direct proportion 정비례	형 proportional 비례의 유 ratio
561	**surgeon** [sə́ːrdʒən]	명 외과 의사 an expert surgeon 외과 전문 의사	
562	**aristocracy** [æ̀rəstɑ́krəsi]	명 귀족정치 the aristocracy 귀족 (사회)	형 aristocratic 귀족의
563	**creature** [kríːtʃər]	명 창조물 Poor creature! 가엾어라!	동 create 만들다 유 living things
564	**frozen** [fróuzn]	형 언, 냉동의 a frozen pond 언 연못	부 frozenly 얼려서, 언 듯이 유 icy
565	**majestic** [mədʒéstik]	형 장엄한	명 majesty 장엄
566	**recur** [rikə́ːr]	동 재발하다, 되풀이되다	명 recurrence 재발
567	**thrust** [θrʌst]	동 밀다 명 밀침 thrust one's way 밀어 제치고 나아가다 *thrust-thrust-thrust*	유 push
568	**bare** [bɛər]	형 발가벗은, 가까스로의 bare feet 맨발	부 barely 간신히 유 naked
569	**demolish** [dimɑ́liʃ]	동 헐다, 파괴하다 demolish several houses 몇 개의 집을 헐다	유 destroy
570	**glance** [glæns]	동 힐끗 보다 명 힐끗 봄 glance about 주위를 힐끗 보다	유 glimpse

✦ 주어진 우리말 문장에 맞도록 알맞은 단어를 넣어 문장을 완성하시오. 정답 p.202

I prefer an ______ seat.
나는 통로 측 좌석을 선호한다.

He didn't know that the picture was a ______.
그는 그 그림이 가짜라는 것을 알지 못했다.

The soldiers are marching in a ______ in front of the president of the country.
군인들이 그 나라 대통령 앞에서 줄을 지어 행진하고 있다.

The new law ______ the importing of Chinese products.
그 새로운 법은 중국제품들의 수입을 금지했다.

The modern birthrate is affecting a ______ of the population.
현대의 출산율은 인구 비율에 영향을 준다.

The ______ removed the boy's brain tumor.
외과 의사가 소년의 뇌종양을 제거했다.

In those days, power rested with the ______.
그 시절에는 귀족들에게 권력이 있었다.

Santa Claus is a ______ of the imagination.
산타클로스는 상상력의 산물이다.

My mother is preparing dinner with ______ food tonight.
엄마는 오늘 밤 냉동 식품으로 저녁식사를 준비하신다.

Mt. Halla in Jeju Island is ______.
제주도에 있는 한라산은 장엄하다.

She has had a ______ nightmare since childhood.
그녀는 어린 시절부터 되풀이되는 악몽을 꿔 왔다.

They ______ him into the back room and tied him up.
그들은 그를 뒷방에 밀치고 묶었다.

Don't walk on that broken glass with your ______ feet.
깨진 유리 위를 맨발로 걷지 마라.

We will ______ these houses first so that the new building can be built.
우리는 새로운 빌딩을 지을 수 있도록 먼저 이 집들을 부술 거예요.

My sister's hobby is to ______ at fashion magazines.
내 동생의 취미는 패션 잡지를 대충 훑어보는 것이다.

DAY 20

DAY 20 표제어 듣기

571 **momentary** [móumәntèri]
형 순식간의 | 명 moment 순간

572 **respective** [rispéktiv]
형 각각의 | 부 respectively 각기, 각각
respective roles of parents 부모 각자의 역할

573 **undiscovered** [ʌ̀ndiskʌ́vәrd]
형 발견되지 않은, 미지의
undiscovered islands 발견되지 않은 섬들

574 **broke** [brouk]
형 파산한 | 동 break 부수다 유 penniless
go broke 파산하다 | *break-broke-broken*

575 **dismiss** [dismís]
동 해고시키다 | 유 fire
be dismissed from a company 회사에서 해고당하다

576 **bustle** [bʌ́sl]
동 분주히 돌아다니다 명 야단법석 | 유 rush
bustle about ~하느라 분주하게 움직이다

577 **hub** [hʌb]
명 중심
a hub of Asia 아시아의 중심

578 **hygiene** [háidʒiːn]
명 위생
public hygiene 공공위생

579 **ignorance** [ígnәrәns]
명 무지 | 동 ignore 무시하다 반 knowledge 지식, 이해
pretend ignorance 모르는 체하다

580 **imaginative** [imǽdʒәnәtiv]
형 상상력이 풍부한 | 동 imagine 상상하다
an imaginative writer 상상력이 풍부한 작가

581 **originate** [әrídʒәnèit]
동 시작되다 | 명 origin 기원, 시작 유 start
originate from ~에서 생기다

582 **shatter** [ʃǽtәr]
동 산산이 부수다
shatter a ship 배를 산산이 부수다

583 **shrink** [ʃriŋk]
동 수축하다, 위축되다 | 유 contract
shrink away 줄어들다

584 **parallel** [pǽrәlèl]
형 평행의 명 평행선
parallel lines 평행선

585 **perception** [pәrsépʃәn]
명 지각 | 동 perceive 지각하다 유 awareness
space perception 공간 지각

✦ 주어진 우리말 문장에 맞도록 알맞은 단어를 넣어 문장을 완성하시오. 정답 p.202

The ______ darkness frightened the children.
순식간의 어둠이 아이들을 겁먹게 했다.

All participants are supposed to bring their ______ partners.
모든 참가자는 각자의 짝을 데려오게 되어 있다.

At last, the miner turned up an ______ gold mine.
결국 광부가 미지의 금광을 발굴했다.

He is flat ______ and cannot find a job anywhere.
그는 완전히 파산했고 어디서도 직업을 찾지 못했다.

He was ______ from the company last month.
그는 지난 달에 회사에서 해고당했다.

My mother ______ around in the kitchen while cooking.
우리 엄마는 요리하는 동안 부엌을 분주히 돌아다니신다.

Korea is the ______ of Asia.
한국은 아시아의 중심이다.

Be extra careful about your personal ______.
개인위생에 특별히 조심해라.

Please forgive my ______.
나의 무지를 용서해 줘.

I like that my son is very ______.
나는 우리 아들이 상상력이 풍부해서 좋아요.

The flames ______ in the kitchen and spread to the other parts of the restaurant.
불길은 부엌에서 시작되어 식당의 다른 부분들로 번졌다.

The strong storm ______ the ship.
강력한 폭풍이 배를 산산이 부수었다.

Wool ______ after washing.
양모는 빨고 나면 수축한다.

These two lines are ______.
이 두 선들은 평행하다.

His ______ of the change came in a flash.
그는 문득 변화를 감지했다. (그의 변화에 대한 인식은 순식간에 일어났다.)

DAY 20

No.	Word	Meaning	Related	Example
586	**snatch** [snætʃ]	동 와락 붙잡다, 낚아채다	형 snatchable 낚아챌 수 있는	snatch a purse 지갑을 낚아채다
587	**accommodation** [əkɑ̀mədéiʃən]	명 숙박시설	유 housing	accommodation for employees 직원들을 위한 숙박시설
588	**comprehensive** [kɑ̀mprihénsiv | kɔ̀m-]	형 포괄적인, 이해하는	동 comprehend 이해하다 유 inclusive	a comprehensive mind 넓은 마음
589	**evolve** [ivɑ́lv | ivɔ́lv]	동 진화하다	명 evolution 진화	evolve into ~로 진화하다
590	**intense** [inténs]	형 강렬한, 극심한	유 fierce	an intense light 강렬한 빛
591	**staple** [stéipl]	형 주요한 명 주요 상품, 주요소		staple foods 주식
592	**content** [kəntént]	형 만족해 하는	명 contentment 만족 유 satisfied	in content 만족하여
593	**inward** [ínwərd]	형 안의, 내적인	반 outward 밖으로 향하는	on the inward side 안쪽에서
594	**stumble** [stʌ́mbl]	동 넘어지다 명 비틀거림	유 trip over	stumble over ~에 걸려 넘어지다
595	**subtle** [sʌ́tl]	형 민감한	유 sensitive	a subtle issue 민감한 이슈
596	**superiority** [səpìəriɔ́(:)rəti]	명 우세, 우월	형 superior 우세한 반 inferiority 열세	overwhelming superiority 압도적인 우세
597	**approximately** [əprɑ́ksəmətli]	부 대략	형 approximate 대략의 유 roughly	approximately estimated figure 대략 추정된 숫자
598	**craftsman** [krǽftsmən]	명 장인	유 master	a skilled craftsman 숙련된 장인
599	**freelance** [frí:læ̀ns]	형 프리랜서로 일하는 명 프리랜서	유 freelancer	a freelance writer 자유기고가
600	**loyalty** [lɔ́iəlti]	명 충성	형 loyal 충성스러운 유 faithfulness	swear one's loyalty 충성을 맹세하다

✦ 주어진 우리말 문장에 맞도록 알맞은 단어를 넣어 문장을 완성하시오. 정답 p.202

He was trying to ______ my handbag.
그가 내 손가방을 낚아채려고 했어요.

The fee includes airfare and ______.
항공료와 숙박료를 포함한 가격입니다.

The ______ report showed what I wanted to know.
그 포괄적인 보고서는 내가 알고 싶어했던 것을 보여 주었다.

All living creatures have ______ since life first began.
살아 있는 모든 생물체들은 생의 시초부터 진화해 왔다.

He was sweating from the ______ heat.
그는 강렬한 열기로 인해 땀을 흘리고 있었다.

Rice is our ______ food.
쌀은 우리의 주식이다.

He was ______ with his work.
그는 그의 일에 만족했다.

She sighed with ______ relief.
그녀는 내심 안도의 한숨을 지었다.

A child ______ over a rock and cried.
한 어린이가 돌에 채어 넘어져서 울었다.

Don't mention any ______ issues.
어떤 민감한 사항들도 언급하지 마라.

America had overwhelming military ______ over Iraq.
미국은 이라크보다 압도적인 군사적 우위를 가졌다.

The number of applicants is ______ a thousand.
신청자 수는 대략 천 명쯤 된다.

The ______ beat the gold into rings.
장인이 금을 두들겨 반지를 만들었다.

She is doing ______ work.
그녀는 프리랜서로 일을 하고 있다.

The soldiers swore their ______ to the country.
군인들은 나라에 충성을 맹세했다.

REVIEW TEST 10 DAY 19 ~ DAY 20

A 우리말과 같은 뜻이 되도록 빈칸에 들어갈 알맞은 단어를 적으시오.

1. ________________ feet (맨발)
2. ________________ foods (주식)
3. ________________ about (주위를 힐끗 보다)
4. ________________ imports (수입을 금지하다)
5. ________________ a purse (지갑을 낚아채다)
6. ________________ over (~에 걸려 넘어지다)
7. ________________ a ship (배를 산산이 부수다)
8. swear one's ________________ (충성을 맹세하다)
9. ________________ one's way (밀어 제치고 나아가다)
10. ________________ several houses (몇 개의 집을 헐다)

B 다음 괄호 안의 지시대로 주어진 단어를 변형시키고 그 뜻을 적으시오.

		변형	뜻
1	originate (명사형으로) →	________	________
2	impersonal (명사형으로) →	________	________
3	acknowledge (명사형으로) →	________	________
4	confess (명사형으로) →	________	________
5	procession (동사형으로) →	________	________
6	majestic (명사형으로) →	________	________
7	momentary (명사형으로) →	________	________
8	snatch (형용사형으로) →	________	________
9	comprehensive (동사형으로) →	________	________
10	approximately (형용사형으로) →	________	________

정답 p.202

C 다음 영영풀이에 해당하는 단어를 보기에서 골라 적으시오.

보기				
distort	inform	aisle	perception	frozen
panic	perish	hub	preference	hygiene

1. having turned into ice → ____________
2. to twist awry or out of shape; make crooked or deformed → ____________
3. a sudden overwhelming fear → ____________
4. to give or impart knowledge of a fact or circumstance to → ____________
5. to die or be destroyed through violence, privation, etc. → ____________
6. the act of preferring → ____________
7. a center of interest, importance, or activity → ____________
8. a condition or practice conducive to the preservation of health, as cleanliness
   → ____________
9. a walkway between or along sections of seats in a theater, classroom, or the like
   → ____________
10. the act or faculty of apprehending by means of the senses or the mind; cognition; understanding → ____________

D 우리말과 같은 뜻이 되도록 주어진 문장의 빈칸을 완성하시오.

1. 미국은 문화적 다양성을 가진 나라이다.
   → America is a country with cultural ____________.
2. 모든 사람들은 어려운 상황을 극복해야 한다.
   → Everyone has to ____________ difficult situations.
3. 그녀는 차가운 방에 들어왔을 때 오슬오슬 떨었다.
   → She ____________ as she walked into the cold room.
4. 외과 의사가 소년의 뇌종양을 제거했다.
   → The ____________ removed the boy's brain tumor.

⑤ 산타클로스는 상상력의 산물이다.

➜ Santa Claus is a ________________ of the imagination.

⑥ 그는 완전히 파산했고 어디서도 직업을 찾지 못했다.

➜ He is flat ________________ and cannot find a job anywhere.

⑦ 나는 우리 아들이 상상력이 풍부해서 좋아요.

➜ I like that my son is very ________________.

⑧ 양모는 빨고 나면 수축한다.

➜ Wool ________________ after washing.

⑨ 살아 있는 모든 생물체들은 생의 시초부터 진화해 왔다.

➜ All living creatures have ________________ since life first began.

⑩ 그녀는 프리랜서로 일을 하고 있다.

➜ She is doing ________________ work.

E 문장의 밑줄 친 부분에 해당하는 유의어 혹은 반의어를 보기에서 골라 적으시오.

보기				
ratio	rush	fired	forbid	inferiority
real	push	outward	satisfied	knowledge

① He didn't know that the picture was a fake. 반의어 ↔ ________________

② The new law prohibited the importing of Chinese products. 유의어 = ________________

③ The modern birthrate is affecting a proportion of the population.

유의어 = ________________

④ They thrust him into the back room and tied him up. 유의어 = ________________

⑤ He was dismissed from the company last month. 유의어 = ________________

⑥ My mother bustles around in the kitchen while cooking. 유의어 = ________________

⑦ Please forgive my ignorance. 반의어 ↔ ________________

⑧ He was content with his work. 유의어 = ________________

⑨ She sighed with inward relief. 반의어 ↔ ________________

⑩ America had overwhelming military superiority over Iraq. 반의어 ↔ ________________

F 영어발음을 듣고 영어단어를 적은 후, 우리말 뜻을 적으시오.

영어단어 듣고 쓰기

	영어	우리말		영어	우리말
❶	________	________	❽	________	________
❷	________	________	❾	________	________
❸	________	________	❿	________	________
❹	________	________	⓫	________	________
❺	________	________	⓬	________	________
❻	________	________	⓭	________	________
❼	________	________	⓮	________	________

G 영어문장을 듣고 빈칸에 들어갈 단어를 채워 문장을 완성하시오.

영어문장 듣고 쓰기

❶ It was ________ his fault.

❷ Everyone considers her a ________ woman.

❸ He is the chief ________ of the company.

❹ In those days, power rested with the ________.

❺ She has had a ________ nightmare since childhood.

❻ At last, the miner turned up an ________ gold mine.

❼ A child ________ over a rock and cried.

❽ The ________ beat the gold into rings.

❾ The soldiers swore their ________ to the country.

❿ The flames ________ in the kitchen and spread to the other parts of the restaurant.

⓫ When you criticize someone, you should be ________.

⓬ The child ________ that he hadn't done his homework.

⓭ The soldiers are marching in a ________ in front of the president of the country.

⓮ The ________ darkness frightened the children.

⓯ The ________ report showed what I wanted to know.

⓰ The number of applicants is ________ a thousand.

601 **reckless** [réklis]
형 무모한 | 명 recklessness 무모함
a reckless attempt 무모한 시도

602 **thrifty** [θrífti]
형 검소한, 절약하는 | 유 frugal
a thrifty habit 검소한 습관

603 **auditorium** [ɔ̀:dətɔ́:riəm]
명 강당
a school auditorium 학교 대강당

604 **definition** [dèfəníʃən]
명 정의 | 동 define 정의를 내리다
give a definition 정의를 내리다

605 **gigantic** [dʒaigǽntik]
형 거대한 | 유 enormous
a gigantic statue 거대한 동상

606 **mock** [mɑk]
동 모방하다 명 흉내 | 유 imitate
mock exactly 정확히 모방하다

607 **requirement** [rikwáiərmənt]
명 요구 | 동 require 요구하다 유 demand
meet the requirements 요구를 충족시키다

608 **ultrasonic** [ʌ̀ltrəsɑ́nik]
형 초음파의 | 유 supersonic
ultrasonic waves 초음파

609 **breakdown** [bréikdàun]
명 (기계의) 고장, (건강의) 쇠약
a mental breakdown 신경쇠약

610 **disappointment** [dìsəpɔ́intmənt]
명 실망 | 동 disappoint 실망시키다
to one's disappointment 실망스럽게도

611 **hijack** [háidʒæ̀k]
동 공중 납치하다, 강탈하다 | 명 hijacker 공중 납치범
plan to hijack 공중 납치를 계획하다

612 **dissatisfied** [dissǽtisfàid]
형 불만을 품은 | 명 dissatisfaction 불만족 반 satisfied 만족한
be dissatisfied with ~에 불만을 품다

613 **numeral** [njú:mərəl]
명 숫자 | 형 numerical 수의
an Arabic numeral 아라비아 숫자

614 **occasion** [əkéiʒən]
명 경우 | 형 occasional 이따금씩의 유 case
on all occasions 모든 경우에

615 **offer** [ɔ́(:)fər]
동 제공하다, 제안하다 명 제공 | 참 offering 헌금, 신청
accept an offer 제안을 승낙하다

✦ 주어진 우리말 문장에 맞도록 알맞은 단어를 넣어 문장을 완성하시오. 정답 p.203

The prisoner made a ________ attempt to escape from prison.
그 죄수는 감옥으로부터 탈출하려고 무모한 시도를 했다.

My mother taught me to be ________.
어머니는 나에게 겸소하라고 가르치셨다.

The ________ was full of people.
강당은 사람들로 가득 찼다.

He gave a different ________ to the theory.
그는 그 이론에 대해 다른 정의를 내렸다.

The building has a ________ frame.
그 건물은 거대한 구조를 가지고 있다.

Children tend to ________ their parents in many ways.
아이들은 많은 면에서 부모를 모방하려는 경향이 있다.

Your application meets our ________.
당신의 지원서는 우리의 요구들을 충족시킵니다.

Since ________ sound has a very high frequency, human beings cannot hear it.
초음파는 고주파이기 때문에 사람은 듣지 못한다.

He suffered continual car ________ during the trip.
그는 여행하는 동안 계속된 차 고장으로 고생했다.

The picnic was a ________.
소풍은 실망스러웠다.

They planned to ________ the plane, but they changed their plan.
그들은 공중납치를 계획했으나 그 계획을 수정했다.

A ________ customer wrote a letter to the manager.
불만을 품은 고객이 매니저에게 편지를 썼다.

Write the ________ which you just heard.
지금 막 들은 숫자들을 적어라.

She only dresses up on special ________.
그녀는 특별한 경우에만 정장차림을 한다.

He ________ me a glass of wine.
그는 나에게 와인 한 잔을 제공했다.

DAY 21

616	**orbit** [ɔ́ːrbit]	명 궤도 the Earth's orbit around the Sun 태양을 도는 지구의 궤도	
617	**sermon** [sə́ːrmən]	명 설교 deliver a sermon 설교하다	동 sermonize 설교하다 유 speech
618	**warfare** [wɔ́ːrfɛ̀ər]	명 전투 trade warfare 무역 전쟁	유 war
619	**signature** [sígnətʃər]	명 서명 imitate a signature 서명을 모방하다	동 sign 서명하다
620	**participation** [pɑːrtìsəpéiʃən]	명 참여 active participation 적극적인 참여	동 participate 참여하다 유 involvement
621	**slack** [slæk]	형 느슨한, 꾸물거리는 명 느슨함, 여유 a slack rope 느슨한 밧줄	유 loose, room
622	**abstract** [ǽbstrækt]	형 추상적인 an abstract idea 추상적 개념	부 abstractly 추상적으로 반 concrete 구체적인
623	**competent** [kɑ́mpətənt]	형 자격이 있는, 유능한 be competent for ~에 적격이다	유 able, capable
624	**evenly** [íːvənli]	부 공평히 evenly distribute 공평히 분배하다	형 even 공평한 유 justly
625	**insulting** [insʌ́ltiŋ]	형 모욕적인 an insulting manner 모욕적인 태도	동 insult 모욕하다
626	**possess** [pəzés]	동 소유하다 possess a house 집을 가지고 있다	명 possession 소유 유 own
627	**advisable** [ədváizəbl]	형 현명한, 바람직한 an advisable solution 현명한 해결책	동 advise 조언하다 유 wise
628	**extraordinary** [ikstrɔ́ːrdənèri]	형 비상한, 비범한 have extraordinary talents 출중한 재주가 있다	반 ordinary 보통의
629	**primary** [práimeri]	형 기본의, 주된 a primary school 초등학교	유 main
630	**analysis** [ənǽləsis]	명 분석 make an analysis on ~에 대해 분석하다	동 analyze 분석하다

✦ 주어진 우리말 문장에 맞도록 알맞은 단어를 넣어 문장을 완성하시오. 정답 p.203

We put an artificial satellite into ________.
우리는 인공위성을 궤도에 진입시켰다.

The principal of our school usually delivers a long ________ to us.
우리 학교의 교장 선생님은 보통 우리에게 오랫동안 설교하신다.

We live in a world of trade ________.
우리는 무역 전쟁의 세계에 살고 있다.

The criminal tried to imitate the ________.
그 범인은 서명을 모방하려고 했다.

The Korean ________ with the peacekeeping forces was highly controversial.
평화유지군에의 한국 참여에 대해 매우 많은 논쟁이 있었다.

There's very little ________ in the budget.
예산에는 여유가 거의 없다.

Pablo Picasso painted ________ and figurative works.
파블로 피카소는 추상적이고 상징적인 작품들을 그렸다.

She is ________ for teaching those children.
그녀는 그 아이들을 가르칠 자격이 있다.

The food was ________ distributed to the poor.
식량은 가난한 사람들에게 공평하게 분배되었다.

Don't speak to others in an ________ manner.
다른 사람에게 모욕적인 태도로 얘기하지 마라.

Eskimos believe every living creature ________ a spirit.
에스키모인들은 모든 생명체가 영혼을 가지고 있다고 믿는다.

It is ________ to book hotels in advance because it's the peak season.
성수기라 호텔을 미리 예약하는 것이 현명하다.

He is full of ________ ideas.
그는 비상한 아이디어들이 많다.

You didn't get the ________ focus of the meeting.
당신은 회의의 주된 관심사를 파악하지 못했다.

An effective ________ can bring a greater change.
효과적인 분석은 더 나은 변화를 가져온다.

DAY 22

631 **apologetic** [əpɑ̀lədʒétik]
형 사과의 명 변명 부 apologetically 변명하여 유 sorry
an apologetic speech 사과의 말

632 **applicant** [ǽplikənt]
명 지원자 동 apply 지원하다

633 **counterbalance** [kàuntərbǽləns]
동 상쇄하다, 평형시키다
counterbalance a problem 문제를 상쇄하다

634 **foretell** [fɔːrtél]
동 예측하다, 예언하다
foretell the future 미래를 예언하다

635 **logic** [lɑ́dʒik]
명 논리학, 논리 형 logical 논리적인
fuzzy logic 알쏭달쏭한 논리

636 **reaction** [riǽkʃən]
명 반응 동 react 반응하다 유 response
an immediate reaction 즉각적인 반응

637 **thermostat** [θə́ːrməstæ̀t]
명 온도 조절 장치 부 thermostatically 온도 조절 장치에 의하여

638 **attain** [ətéin]
동 달성하다 명 attainment 달성 유 achieve
attain a goal 목표를 달성하다

639 **decorate** [dékərèit]
동 장식하다 명 decoration 장식
decorate with ~으로 장식하다

640 **genuine** [dʒénjuin]
형 진짜의 부 genuinely 진정으로 유 authentic
genuine writing 진필

641 **minimize** [mínəmàiz]
동 최소화하다 형 minimal 최소한의 반 maximize 최대화하다
minimize the expense 비용을 최소화하다

642 **representative** [rèprizéntətiv]
명 대표자, 대리인 동 represent 대표하다
a diplomatic representative 외교관

643 **troop** [truːp]
명 군대, 병력
command troops 군대를 지휘하다

644 **boundary** [báundəri]
명 경계 유 border
a boundary line 경계선

645 **diligent** [dílədʒənt]
형 부지런한 명 diligence 근면
a diligent worker 근면한 사람

✦ 주어진 우리말 문장에 맞도록 알맞은 단어를 넣어 문장을 완성하시오. 정답 p.203

I am ＿＿＿＿＿＿ about the mistake I made yesterday.
어제 제가 저지른 실수에 대해 사과드립니다.

He was an ＿＿＿＿＿＿ to that company.
그는 저 회사의 지원자였다.

She put in some honey to ＿＿＿＿＿＿ the acidity.
그녀는 산을 상쇄하기 위해 꿀을 조금 넣었다.

The outcome of the war is hard to ＿＿＿＿＿＿.
전쟁의 결과는 예측하기 힘들다.

He thinks my ＿＿＿＿＿＿ is wrong.
그는 나의 논리가 틀렸다고 생각한다.

I opened my eyes wide as a ＿＿＿＿＿＿ to the news.
나는 그 소식에 대한 반응으로 내 눈을 크게 떴다. (그 소식을 듣고 놀랐다.)

The ＿＿＿＿＿＿ in our office is not working well.
사무실에 있는 온도조절장치가 제대로 작동하지 않는다.

We have to work hard to ＿＿＿＿＿＿ our goal.
우리는 목표를 달성하기 위해 열심히 일해야 한다.

She ＿＿＿＿＿＿ her room with pictures of her favorite singer.
그녀는 방을 자신이 가장 좋아하는 가수의 사진으로 장식했다.

The ring is ＿＿＿＿＿＿ gold.
그 반지는 진짜 금이다.

We need to ＿＿＿＿＿＿ expenses and maximize profits.
우리는 비용을 최소화하고 이득을 최대화시켜야 한다.

He is a student ＿＿＿＿＿＿ of our school who will go to Canada.
그가 우리 학교의 학생 대표로 캐나다에 갈 것이다.

My brother commands 60 ＿＿＿＿＿＿.
내 남동생은 60명의 병력을 지휘한다.

Don't go over the ＿＿＿＿＿＿ line.
경계선을 넘지 마라.

He is a ＿＿＿＿＿＿ worker.
그는 부지런히 일하는 사람이다.

DAY 22

646	**haste** [heist]	명 급함, 서두름 make haste 서두르다	동 hasten 재촉하다
647	**near-sighted** [níərsàitid]	형 근시안의 a near-sighted person 근시인 사람	반 long-sighted 원시안의
648	**horizontal** [hɔ̀:rəzɑ́ntl]	형 수평의 명 수평물 a horizontal position 수평 자세	부 horizontally 수평으로
649	**scatter** [skǽtər]	동 흩어버리다	명 scatteredness 산재함
650	**scratch** [skrætʃ]	동 긁다, 할퀴다 scratch a person where he itches 가려운 곳을 긁어 주다	
651	**segment** [ségmənt]	명 구획, 단편 a line segment (수학의) 선분	형 segmental 부분의 유 section
652	**sensation** [senséiʃən]	명 감각, 느낌 a keen sensation 예리한 감각	형 sensational 감각의, 지각의
653	**vocation** [voukéiʃən]	명 직업 select a vocation 직업을 선택하다	형 vocational 직업의 유 occupation
654	**circular** [sə́:rkjulər]	형 원의 a circular cone 원뿔	명 circle 원
655	**warm-hearted** [wɔ:rmhɑ́:rtid]	형 마음이 따뜻한, 인정 많은 a warm-hearted person 마음이 따뜻한 사람	명 warm-heartedness 인정 반 cold-hearted 냉정한
656	**particle** [pɑ́:rtikl]	명 입자 a particle of dust 먼지 입자	
657	**abound** [əbáund]	동 많이 있다, 풍부하다 abound in[on] ~이 많다	형 abundant 풍부한
658	**commonplace** [kɑ́mənplèis]	명 평범한 것 형 평범한 a commonplace remark 진부한 말	반 rare
659	**errand** [érənd]	명 심부름 an errand boy 심부름꾼	참 task 임무, chore 잡일
660	**inspiration** [ìnspəréiʃən]	명 영감, 격려 moral inspiration 도덕적 영감	동 inspire 영감을 주다 유 stimulus

1회독	월	일
2회독	월	일

✦ 주어진 우리말 문장에 맞도록 알맞은 단어를 넣어 문장을 완성하시오. 정답 p.203

In my ______, I forgot to lock the door.
서두른 나머지 나는 문 잠그는 것을 잊었다.

My son is dreadfully ______.
내 아들은 심각한 근시이다.

The design has ______ and vertical patterns.
그 디자인은 수평과 수직의 패턴으로 되어 있다.

The broken pieces of the vase are ______ all over the floor.
깨진 꽃병의 조각들이 바닥에 흩어져 있다.

Would you ______ my back? I've got an itch.
등 좀 긁어 줄래? 가려워.

Another ______ is painted differently.
다른 구획은 다르게 칠해진다.

I had the weird ______ that someone was watching me.
누군가 나를 지켜보고 있다는 이상한 느낌이 들었다.

Selecting a ______ suitable for me is really hard.
나에게 맞는 직업을 선택하는 것은 정말 어렵다.

There are lots of ______ buildings in the city.
그 도시에는 둥근 모양의 건물들이 많이 있다.

It is natural for a ______ person to be loved by everyone.
마음이 따뜻한 사람이 모든 이에게 사랑을 받는 것은 당연하다.

You can study about ______ in physics.
물리학에서 입자에 대해 공부할 수 있다.

Information ______ on the Internet these days.
근래에는 인터넷에 정보가 풍부하다.

Air travel has now become ______.
비행기 여행은 이제 평범한 것이 되었다.

She went on an ______. Do you want me to take a message for you?
그녀는 심부름 갔어. 메시지 남겨 줄까?

He got his ______ from the singer and tried to become a singer himself.
그는 그 가수에게서 영감을 얻어 자신도 가수가 되려고 했다.

REVIEW TEST 11 DAY 21 ~ DAY 22

A 우리말과 같은 뜻이 되도록 빈칸에 들어갈 알맞은 단어를 적으시오.

1. make ______________ (서두르다)
2. ______________ a sermon (설교하다)
3. on all ______________ (모든 경우에)
4. a diplomatic ______________ (외교관)
5. a ______________ of dust (먼지 입자)
6. a ______________ attempt (무모한 시도)
7. ______________ distribute (공평히 분배하다)
8. ______________ the future (미래를 예언하다)
9. an immediate ______________ (즉각적인 반응)
10. ______________ a person where he itches (가려운 곳을 긁어 주다)

B 다음 괄호 안의 지시대로 주어진 단어를 변형시키고 그 뜻을 적으시오.

		변형	뜻
1. circular (명사형으로)	→	______________	______________
2. sermon (동사형으로)	→	______________	______________
3. reckless (명사형으로)	→	______________	______________
4. definition (동사형으로)	→	______________	______________
5. occasion (형용사형으로)	→	______________	______________
6. participation (동사형으로)	→	______________	______________
7. apologetic (부사형으로)	→	______________	______________
8. genuine (부사형으로)	→	______________	______________
9. sensation (형용사형으로)	→	______________	______________
10. logic (형용사형으로)	→	______________	______________

정답 p.203

C 다음 영영풀이에 해당하는 단어를 보기에서 골라 적으시오.

보기				
requirement	warfare	diligent	scatter	applicant
disappointment	reaction	horizontal	numeral	attain

1. that which is required; a thing demanded or obligatory → ______________
2. sadness caused by the non-fulfillment of one's hope → ______________
3. of, pertaining to, or consisting of a number or numbers → ______________
4. a person who applies for or requests something; a candidate → ______________
5. to reach, achieve, or accomplish; gain; obtain → ______________
6. constant in effort to accomplish something → ______________
7. at right angles to the vertical; parallel to level ground → ______________
8. to throw loosely about; distribute at irregular intervals → ______________
9. the process of military struggle between two nations or groups of nations; war
   → ______________
10. something you say, feel, or do because of something that has happened
   → ______________

D 우리말과 같은 뜻이 되도록 주어진 문장의 빈칸을 완성하시오.

1. 어머니는 나에게 겸소하라고 가르치셨다.
   → My mother taught me to be ______________.
2. 그 건물은 거대한 구조를 가지고 있다.
   → The building has a ______________ frame.
3. 아이들은 많은 면에서 부모를 모방하려는 경향이 있다.
   → Children tend to ______________ their parents in many ways.
4. 우리는 인공위성을 궤도에 진입시켰다.
   → We put an artificial satellite into ______________.

5 그 범인은 서명을 모방하려고 했다.
→ The criminal tried to imitate the ______________.

6 에스키모인들은 모든 생명체가 영혼을 가지고 있다고 믿는다.
→ Eskimos believe every living creature ______________ a spirit.

7 당신은 회의의 주된 관심사를 파악하지 못했다.
→ You didn't get the ______________ focus of the meeting.

8 그녀는 방을 자신이 가장 좋아하는 가수의 사진으로 장식했다.
→ She ______________ her room with pictures of her favorite singer.

9 마음이 따뜻한 사람이 모든 이에게 사랑을 받는 것은 당연하다.
→ It is natural for a ______________ person to be loved by everyone.

10 그는 그 가수에게서 영감을 얻어 자신도 가수가 되려고 했다.
→ He got his ______________ from the singer and tried to become a singer himself.

E 문장의 밑줄 친 부분에 해당하는 유의어 혹은 반의어를 보기에서 골라 적으시오.

보기				
room	ordinary	capable	concrete	satisfied
rare	maximize	long-sighted	occupation	wise

1 A dissatisfied customer wrote a letter to the manager. 반의어 ↔ ______________

2 There's very little slack in the budget. 유의어 = ______________

3 Pablo Picasso painted abstract and figurative works. 반의어 ↔ ______________

4 She is competent at teaching those children. 유의어 = ______________

5 It is advisable to book hotels in advance because it's the peak season.
유의어 = ______________

6 He is full of extraordinary ideas. 반의어 ↔ ______________

7 We need to minimize expenses and maximize profits. 반의어 ↔ ______________

8 My son is dreadfully near-sighted. 반의어 ↔ ______________

9 Selecting a vocation suitable for me is really hard. 유의어 = ______________

10 Air travel has now become commonplace. 반의어 ↔ ______________

F 영어발음을 듣고 영어단어를 적은 후, 우리말 뜻을 적으시오.

영어단어 듣고 쓰기

	영어	우리말		영어	우리말
❶	________	________	❽	________	________
❷	________	________	❾	________	________
❸	________	________	❿	________	________
❹	________	________	⓫	________	________
❺	________	________	⓬	________	________
❻	________	________	⓭	________	________
❼	________	________	⓮	________	________

G 영어문장을 듣고 빈칸에 들어갈 단어를 채워 문장을 완성하시오.

영어문장 듣고 쓰기

❶ Since ________ sound has a very high frequency, human beings cannot hear it.

❷ He suffered continual car ________ during the trip.

❸ She put in some honey to ________ the acidity.

❹ The ________ in our office is not working well.

❺ Another ________ is painted differently.

❻ Information ________ on the Internet these days.

❼ She went on an ________. Do you want me to take a message for you?

❽ There are lots of ________ buildings in the city.

❾ He ________ me a glass of wine.

❿ The prisoner made a ________ attempt to escape from prison.

⓫ He gave a different ________ to the theory.

⓬ The Korean ________ with the peacekeeping forces was highly controversial.

⓭ I am ________ about the mistake I made yesterday.

⓮ I had the weird ________ that someone was watching me.

⓯ He thinks my ________ is wrong.

⓰ They planned to ________ the plane, but they changed their plan.

DAY 23

661 **populate** [pɑ́pjulèit]
동 거주하다 명 population 인구
densly populated 인구 밀도가 높은

662 **squish** [skwiʃ]
동 찌부러뜨리다, 으깨다
squish cans 깡통을 찌부러뜨리다

663 **consult** [kənsʌ́lt]
동 의견을 듣다, 상담하다 명 consultation 상담 유 confer
consult with ~와 상의하다

664 **intricate** [íntrikət]
형 얽힌, 복잡한 유 complicated
an intricate knot 엉클어진 매듭

665 **sting** [stiŋ]
동 쏘다, 찌르다 형 stingy 쏘는 유 tingle
be stung on the arm 팔을 쏘이다 *sting-stung-stung*

666 **coordinate** [kouɔ́:rdənèit]
동 조정하다 명 coordination 조정
coordinate a schedule 스케줄을 조정하다

667 **corporation** [kɔ̀:rpəréiʃən]
명 주식회사 형 corporate 법인 조직의
a trading corporation 무역 회사

668 **cosmetic** [kɑzmétik]
형 화장의 명 *pl.* 화장품
a cosmetic bag 화장품 가방

669 **fluency** [flú:ənsi]
명 유창함 형 fluent 유창한 유 eloquence
language fluency 언어의 유창함

670 **lining** [láiniŋ]
명 안감
a silver lining 구름의 흰 가장자리, 불행 속 한가닥 희망

671 **ragged** [rǽgid]
형 남루한, 초라한 유 tatty
a ragged child 남루한 아이

672 **tension** [ténʃən]
명 긴장 형 tensional 긴장의 유 pressure
racial tension 인종적인 긴장감

673 **assumption** [əsʌ́mpʃən]
명 가정 동 assume 가정하다 유 supposition
a mere assumption 단순한 가정

674 **daylight** [déilàit]
명 일광, 햇빛, 낮 유 sunlight
in broad daylight 대낮에

675 **generalization** [dʒènərəlizéiʃən | -laiz-]
명 일반화, 보편화 동 generalize 일반화하다
a generalization of patterns 패턴의 일반화

✦ 주어진 우리말 문장에 맞도록 알맞은 단어를 넣어 문장을 완성하시오. 정답 p.204

The central part of the city is densely ______.
도시의 중심부는 인구 밀도가 높다.

They ______ the tomatoes to make ketchup.
그들은 케첩을 만들기 위해 토마토를 으깼다.

He needed to ______ with a lawyer.
그는 변호사와 상의할 필요가 있었다.

The ______ machine requires a skilled operator.
복잡한 기계는 숙련된 조작자를 필요로 한다.

A bee ______ me on my left leg.
벌이 내 왼쪽 다리를 쏘았다.

Let me contact him and ______ our schedules.
내가 그에게 연락해서 우리 일정을 조정할게요.

This company is a multinational ______.
이 회사는 다국적 주식회사이다.

She is wearing a uniform and has a ______ bag in her right hand.
그녀는 유니폼을 입고 오른손엔 화장품 가방을 들고 있다.

You need ______ in at least one foreign language to be a translator.
통역사가 되기 위해서는 최소한 한 개의 외국어에 능통해야 한다.

The ______ of my coat is torn.
내 코트의 안감이 찢어졌다.

Maybe she was ashamed of her ______ clothes.
아마도 그녀는 자신의 남루한 옷차림이 부끄러웠을 것이다.

Violence can be caused by ______ between people.
폭력은 사람들 사이의 긴장감에 의해 일어날 수 있다.

His false ______ often leads him to answer negatively.
그의 잘못된 가정은 종종 그를 부정적으로 대답하게 한다.

The incident happened in broad ______.
그 사건은 대낮에 일어났다.

The evaluation of the survey involved some amount of ______.
설문조사의 평가는 어느 정도의 일반화가 포함되어 있었다.

DAY 23

No.	Word	Pronunciation	Meaning	Related	Example
676	**messy**	[mési]	형 어질러진	명 mess 난잡 반 tidy 깔끔한	in a messy way 지저분하게
677	**Renaissance**	[rènəsɑ́:ns ǀ rənéisəns]	명 문예부흥기, 르네상스	유 rebirth	Renaissance painters 르네상스 화가들
678	**treadmill**	[trédmìl]	명 러닝머신		use a treadmill 러닝머신을 이용하다
679	**blockade**	[blɑkéid]	명 봉쇄, 차단 동 봉쇄하다	유 obstruction	break a blockade 봉쇄를 뚫다
680	**devastate**	[dévəstèit]	동 황폐시키다	명 devastation 황폐	devastate a land 땅을 황폐시키다
681	**habitat**	[hǽbitæ̀t]	명 서식지		a natural habitat 자연 서식지
682	**nationality**	[næ̀ʃənǽləti]	명 국적	형 national 국가의	dual nationality 이중 국적
683	**riot**	[ráiət]	명 폭동	유 uprising	A riot breaks out. 폭동이 일어나다.
684	**neighboring**	[néibəriŋ]	형 이웃의, 근접해 있는	유 adjoining	neighboring countries 이웃 나라
685	**vacancy**	[véikənsi]	명 빈자리, 빈방	형 vacant 비어 있는	
686	**ventilate**	[véntəlèit]	동 환기시키다		ventilate a room 방을 환기시키다
687	**viewpoint**	[vjú:pɔ̀int]	명 견해		a difference of viewpoints 견해의 차이
688	**visualize**	[víʒuəlàiz]	동 시각화하다	형 visual 시각적인	Visualize what you want. 당신이 원하는 것을 시각화하세요.
689	**chaotic**	[keiɑ́tik]	형 혼돈된	유 disordered	be in a chaotic state 혼돈 상태에 있다
690	**circulate**	[sə́:rkjulèit]	동 순환하다	명 circulation 순환 유 spread	Blood circulates. 혈액이 순환하다.

1회독	월	일
2회독	월	일

✦ 주어진 우리말 문장에 맞도록 알맞은 단어를 넣어 문장을 완성하시오. 정답 p.204

I can't find anything on this ________ desk.
나는 이렇게 어질러진 책상에서는 아무것도 찾을 수 없다.

The style of painting in the ________ was much like the style in Greece and Rome.
르네상스 시대의 화풍은 그리스와 로마 시대의 화풍과 매우 닮아 있었다.

Some people are using the ________ in the gym.
여러 사람들이 체육관에서 러닝머신을 사용하고 있다.

America imposed an economic ________ on China.
미국은 중국에 경제적인 봉쇄를 가했다.

The development of the land ________ everything.
그 땅의 개발이 모든 것을 황폐시켰다.

Animals are losing their natural ________ because of human civilization.
인간의 문명 때문에 동물들은 자연 서식지를 잃고 있다.

He is of British ________.
그의 국적은 영국이다.

Many people are gathered here to plan the ________.
많은 이들이 폭동을 계획하기 위해 이 곳에 모였다.

A ________ house was built 100 years ago.
한 이웃집은 100년 전에 지어졌다.

I'm sorry, but we have no ________.
죄송합니다만, 빈방이 없습니다.

This room seems badly ________.
이 방은 환기가 잘 안 되는 것 같다.

This is entirely wrong from my ________.
내 견해로는 이건 완전히 틀렸다.

________ your dream is the first step to bring you success.
당신의 꿈을 시각화하는 것이 성공을 가져다 주는 첫 번째 관문이다.

It was a ________ age in the history of Europe.
그 당시는 유럽 역사에서 혼란스러운 시기였다.

This medicine helps your blood ________.
이 약은 당신의 피가 순환하는 것을 도와줍니다.

DAY 24

691 **weary** [wíəri]
형 피곤한 유 tired
weary eyes 피곤한 눈

692 **significance** [signífikəns]
명 중요성 형 significant 중요한 유 importance
of no significance 중요하지 않은

693 **comet** [kámit]
명 혜성 형 cometary 혜성 같은
Halley's Comet 핼리혜성

694 **equation** [ikwéiʃən]
명 동등, 등식, 방정식 형 equational 균등한, 방정식의
a chemical equation 화학 방정식

695 **inquire** [inkwáiər]
동 문의하다 명 inquiry 문의
inquire how to get A A에 가는 방법을 문의하다

696 **poke** [pouk]
동 쿡쿡 찌르다 명 찌르기

697 **spotless** [spátlis]
형 결백한, 흠 없는 명 spotlessness 결백 유 innocent
a spotless person 결백한 사람

698 **adrenaline** [ədrénəlin]
명 아드레날린

699 **exposure** [ikspóuʒər]
명 노출, 발각 동 expose 노출시키다 유 revelation
ultraviolet exposure 자외선 노출

700 **preservation** [prèzərvéiʃən]
명 보존 동 preserve 보존하다
environmental preservation 환경 보전

701 **ambition** [æmbíʃən]
명 야망 형 ambitious 야망을 품은
have great ambition 원대한 포부를 지니다

702 **fate** [feit]
명 운명, 비운 유 destiny
accept one's fate 운명을 받아들이다

703 **feedback** [fíːdbæ̀k]
명 피드백, 반응, 조사 결과
negative feedback 부정적인 피드백

704 **fistful** [fístfùl]
명 한 주먹, 다수
a fistful of sand 한 주먹 분량의 모래

705 **legend** [lédʒənd]
명 전설 형 legendary 전설상의
an urban legend 도시의 괴담

✦ 주어진 우리말 문장에 맞도록 알맞은 단어를 넣어 문장을 완성하시오. 정답 p.204

He looked at me with ________ eyes.
그는 피곤한 눈으로 나를 바라보았다.

Parents should realize the ________ of education in the family.
부모들은 가정 교육의 중요성을 인식해야 한다.

Halley's ________ is going to come back in 2061.
핼리혜성은 2061년에 다시 올 것이다.

Nobody in the class solved the ________.
교실 안의 누구도 그 방정식을 풀지 못했다.

I want to ________ about how to get a credit card.
신용카드를 어떻게 발급받는지 문의하고 싶어요.

He ________ her in the ribs with his finger over and over.
그는 손가락으로 계속해서 그녀의 옆구리를 쿡쿡 찔렀다.

I like a man who is ________.
나는 결백한 사람을 좋아한다.

Have you ever heard of ________?
아드레날린에 대해서 들어본 적 있니?

Skin gets dry after sun ________.
피부는 햇빛에 노출되면 건조해진다.

The old building is in a good state of ________.
낡은 건물이 잘 보전되어 있다.

His ________ is limitless.
그의 야망은 끝이 없다.

She decided not to accept her ________.
그녀는 자신의 운명을 받아들이지 않기로 결심했다.

I thank you for giving me positive ________ on my work.
제 작업에 대해 긍정적인 피드백을 주셔서 감사합니다.

He put a ________ of sand in the bucket.
그는 바구니 안에 한 주먹 분량의 모래를 넣었다.

The play was based on the ________ of King Arthur.
그 연극은 아더왕의 전설에 기초를 두고 있었다.

DAY 24

706	**quit** [kwit]	동 그만두다 quit drinking 술을 끊다	반 continue 계속하다
707	**temper** [témpər]	명 기질, 성질 an even temper 고른 성질	참 mood 기분
708	**asset** [ǽset]	명 자산 assets and liabilities 자산과 부채	유 property
709	**currency** [kə́:rənsi]	명 통화 paper currency 지폐	형 current 통화의
710	**fuss** [fʌs]	명 야단법석 make a fuss about ~에 대해 야단스럽게 떠들어대다	형 fussy 야단법석인
711	**meditate** [médətèit]	동 명상하다 meditate on ~에 관하여 명상하다	명 meditation 명상 유 ponder
712	**reliable** [riláiəbl]	형 신뢰할 수 있는 from a reliable source 믿을 만한 출처로부터	동 rely 의지하다 반 unreliable 신뢰할 수 없는
713	**tragic** [trǽdʒik]	형 비극의 a tragic actor 비극 배우	명 tragedy 비극 반 comedic 희극의
714	**blade** [bleid]	명 칼날 a razor blade 면도칼	
715	**destiny** [déstəni]	명 운명 work out one's own destiny 자신의 운명을 개척하다	동 destine 운명 짓다 유 fate
716	**grim** [grim]	형 엄한, 엄숙한 a grim face 엄숙한 얼굴	
717	**nap** [næp]	명 낮잠 take a nap 낮잠을 자다	
718	**revolutionize** [rèvəlú:ʃənàiz]	동 대변혁을 일으키다 revolutionize an activity 행동을 변혁시키다	
719	**unlimited** [ʌ̀nlímitid]	형 제한 없는 an unlimited challenge 무한한 도전	반 limited 제한된
720	**sake** [seik]	명 이익, 목적 for the sake of ~을 위하여	

✦ 주어진 우리말 문장에 맞도록 알맞은 단어를 넣어 문장을 완성하시오. 정답 p.204

I've ________ my job.
나 직장 그만뒀어.

He has such a quick ________.
그는 매우 급한 성미를 가졌다.

It is a very important cultural ________ for us.
그것은 우리에게 아주 중요한 문화적 자산이다.

The trading companies trade their goods in foreign ________.
무역 회사들은 외화로 그들의 상품들을 거래한다.

Don't make a ________ about the matter.
그 상황에 대해 야단스럽게 떠들어대지 마라.

Monks ________ in temples every day.
승려들은 매일 사원에서 명상한다.

It's not ________ to judge a man only by his looks.
사람을 외모로만 판단하는 것은 신뢰할 수 없다.

Watching ________ dramas makes me gloomy.
비극적인 드라마를 보면 우울해진다.

I am going to ask them to bring some new ________.
나는 그들에게 새 칼날 몇 개를 보내달라고 요구할 것이다.

We want to be in control of our own ________.
우리는 우리 자신의 운명을 통제하고 싶어한다.

His ________ way of talking to others makes me angry.
다른 사람들에게 엄하게 말하는 그의 방식이 나를 화나게 만든다.

In the afternoon, she would take a ________.
오후에 그녀는 낮잠을 자곤 했다.

Automation has ________ the industry.
자동화는 산업을 크게 변혁시켰다.

What people want is ________.
사람들이 원하는 것은 한계가 없다.

They fight all the time for the ________ of money.
그들은 돈 때문에 항상 싸운다.

REVIEW TEST 12 DAY 23 ~ DAY 24

A 우리말과 같은 뜻이 되도록 빈칸에 들어갈 알맞은 단어를 적으시오.

1. a razor ________________ (면도칼)
2. in broad ________________ (대낮에)
3. take a ________________ (낮잠을 자다)
4. ________________ drinking (술을 끊다)
5. for the ________________ of (~을 위하여)
6. ________________ countries (이웃 나라)
7. ________________ a room (방을 환기시키다)
8. be ________________ on the arm (팔이 쏘이다)
9. a ________________ of sand (한 주먹 분량의 모래)
10. make a ________________ about (~에 대해 야단스럽게 떠들어대다)

B 다음 괄호 안의 지시대로 주어진 단어를 변형시키고 그 뜻을 적으시오.

		변형	뜻
1	equation (형용사형으로) →	________________	________________
2	populate (명사형으로) →	________________	________________
3	consult (명사형으로) →	________________	________________
4	coordinate (명사형으로) →	________________	________________
5	assumption (동사형으로) →	________________	________________
6	devastate (명사형으로) →	________________	________________
7	significance (형용사형으로) →	________________	________________
8	comet (형용사형으로) →	________________	________________
9	spotless (명사형으로) →	________________	________________
10	legend (형용사형으로) →	________________	________________

정답 p.204

C 다음 영영풀이에 해당하는 단어를 보기에서 골라 적으시오.

보기				
nationality	riot	feedback	expose	corporation
ragged	currency	blockade	circulate	ambition

1. torn or worn to rags; tattered → ______________
2. any obstruction of passage or progress → ______________
3. to move in a circle or circuit → ______________
4. to leave without protection → ______________
5. a desire to be successful or famous → ______________
6. a reaction or response to a particular process or activity → ______________
7. something that is used as a medium of exchange; money → ______________
8. a business firm whose articles of incorporation have been approved in some state
   → ______________
9. the status of belonging to a particular nation, whether by birth or naturalization
   → ______________
10. a noisy, violent public disorder caused by a group or crowd of people
   → ______________

D 우리말과 같은 뜻이 되도록 주어진 문장의 빈칸을 완성하시오.

1. 통역사가 되기 위해서는 최소한 한 개의 외국어에 능통해야 한다.
   → You need ______________ in at least one foreign language to be a translator.
2. 폭력은 사람들 사이의 긴장감에 의해 일어날 수 있다.
   → Violence can be caused by ______________ between people.
3. 여러 사람들이 체육관에서 러닝머신을 사용하고 있다.
   → Some people are using the ______________ in the gym.
4. 인간의 문명 때문에 동물들은 자연 서식지를 잃고 있다.
   → Animals are losing their natural ______________ because of human civilization.

⑤ 죄송합니다만, 빈방이 없습니다.

➔ I'm sorry, but we have no ________________.

⑥ 신용카드를 어떻게 발급받는지 문의하고 싶어요.

➔ I want to ________________ about how to get a credit card.

⑦ 그는 손가락으로 계속해서 그녀의 옆구리를 쿡쿡 찔렀다.

➔ He ________________ her in the ribs with his finger over and over.

⑧ 낡은 건물이 잘 보전되어 있다.

➔ The old building is in a good state of ________________.

⑨ 그것은 우리에게 아주 중요한 문화적 자산이다.

➔ It is a very important cultural ________________ for us.

⑩ 승려들은 매일 사원에서 명상한다.

➔ Monks ________________ in temples every day.

E 문장의 밑줄 친 부분에 해당하는 유의어 혹은 반의어를 보기에서 골라 적으시오.

보기				
confer	disordered	limited	sunlight	fate
tired	unreliable	comedic	adjoining	tidy

① The incident happened in broad daylight. 유의어 = ________________

② I can't find anything on this messy desk. 반의어 ↔ ________________

③ He looked at me with weary eyes. 유의어 = ________________

④ A neighboring house was built 100 years ago. 유의어 = ________________

⑤ It was a chaotic age in the history of Europe. 유의어 = ________________

⑥ He needed to consult with a lawyer. 유의어 = ________________

⑦ It's not reliable to judge a man only by his looks. 반의어 ↔ ________________

⑧ Watching tragic dramas makes me gloomy. 반의어 ↔ ________________

⑨ What people want is unlimited. 반의어 ↔ ________________

⑩ We want to be in control of our own destinies. 유의어 = ________________

F 영어발음을 듣고 영어단어를 적은 후, 우리말 뜻을 적으시오.

영어단어 듣고 쓰기 

	영어	우리말		영어	우리말
❶	______	______	❽	______	______
❷	______	______	❾	______	______
❸	______	______	❿	______	______
❹	______	______	⓫	______	______
❺	______	______	⓬	______	______
❻	______	______	⓭	______	______
❼	______	______	⓮	______	______

G 영어문장을 듣고 빈칸에 들어갈 단어를 채워 문장을 완성하시오.

영어문장 듣고 쓰기

❶ They ______ the tomatoes to make ketchup.

❷ She is wearing a uniform and has a ______ bag in her right hand.

❸ The evaluation of the survey involved some amount of ______.

❹ ______ your dream is the first step to bring you success.

❺ Have you ever heard of ______?

❻ He put a ______ of sand in the bucket.

❼ He has such a quick ______.

❽ I am going to ask them to bring some new ______.

❾ Automation has ______ the industry.

❿ She decided not to accept her ______.

⓫ The central part of the city is densely ______.

⓬ Let me contact him and ______ our schedules.

⓭ His false ______ often leads him to answer negatively.

⓮ The development of the land ______ everything.

⓯ Halley's ______ is going to come back in 2061.

⓰ I like a man who is ______.

721 **cape** [keip]
명 망토
a bullfighter's cape 투우사의 망토

722 **carefree** [kέərfrìː]
형 근심이 없는 명 carefreeness 태평함
a carefree school life 걱정이 없는 학교 생활

723 **categorize** [kǽtəgəràiz]
동 분류하다 명 categorization 분류 유 classify
categorize information 정보를 분류하다

724 **cease** [siːs]
동 중지하다 유 stop
Cease fire! 사격 중지!

725 **elaborate** [ilǽvərət]
형 공들인, 고심한 명 elaboration 공들여 만듦
an elaborate dinner 공들인 만찬

726 **citizenship** [sítəzənʃip]
명 시민권
acquire citizenship 국적을 취득하다

727 **weird** [wiərd]
형 기묘한, 이상한 반 normal 평범한
a weird costume 이상한 복장

728 **simplify** [símpləfài]
동 간단히 하다 명 simplification 간소화
simplify one's explanation 설명을 간단하게 하다

729 **ensure** [inʃúər]
동 확실히 하다, 지키다 유 guarantee
ensure a person against ~으로부터 누군가를 지키다

730 **inherit** [inhérit]
동 상속하다, 유전하다 명 inheritance 유산, 유전
an inherited quality 유전 형질

731 **plague** [pleig]
명 전염병 유 epidemic
a cholera plague 콜레라 전염병

732 **spectacular** [spektǽkjulər]
형 장관인, 볼 만한 명 spectacle 장관 유 striking
a spectacular scene 장엄한 광경

733 **adjustment** [ədʒʌ́stmənt]
명 적응 동 adjust 적응하다 유 adaptation
make an adjustment 적응하다

734 **consistent** [kənsístənt]
형 일관된 명 consistency 일관성 유 coherent
a consistent policy 일관된 정책

735 **interpretation** [intə̀ːrprətéiʃən]
명 해석, 이해 동 interpret 해석하다 유 translation
put one's own interpretation on ~을 나름대로 해석하다

✦ 주어진 우리말 문장에 맞도록 알맞은 단어를 넣어 문장을 완성하시오. 정답 p.205

She always wears a ______ when she goes out in winter.
그녀는 겨울에 밖에 나갈 때 항상 망토를 입는다.

My daughter had a ______ school life.
내 딸은 근심 없는 학교 생활을 보냈다.

We ______ the songs by genre.
우리는 노래를 장르별로 분류했다.

She never ______ telling me about her troubles.
그녀는 나에게 끊임 없이(결코 중단하지 않고) 자신의 문제를 이야기한다.

It is seemingly true that their report was more ______ than ours.
그들의 보고서는 우리의 것에 비해 훨씬 공들인 것처럼 보이는 게 사실이다.

She took Canadian ______ in 2002.
그녀는 2002년에 캐나다 시민권을 취득했다.

He has some ______ ideas.
그는 좀 이상한 생각을 한다.

Let me ______ the explanation.
설명을 간단하게 할게요.

I want to ______ they will refund my money in case I'm not satisfied with my purchase. 구매가 만족스럽지 않을 경우에 제 돈을 환불해 주신다는 것을 확실히 하고 싶어요.

He ______ his father's farm.
그는 아버지의 농장을 물려받았다.

A cholera ______ raged throughout the entire European nation.
콜레라 전염병이 유럽 전역에 거세게 퍼졌다.

People were amazed by the ______ views before their eyes.
사람들은 그들 눈 앞에 펼쳐진 장엄한 광경에 놀랐다.

He tried to make an ______ to American culture.
그는 미국 문화에 적응하려고 애썼다.

What we need is a ______ policy.
우리가 필요한 것은 일관된 정책이다.

Language ______ is the point of reading.
언어 해석이 독서의 핵심이다.

DAY 25

736	**stiff** [stif]	형 뻣뻣한, 딱딱한 have stiff shoulders 어깨가 뻐근하다	동 stiffen 뻣뻣해지다 반 flexible 유연한
737	**controversy** [kɑ́ntrəvə̀ːrsi]	명 논쟁 have a controversy with ~와 논쟁하다	형 controversial 논쟁의 유 argument
738	**itch** [itʃ]	동 가렵다 My back itches. 등이 가렵다.	형 itchy 가려운
739	**landfill** [lǽndfil]	명 매립식 쓰레기 처리, 쓰레기 매립지 a landfill site 매립식 쓰레기 처리 장소	
740	**leadership** [líːdərʃip]	명 지도력 leadership training 지도력 훈련	
741	**python** [páiθɑn]	명 구렁이, 비단뱀 a deadly python 치명적인 뱀	
742	**tact** [tækt]	명 재치, 요령 with tact 재치 있게	형 tactful 재치 있는
743	**ascend** [əsénd]	동 오르다, 올라가다 ascend the throne 왕위에 오르다	형 ascendant 상승하는 유 climb
744	**crucial** [krúːʃəl]	형 중요한 a crucial role 중대한 역할	유 important
745	**fund** [fʌnd]	명 기금, 자금 동 자금을 대다 a relief fund 구호 기금	
746	**masterpiece** [mǽstərpìːs]	명 걸작 an immortal masterpiece 불후의 명작	
747	**regulate** [régjulèit]	동 통제하다, 규정하다 regulate traffic 교통을 통제하다	명 regulation 규정 유 govern
748	**toll** [toul]	동 (종, 시계를) 울리다, (시간을) 알리다 toll a bell 종을 치다	참 toll 사용료
749	**beware** [biwɛ́ər]	동 조심하다 Beware of the dog! 개조심!	유 be careful
750	**depiction** [dipíkʃən]	명 묘사, 서술 a realistic depiction 사실적인 묘사	동 depict 묘사하다 유 description

✦ 주어진 우리말 문장에 맞도록 알맞은 단어를 넣어 문장을 완성하시오. 정답 p.205

He has a ______ manner of speaking.
그는 딱딱한 말투를 가지고 있다.

These are the facts that are beyond ______.
이것들은 논쟁할 여지가 없는 사실들이다.

The mosquito bite ______.
모기에 물린 곳이 가렵다.

The city is looking for a suitable site for the new ______.
그 도시는 새로운 매립식 쓰레기 처리를 위한 적당한 장소를 찾고 있다.

Her ______ skills are beyond my expectations.
그녀의 지도력은 내 기대 이상이다.

A ______ kills animals by squeezing them with its body.
구렁이는 동물을 몸으로 감아서 죽인다.

A diplomat must have ______.
외교관은 재치가 있어야 한다.

The smoke slowly ______ to the sky.
연기가 천천히 하늘로 올라갔다.

It is ______ that we go over those documents again.
우리가 그 서류들을 다시 점검하는 것이 매우 중요하다.

The charity has raised money for a disaster relief ______ since last month.
그 자선단체는 지난 달부터 재난 구호 기금을 모금해 오고 있다.

The museum has Picasso's ______.
그 박물관은 피카소의 걸작들을 소장하고 있다.

The government ______ excessive competition among companies.
정부는 기업 간의 과도한 경쟁을 규제한다.

The church bell ______ the hour.
교회종이 울리며 시간을 알렸다.

You must ______ of strangers.
낯선 사람을 조심해야 한다.

One of the things I like in his painting is the realistic ______ of life.
그의 그림에서 내가 좋아하는 점 중 하나는 삶에 대한 사실적인 묘사이다.

DAY 26

751 **gorgeous** [gɔ́ːrdʒəs]
형 멋진 | 부 gorgeously 멋지게 | 유 splendid
a gorgeous girl 멋진 여자아이

752 **mount** [maunt]
동 (산이나 왕위 등에) 오르다 | 유 ascend
mount a hill 언덕에 오르다

753 **retrospect** [rétrəspèkt]
명 회고, 회상 동 회고하다 | 반 prospect 예상, 기대
in retrospect 돌이켜보면

754 **unidentifiable** [ʌ̀naidéntifáiəbl]
형 식별불능의, 증명할 수 없는
unidentifiable noises 식별할 수 없는 소음

755 **bureau** [bjúərou]
명 (관청의) 국, 안내소 | 유 department
the Exit and Entry Control Bureau 출입국 관리국

756 **unwilling** [ʌ̀nwíliŋ]
형 마지못해 하는 | 명 unwillingness 마지못해 함 | 유 reluctant
be unwilling to+**동사원형** ~하고 싶어하지 않다

757 **distribution** [dìstrəbjúːʃən]
명 분배, 분포 | 동 distribute 분배하다 | 유 division
the distribution of wealth 부의 분배

758 **domestic** [dəméstik]
형 국내의 | 동 domesticate 길들이다
a domestic product 국산품

759 **drawing** [drɔ́ːiŋ]
명 그림 | 동 draw 그리다 | 유 picture
a watercolor drawing 수채화

760 **effective** [iféktiv]
형 효과적인 | 명 effect 효과, 결과 | 반 ineffective 효과 없는
effective teaching methods 효과적인 교수법

761 **impolite** [ìmpəláit]
형 예의 없는 | 반 polite 예의 바른
impolite behavior 예의 없는 행동

762 **civilization** [sìvəlizéiʃən | -lai-]
명 문명(화) | 동 civilize 문명화하다 | 유 culture
Western civilization 서양 문명

763 **wholesome** [hóulsəm]
형 건강에 좋은 | 유 healthy
a wholesome environment 건강에 좋은 환경

764 **informed** [infɔ́ːrmd]
형 정보통의, 유식한
an informed man 박식한 사람

765 **physician** [fizíʃən]
명 의사, 내과 의사 | 유 doctor | 참 surgeon 외과 의사
a physician's prescription 의사의 처방

✦ 주어진 우리말 문장에 맞도록 알맞은 단어를 넣어 문장을 완성하시오. 정답 p.205

He saw a ______ woman passing by him.
그는 한 멋진 여자가 옆을 지나가는 것을 보았다.

Do not ______ that horse.
저 말에 타지 마세요.

In ______, he had no choice but to sign the contract.
돌이켜보면 그는 계약에 서명하지 않을 수 없었다.

He gave his views on the ______ origin of the universe.
그는 증명할 수 없는 우주의 기원에 대한 자신의 견해를 설명했다.

He was employed in a tourist ______.
그는 관광청에서 일했다.

They are ______ to give us any more detailed information.
그들은 우리에게 더 이상 자세한 정보를 주고 싶어하지 않는다.

They studied the ______ of this odd species across the country.
그들은 전국에 걸쳐 이 특이한 종의 분포를 연구했다.

We should try to buy ______ products.
우리는 국산품을 사려고 노력해야 한다.

As a child, his interest was ______.
어릴 적 그의 관심은 그림이었다.

The medicine is an ______ cure for headaches.
그 약은 두통에 효과적인 치료제이다.

I cannot take his ______ behavior any more.
나는 더 이상 그의 예의 없는 행동을 견딜 수 없다.

Western ______ heavily influences Eastern countries.
서양 문명은 동양에 막대한 영향을 끼친다.

Homemade food is ______.
가정식은 건강에 좋다.

______ people knew the company was shaky.
정보에 밝은 사람들은 그 회사가 흔들리고 있다는 것을 알았다.

The ______ prescribed him some medicine.
의사가 그에게 몇 가지 약을 처방하였다.

DAY 26

No.	Word	Pronunciation	Meaning	Related	Example
766	**sow**	[sou]	동 씨를 뿌리다	유 scatter 참 saw 바느질하다	sow the seeds of ~의 씨를 뿌리다
767	**activate**	[ǽktəvèit]	동 활성화하다	명 activation 활성화	activate the server 서버를 활성화하다
768	**confirm**	[kənfə́ːrm]	동 확실히 하다, 확인하다	형 confirmative 확실히 하는 유 prov	confirm one's suspicions 의혹을 확인하다
769	**exert**	[igzə́ːrt]	동 (힘·지식 등을) 쓰다, 발휘하다	명 exertion 노력	exert an effort 노력을 기울이다
770	**preliminary**	[prilímənèri]	형 예비의, 준비의 명 준비	유 preparatory	a preliminary test 예비시험
771	**alertness**	[ələ́ːrtnis]	명 방심하지 않음, 경각심	형 alert 방심 않는, 빈틈 없는 유 vigilance	a lack of alertness 경각심 부족
772	**falsehood**	[fɔ́ːlshùd]	명 허위	반 truth 진실	tell a falsehood 거짓말하다
773	**professional**	[prəféʃənl]	형 전문적인	유 qualified, skilled	a professional actor 전문 배우
774	**prominent**	[prámənənt]	형 눈에 띄는, 중요한	명 prominence 현저함 유 outstanding	a prominent leader 중요한 지도자
775	**prospect**	[práspekt]	명 전망	형 prospective 예상되는 유 view	prospect of one's job 직업의 전망
776	**swarm**	[swɔːrm]	명 떼	유 herd	a swarm of 다수의
777	**arithmetic**	[əríθmətik]	명 산수 형 산수상의		mental arithmetic 암산
778	**creek**	[kriːk]	명 시내, 지류	유 stream	the Cheonggye creek 청계천
779	**fruitless**	[frúːtlis]	형 결실이 없는	반 fruitful 결실의	a fruitless effort 결실 없는 노력 [헛수고]
780	**management**	[mǽnidʒmənt]	명 경영	동 manage 경영하다 유 administration	hotel management 호텔 경영

1회독	월	일
2회독	월	일

✦ 주어진 우리말 문장에 맞도록 알맞은 단어를 넣어 문장을 완성하시오. 정답 p.205

My mom ________ flower seeds in our garden this spring.
올 봄에 엄마가 우리 정원에 꽃씨를 뿌리셨다.

The telephone was ________.
그 전화는 활성화되었다.

I ________ that he stole my wallet yesterday.
나는 그가 어제 내 지갑을 훔쳤다는 것을 확인했다.

The government will ________ an effort to restore the facility.
정부는 그 시설을 복구하기 위해 노력을 기울일 것이다.

Some ________ polls showed that he would win the election.
몇몇 예비선거는 그가 선거에서 이길 것이라는 것을 보여 주었다.

The drug improved mental ________.
그 약은 정신적 각성을 증진시켰다.

Truth, if exaggerated, may become ________.
진실도 과장된다면 거짓이 될 수 있다.

When she was 17, she became a ________ actress.
그녀가 17살이었을 때, 전문 배우가 되었다.

He played a ________ role in making the decision.
그는 결정하는 데 중요한 역할을 했다.

It isn't easy to predict the ________ of my new job.
나의 새로운 직업의 전망을 예측하기란 쉽지 않다.

A large ________ of locusts ate all the crops.
많은 메뚜기 떼가 곡물을 다 먹어 치웠다.

Practice mental ________ when shopping.
쇼핑을 할 때는 암산을 해라.

Factory waste has polluted the ________.
공장 폐기물이 지류를 오염시켰다.

I couldn't believe that all our efforts had been ________.
나는 모든 노력이 헛된 것이란 걸 믿을 수 없었다.

The bad ________ of the company was criticized by the workers.
그 회사의 형편없는 경영은 노동자들에 의해 비난을 받았다.

REVIEW TEST 13 DAY 25 ~ DAY 26

A 우리말과 같은 뜻이 되도록 빈칸에 들어갈 알맞은 단어를 적으시오.

1. a relief ________________ (구호 기금)
2. a ________________ product (국산품)
3. make an ________________ (적응하다)
4. an ________________ man (박식한 사람)
5. a ________________ scene (장엄한 광경)
6. a ________________ costume (이상한 복장)
7. ________________ traffic (교통을 통제하다)
8. an immortal ________________ (불후의 명작)
9. ________________ one's suspicions (의혹을 확인하다)
10. ________________ teaching methods (효과적인 교수법)

B 다음 괄호 안의 지시대로 주어진 단어를 변형시키고 그 뜻을 적으시오.

		변형	뜻
1. inherit (명사형으로)	→		
2. effective (명사형으로)	→		
3. adjustment (동사형으로)	→		
4. consistent (명사형으로)	→		
5. stiff (동사형으로)	→		
6. controversy (형용사형으로)	→		
7. depiction (동사형으로)	→		
8. domestic (동사형으로)	→		
9. exert (명사형으로)	→		
10. prominent (명사형으로)	→		

정답 p.205

C 다음 영영풀이에 해당하는 단어를 보기에서 골라 적으시오.

보기				
simplify	landfill	falsehood	elaborate	toll
ensure	management	activate	mount	tact

1. to make sure or certain → ______
2. worked out with great care and attention to detail → ______
3. to make less complex or complicated → ______
4. a system in which waste materials are buried underground → ______
5. a keen sense of what to say or do to avoid giving offense → ______
6. to make something known by ringing → ______
7. to rise or go to a higher position, level, degree, etc.; ascend → ______
8. to make active; cause to function or act → ______
9. a false statement; lie → ______
10. the act or manner of managing; handling, direction, or control → ______

D 우리말과 같은 뜻이 되도록 주어진 문장의 빈칸을 완성하시오.

1. 내 딸은 근심 없는 학교 생활을 보냈다.
   → My daughter had a ______ school life.
2. 그녀는 나에게 끊임 없이(결코 중단하지 않고) 자신의 문제를 이야기한다.
   → She never ______ telling me about her troubles.
3. 언어 해석이 독서의 핵심이다.
   → Language ______ is the point of reading.
4. 모기에 물린 곳이 가렵다.
   → The mosquito bite ______.

⑤ 그녀의 지도력은 내 기대 이상이다.

→ Her ______________ skills are beyond my expectations.

⑥ 연기가 천천히 하늘로 올라갔다.

→ The smoke slowly ______________ to the sky.

⑦ 낯선 사람을 조심해야 한다.

→ You must ______________ of strangers.

⑧ 그는 관광청에서 일했다.

→ He was employed in a tourist ______________.

⑨ 가정식은 건강에 좋다. → Homemade food is ______________.

⑩ 올 봄에 엄마가 우리 정원에 꽃씨를 뿌리셨다.

→ My mom ______________ flower seeds in our garden this spring.

E 문장의 밑줄 친 부분에 해당하는 유의어 혹은 반의어를 보기에서 골라 적으시오.

보기				
epidemic	splendid	reluctant	herd	normal
vigilance	govern	fruitful	prospect	culture

① He has some weird ideas. 반의어 ↔ ______________

② A cholera plague raged throughout the entire European nation.

유의어 = ______________

③ The government regulates excessive competition among companies.

유의어 = ______________

④ He saw a gorgeous woman passing by him. 유의어 = ______________

⑤ In retrospect, he had no choice but to sign the contract. 반의어 ↔ ______________

⑥ They are unwilling to give us any more detailed information. 유의어 = ______________

⑦ Western civilization heavily influences Eastern countries. 유의어 = ______________

⑧ The drug improved mental alertness. 유의어 = ______________

⑨ A large swarm of locusts ate all the crops. 유의어 = ______________

⑩ I couldn't believe that all our efforts had been fruitless. 반의어 ↔ ______________

F 영어발음을 듣고 영어단어를 적은 후, 우리말 뜻을 적으시오.

영어단어 듣고 쓰기 

	영어	우리말		영어	우리말
❶	________	________	❽	________	________
❷	________	________	❾	________	________
❸	________	________	❿	________	________
❹	________	________	⓫	________	________
❺	________	________	⓬	________	________
❻	________	________	⓭	________	________
❼	________	________	⓮	________	________

G 영어문장을 듣고 빈칸에 들어갈 단어를 채워 문장을 완성하시오.

영어문장 듣고 쓰기

❶ She always wears a ________ when she goes out in winter.

❷ A ________ kills animals by squeezing them with its body.

❸ The charity has raised money for a disaster relief ________ since last month.

❹ He gave his views on the ________ origin of the universe.

❺ The ________ prescribed him some medicine.

❻ I ________ that he stole my wallet yesterday.

❼ When she was 17, she became a ________ actress.

❽ Practice mental ________ when shopping.

❾ He ________ his father's farm.

❿ The medicine is an ________ cure for headaches.

⓫ He tried to make an ________ to American culture.

⓬ What we need is a ________ policy.

⓭ He has a ________ manner of speaking.

⓮ These are the facts that are beyond ________.

⓯ One of the things I like in his painting is the realistic ________ of life.

⓰ The government will ________ an effort to restore the facility.

781 **recyclable** [ri:sáikləbl]
형 재활용할 수 있는 명 recycling 재활용
recyclable paper 재활용할 수 있는 종이

782 **tickle** [tíkl]
동 간지럽히다 명 간지럼, 간지러움
be tickled to death 포복절도하다

783 **barefoot** [bɛ́ərfùt]
형 맨발의
walk barefoot 맨발로 걷다

784 **density** [dénsəti]
명 밀도 형 dense 조밀한
traffic density 교통량

785 **glaze** [gleiz]
명 유약, 광택제
a tile with glaze 유약칠이 되어 있는 타일

786 **monk** [mʌŋk]
명 수도자, 성직자 형 monkish 수도사의
a Buddhist monk 승려

787 **respiration** [rèspəréiʃən]
명 호흡 동 respire 호흡하다 유 breath
respiration system 호흡기관

788 **undo** [ʌndú:]
동 원상태로 되돌리다, 취소하다
undo the past 과거를 되돌리다

789 **bruise** [bru:z]
명 타박상, 멍 동 멍들게 하다
cuts and bruises 베이고 멍든 상처

790 **dispose** [dispóuz]
동 처리하다, 배치하다 명 disposal 처분
dispose of ~을 처분하다

791 **cabinet** [kǽbənit]
명 진열장 유 locker
look in a cabinet 진열장 안을 보다

792 **humble** [hʌ́mbl]
형 겸손한 부 humbly 겸손하게 유 modest
a humble heart 겸손한 마음

793 **hymn** [him]
명 찬송가
sing a hymn 찬송가를 부르다

794 **illuminate** [ilú:mənèit]
동 밝게 하다 유 brighten
be poorly illuminated 조명이 나쁘다

795 **immigration** [ìməgréiʃən]
명 이민 동 immigrate 이주하다
immigration office 출입국 관리소

✦ 주어진 우리말 문장에 맞도록 알맞은 단어를 넣어 문장을 완성하시오. 정답 p.206

The paper you are holding is ______________.
당신이 들고 있는 종이는 재활용할 수 있다.

I was ______________ him, and he was giggling.
나는 그를 간지럽히고 있었고, 그는 킥킥거리며 웃고 있었다.

Strangely enough, she was ______________ in a white dress.
정말 이상하게도, 그녀는 맨발에 하얀 드레스를 입고 있었다.

This area had a population ______________ of ten people per square mile.
이 지역은 평방 마일당 인구밀도가 10명이었다.

I bought the hand-painted French tiles with the decorative ______________.
나는 사람 손으로 장식 유약을 칠한 프랑스식 타일을 샀다.

When I went to Thailand, it was easy to see ______________ on the street.
태국에 갔을 때 거리에서 승려들을 심심치 않게 보았다.

We should check our ______________ system regularly.
호흡기관을 정기적으로 검사해야 한다.

She knew it would be difficult to ______________ the damage.
그녀는 피해를 원상으로 되돌리는 것이 어려울 거라는 것을 알고 있었다.

The little girl fell and ______________ her knees.
어린 소녀는 넘어져서 무릎에 멍이 들었다.

______________ of these old books.
이 낡은 책들을 처분해라.

Carrying the ______________ will be the hardest thing, I guess.
추측하건대, 진열장을 옮기는 것이 제일 어려운 일이 될 거에요.

To learn from others, you need a ______________ manner.
다른 사람들로부터 배우기 위해서는 겸손한 태도가 필요하다.

I practiced singing a ______________.
나는 찬송가 부르는 것을 연습했다.

Brightly colored pictures ______________ the hall.
밝게 칠해진 그림들이 복도를 밝게 했다.

The ______________ officer stamped my passport.
출입국 관리 직원이 내 여권에 도장을 찍었다.

DAY 27

796 **outlaw** [áutlɔ̀ː]
명 무법자
an infamous outlaw 악명 높은 무법자

797 **civilize** [sívəlàiz]
동 개화시키다 명 civilization 문명

798 **wicked** [wíkid]
형 악한 명 wickedness 사악함
a wicked person 악한 사람

799 **perfection** [pərfékʃən]
명 완벽, 완전 형 perfect 완벽한
bring to perfection 완성시키다

800 **sniff** [snif]
동 코를 킁킁거리다, 콧방귀를 뀌다
sniff danger 위험을 감지하다

801 **accumulate** [əkjúːmjulèit]
동 모으다 명 accumulation 축적 유 collect
accumulate a fortune 재산을 모으다

802 **compression** [kəmpréʃən]
명 압축 동 compress 압축하다 반 enlargement 확대
hardware compression 하드웨어 압축

803 **exaggerate** [igzǽdʒərèit]
동 과장해서 말하다 명 exaggeration 과장 반 understate 억제해서 말하다
exaggerate one's own importance 자만하다

804 **intensive** [inténsiv]
형 집중적인 명 intension 집중 반 extensive 광범위한
an intensive course 특강, 집중 과정

805 **starry** [stáːri]
형 별이 많은
a starry night 별이 많이 보이는 밤

806 **context** [kántekst]
명 문맥, 전후관계 형 contextual 문맥상의, 전후관계의
in this context 이와 관련하여

807 **irresistible** [ìrizístəbl]
형 저항할 수 없는 유 overwhelming
an irresistible force 불가항력

808 **stun** [stʌn]
동 기절시키다 형 stunning 굉장히 멋진, stunned 정신이 멍한 유 shock
stun the bear 곰을 기절시키다

809 **succession** [səkséʃən]
명 연속 형 successive 연속적인 유 series
two years in succession 2년 연속으로

810 **superlative** [səpə́ːrlətiv]
형 최상급의, 최고의 유 excellent

✦ 주어진 우리말 문장에 맞도록 알맞은 단어를 넣어 문장을 완성하시오. 정답 p.206

The story is about an American ______ from a long time ago.
그 이야기는 오래 전 미국의 무법자에 대한 것이다.

The missionaries tried to ______ the natives of Africa.
선교사들이 아프리카의 원주민들을 개화시키려고 했다.

Stay away from ______ people.
악한 사람들로부터 떨어져 있어라.

He played Hamlet in the play to ______.
그는 연극에서 햄릿을 완벽하게 연기했다.

The dog ______ at the stranger.
개가 킁킁거리며 낯선 사람의 냄새를 맡았다.

Your way to ______ a million dollars is very unique.
당신이 백만 불을 모으는 방법은 매우 독특하군요.

Increase your available storage space by hardware ______.
하드웨어 압축으로 저장 가능 공간을 늘리세요.

He tends to ______ that he has too much homework.
그는 숙제가 너무 많다고 과장해서 말하는 경향이 있다.

I'm planning to take the ______ course during vacation.
나는 방학 동안에 특강을 수강할 계획이다.

The sky was deep blue and ______.
하늘은 짙은 파랑색이고 별이 많았다.

Without a ______, I assume it was torn on purpose.
전후관계가 없었다면 그것은 일부러 찢어진 것이라고 생각한다.

I cannot refuse this offer; it is ______.
나는 이 제안을 거절할 수 없다. 그것은 저항할 수 없을 만큼 매혹적이기 때문이다.

The view of the city from the tower almost ______ me.
타워에서의 도시의 정경은 거의 나를 기절시켰다(놀라게 했다).

This area is known as a dangerous place due to a ______ of traffic accidents.
이 지역은 교통사고의 연발로 위험한 곳으로 알려져 있다.

She took us to a ______ hotel.
그녀는 우리를 최상급 호텔로 데려갔다.

811 **apt** [æpt]
형 ~하기 쉬운, 적절한
be apt to+동사원형 ~하기 쉽다

812 **cram** [kræm]
동 억지로 채워 넣다
cram oneself with food 잔뜩 먹다

813 **frequency** [fríːkwənsi]
명 빈번, 빈도, 주파수 형 frequent 자주 일어나는
an audible frequency 가청 주파수

814 **luxurious** [lʌgʒúəriəs]
형 화려한 명 luxury 사치, 호사
luxurious food 화려한 음식

815 **reconcile** [rékənsàil]
동 화해시키다, 화해하다 명 reconciliation 화해 반 quarrel 싸우다
reconcile A with B A를 B와 화해시키다

816 **thrilling** [θríliŋ]
형 떨리는 유 exciting
a thrilling experience 떨리는 경험

817 **auxiliary** [ɔːgzíljəri]
형 보조의
an auxiliary verb 조동사

818 **defrost** [di(ː)frɔ́ːst]
동 얼음을 제거하다, 해동하다
defrost the freezer 냉동실의 얼음을 제거하다

819 **glacier** [gléiʃər | glǽsjə]
명 빙하
an alpine glacier 고산성 빙하

820 **moderate** [mɑ́dərət]
형 알맞은 명 moderation 알맞음, 중용
a moderate price 알맞은 가격

821 **resemble** [rizémbl]
동 닮다 명 resemblance 닮음 유 look like
resemble A closely A를 꼭 닮다

822 **unarmed** [ʌnɑ́ːrmd]
형 무기를 지니지 않은 반 armed 무장한
an unarmed person 무기를 지니지 않은 사람

823 **breed** [briːd]
동 양육하다, 일으키다 유 raise
breed disbelief among people 사람들 사이에 불신을 키우다

824 **disclose** [disklóuz]
동 밝히다, 폭로하다 유 reveal
disclose a secret 비밀을 폭로하다

825 **hire** [háiər]
동 고용하다 유 employ
hire a clerk 점원을 고용하다

✦ 주어진 우리말 문장에 맞도록 알맞은 단어를 넣어 문장을 완성하시오. 정답 p.206

Children are ______ to act impatiently.
아이들은 참을성 없게 행동하기 쉽다.

She ______ her bag with books.
그녀는 가방에 책을 잔뜩 채워 넣었다.

This radio station broadcasts on three different ______.
라디오 방송국에서 세 개의 다른 주파수로 방송을 한다.

The interior of this room is too ______.
이 방의 인테리어는 너무 화려하다.

My friend and I ______ after he apologized to me.
친구가 내게 사과를 해 우리는 화해했다.

Going on a trip alone was a ______ experience for me.
혼자서 여행을 갔던 것은 나에게 떨리는 경험이었다.

Today, we studied ______ verbs in our grammar class.
오늘 우리는 문법 시간에 조동사에 대해서 공부했다.

She put the bread into the microwave oven to ______ it.
그녀는 해동시키기 위해 빵을 전자레인지에 넣었다.

The longest valley ______ extends 10km.
가장 긴 계곡 빙하는 10km에 달한다.

Visit our site for a ______ annual fee.
적절한 연회비를 내고 우리 사이트를 방문하세요.

I don't ______ my parents in appearance at all.
외모상 나는 부모님을 전혀 닮지 않았다.

The police found that the criminal was ______.
경찰은 그 범인이 무기를 지니지 않았다는 것을 발견했다.

The cruel situation may ______ disbelief among people.
그 잔혹한 상황은 사람들 사이에 불신을 키울지도 모른다.

The company ______ that he will retire this year.
회사는 그가 올해 퇴임할 것이라고 밝혔다.

They ______ a new employee.
그들은 새로운 직원을 고용했다.

DAY 28

826	**dissimilar** [dissímələr]	형 다른 dissimilar in character 성질이 다른	부 dissimilarly 다르게 반 similar 비슷한
827	**numerous** [njúːmərəs]	형 매우 많은 too numerous to count 셀 수 없을 만큼 많이	부 numerously 많이 유 many
828	**odd** [ɑd]	형 이상한	유 strange
829	**official** [əfíʃəl]	형 공식적인 an official visit 공식 방문	반 unofficial 비공식적인
830	**organic** [ɔːrgǽnik]	형 유기체의 an organic body 유기물	동 organize 조직하다
831	**session** [séʃən]	명 수업, 학기 the afternoon session 오후 수업	
832	**eliminate** [ilímənèit]	동 제거하다 eliminate A from B B에서 A를 제거하다	명 elimination 제거 유 get rid of
833	**classification** [klæ̀səfikéiʃən]	명 분류 a complicated classification 복잡한 분류	동 classify 분류하다 유 categorization
834	**sleet** [sliːt]	명 진눈깨비 동 진눈깨비가 내리다 There is sleet coming down. 진눈깨비가 내린다.	
835	**abuse** 동 [əbjúːz] 명 [əbjúːs]	동 남용하다, 학대하다 명 남용, 학대 abuse one's authority 직권을 남용하다	
836	**completion** [kəmplíːʃən]	명 완성 be near completion 완성에 가깝다	동 complete 완성하다 유 finishing
837	**eventful** [ivéntfəl]	형 사건이 많은, 다사다난한 an eventful year 다사다난한 해	명 event 사건, 행사
838	**insure** [inʃúər]	동 보험을 들다, 보증하다 insure against ~에 대해 보험을 들다	명 insurance 보험 유 assure
839	**precaution** [prikɔ́ːʃən]	명 조심 take precautions to ~에 조심하다	유 caution
840	**affectionate** [əfékʃənət]	형 애정이 깊은 an affectionate person 애정이 많은 사람	명 affection 애정

✦ 주어진 우리말 문장에 맞도록 알맞은 단어를 넣어 문장을 완성하시오. 정답 p.206

Even though they are sisters, they are ________ in appearance.
자매임에도 그들의 외모는 매우 달랐다.

The advantages of this online program are too ________ to mention.
이 온라인 프로그램의 장점들은 언급하기에 너무 많다.

Sometimes, his ________ behavior is annoying.
때때로 그의 이상한 행동이 성가실 때가 있다.

You should write in black on ________ letterhead.
공식적인 편지지는 검정색으로 작성해야 한다.

Mothers prefer ________ foods for their babies.
어머니들은 아기를 위해서 유기농 식품을 선호한다.

The morning ________ will start at 9 o'clock.
아침 수업은 9시에 시작될 것이다.

The government has tried to ________ poverty from the country.
정부는 나라의 가난을 없애려고 노력해왔다.

The ________ of animals is very complicated to do.
동물을 분류하는 것은 하기에 너무 복잡하다.

________ is freezing rain.
진눈깨비는 얼어붙은 비이다.

His boss ________ his authority.
그의 상사는 자신의 지위를 남용했다.

The teacher retired at the ________ of the school year.
선생님은 학교 정년을 채우시고 은퇴하셨다.

Last year was really ________ for me.
작년은 나에게 매우 다사다난한 해였다.

My father ________ himself against death.
우리 아버지는 생명보험을 들었다.

You should take ________ to prevent car accidents.
자동차 사고가 일어나지 않도록 조심해야 한다.

The woman is an ________ person.
그 여자는 애정이 많은 사람이다.

REVIEW TEST 14

DAY 27 ~ DAY 28

A 우리말과 같은 뜻이 되도록 빈칸에 들어갈 알맞은 단어를 적으시오.

1. a Buddhist ________________ (승려)
2. a ________________ heart (겸손한 마음)
3. walk ________________ (맨발로 걷다)
4. ________________ a secret (비밀을 폭로하다)
5. sing a ________________ (찬송가를 부르다)
6. ________________ against (~에 대해 보험을 들다)
7. a ________________ experience (떨리는 경험)
8. a complicated ________________ (복잡한 분류)
9. an ________________ person (무기를 지니지 않은 사람)
10. ________________ the freezer (냉동실의 얼음을 제거하다)

B 다음 괄호 안의 지시대로 주어진 단어를 변형시키고 그 뜻을 적으시오.

		변형	뜻
1	accumulate (명사형으로) →		
2	civilize (명사형으로) →		
3	completion (동사형으로) →		
4	context (형용사형으로) →		
5	density (형용사형으로) →		
6	dispose (명사형으로) →		
7	frequency (형용사형으로) →		
8	insure (명사형으로) →		
9	stun (형용사형으로) →		
10	succession (형용사형으로) →		

정답 p.206

C 다음 영영풀이에 해당하는 단어를 보기에서 골라 적으시오.

보기				
eliminate	illuminate	recyclable	wicked	cram
abuse	affectionate	superlative	bruise	monk

1. to use wrongly or improperly; misuse → ____________
2. showing, indicating, or characterized by affection or love → ____________
3. a painful area on your skin caused by an injury → ____________
4. to fill something by force with more than it can easily hold → ____________
5. to remove or get rid of, especially as being in some way undesirable → ____________
6. to supply or brighten with light; light up → ____________
7. capable of being used again → ____________
8. evil or morally bad in principle or practice; sinful → ____________
9. of the highest kind, quality, or order; surpassing all else or others; supreme → ____________
10. a male religious living in a cloister and devoting himself to contemplation and prayer and work → ____________

D 우리말과 같은 뜻이 되도록 주어진 문장의 빈칸을 완성하시오.

1. 하드웨어 압축으로 저장 가능 공간을 늘리세요.
   → Increase your available storage space by hardware ____________.
2. 작년은 나에게 매우 다사다난한 해였다.
   → Last year was really ____________ for me.
3. 가장 긴 계곡 빙하는 10km에 달한다.
   → The longest valley ____________ extends 10km.
4. 나는 사람 손으로 장식 유약을 칠한 프랑스식 타일을 샀다.
   → I bought the hand-painted French tiles with the decorative ____________.

⑤ 이 방의 인테리어는 너무 화려하다.

➔ The interior of this room is too ______________.

⑥ 이 온라인 프로그램의 장점들은 언급하기에 너무 많다.

➔ The advantages of this online program are too ______________ to mention.

⑦ 때때로 그의 이상한 행동이 성가실 때가 있다.

➔ Sometimes, his ______________ behavior is annoying.

⑧ 외모상 나는 부모님을 전혀 닮지 않았다.

➔ I don't ______________ my parents in appearance at all.

⑨ 나는 찬송가 부르는 것을 연습했다.

➔ I practiced singing a ______________.

⑩ 개가 킁킁거리며 낯선 사람의 냄새를 맡았다.

➔ The dog ______________ at the stranger.

E 문장의 밑줄 친 부분에 해당하는 유의어 혹은 반의어를 보기에서 골라 적으시오.

보기				
similar	caution	unofficial	extensive	quarrel
reveal	employ	overwhelming	understate	breath

① The company disclosed that he will retire this year. 유의어 = ______________

② Even though they are sisters, they are dissimilar in appearance. 반의어 ↔ ______________

③ He tends to exaggerate that he has too much homework. 반의어 ↔ ______________

④ They hired a new employee. 유의어 = ______________

⑤ I'm planning to take the intensive course during vacation. 반의어 ↔ ______________

⑥ I cannot refuse this offer; it is irresistible. 유의어 = ______________

⑦ You should write in black on official letterhead. 반의어 ↔ ______________

⑧ You should take precautions to prevent car accidents. 유의어 = ______________

⑨ My friend and I reconciled after he apologized to me. 반의어 ↔ ______________

⑩ We should check our respiration system regularly. 유의어 = ______________

F 영어발음을 듣고 영어단어를 적은 후, 우리말 뜻을 적으시오.

	영어	우리말
1		
2		
3		
4		
5		
6		
7		
8		
9		
10		
11		
12		
13		
14		

G 영어문장을 듣고 빈칸에 들어갈 단어를 채워 문장을 완성하시오.

영어문장
듣고 쓰기

1. Children are ________________ to act impatiently.
2. To learn from others, you need a ________________ manner.
3. The ________________ officer stamped my passport.
4. Visit our site for a ________________ annual fee.
5. Mothers prefer ________________ food for their babies.
6. The story is about an American ________________ from a long time ago.
7. The sky was deep blue and ________________.
8. She knew it would be difficult to ________________ the damage.
9. The missionaries tried to ________________ the natives of Africa.
10. Without a ________________, I assume it was torn on purpose.
11. This area had a population ________________ of ten people per square mile.
12. ________________ of these old books.
13. This radio station broadcasts on three different ________________.
14. My friend is working for the insurance company that ________________ my father against death.
15. This area is known as a dangerous place due to a ________________ of traffic accidents.
16. His boss ________________ his authority.

DAY 29

841 **facility** [fəsíləti]
명 설비, 시설
education facilities 교육기관

842 **primitive** [prímətiv]
형 원시의 반 modern 현대의
a primitive society 원시 사회

843 **anthropology** [æ̀nθrəpɑ́lədʒi]
명 인류학
cultural anthropology 문화 인류학

844 **apparent** [əpǽrənt]
형 분명한 부 apparently 분명히 유 obvious
apparent to everybody 누구에게나 분명한

845 **courageous** [kəréidʒəs]
형 용기 있는 명 courage 용기 반 cowardly 겁이 많은
courageous behavior 용기 있는 행동

846 **formulate** [fɔ́ːrmjulèit]
동 명확하게 말하다, 공식화하다 명 formulation 공식화
formulate an idea 생각을 명확하게 말하다

847 **loosen** [lúːsn]
동 풀다, 늦추다 형 loose 헐거운 유 untie
loosen one's belt 벨트를 느슨하게 하다

848 **realization** [rìːəlizéiʃən | rìːəlɑi-]
명 깨달음 동 realize 깨닫다 유 awareness
the realization of what you are 당신이 누구인지 깨닫는 것

849 **thigh** [θai]
명 넓적다리
a chicken thigh 닭의 넓적다리

850 **attendance** [əténdəns]
명 참석 동 attend 참석하다 유 presence
an attendance book 출석부

851 **dedicate** [dédikèit]
동 바치다 명 dedication 헌신 유 devote
dedicate oneself to ~에 전념하다

852 **geographical** [dʒìːəgrǽfikəl]
형 지리적인 명 geography 지리
geographical features 지형

853 **minister** [mínəstər]
명 성직자, 장관
the Minister of Defense 국방 장관

854 **reproduction** [rìːprədʌ́kʃən]
명 재생, 재현 유 copy
a photographic reproduction 사진에 의한 재생

855 **trout** [traut]
명 송어 동 송어를 낚다
trout fishing 송어 잡이

✦ 주어진 우리말 문장에 맞도록 알맞은 단어를 넣어 문장을 완성하시오. 정답 p.207

We have ______ for the babies as well.
우리는 아이들을 위한 시설도 갖추고 있어요.

______ people often lived in caves.
원시인들은 주로 동굴에서 살았다.

Social ______ is one of the social sciences.
사회 인류학은 사회 과학의 한 영역이다.

It is ______ that they are all true.
그것들이 모두 사실이라는 것은 분명하다.

Her ______ behavior is to be praised.
그녀의 용기 있는 행동은 칭송 받아야만 한다.

The faculty was all impressed by his way of ______ his ideas.
임원들은 생각을 명확하게 말하는 그의 태도에 감명 받았다.

By degrees, her tongue became ______, and she began to speak more freely.
점차 그녀의 혀가 풀려서 그녀는 더 자유롭게 말을 하기 시작했다.

The ______ of the fact was impossible for him.
그가 그 사실을 깨닫기란 불가능한 것이었다.

Chicken ______ are very delicious.
닭의 넓적다리는 아주 맛있다.

______ at class is compulsory.
수업에 참석하는 것은 의무이다.

I would like to ______ myself to playing instruments.
나는 악기 연주에 전념하고 싶다.

Many birds follow major ______ features.
많은 새들이 주요 지형을 따른다.

The prime ______ gave a vague answer.
총리는 모호한 대답을 했다.

The ______ of a literary work into a film is not always easy.
문학 작품을 영화로 재현하는 것은 항상 쉽지만은 않다.

We had ______ for dinner yesterday, and it was very delicious.
우리는 어제 저녁 식사로 송어를 먹었는데 아주 맛있었다.

DAY 29

856	**boycott** [bɔ́ikɑt]	동 ~을 사지 않다 명 불매 동맹 boycott a product 상품을 사지 않다	유 ban 금지하다
857	**dim** [dim]	형 어렴풋한, 희미한	부 dimly 어렴풋이
858	**hazardous** [hǽzərdəs]	형 위험한 hazardous employment 위험한 직업	명 hazard 위험 유 risky
859	**horror** [hɔ́:rər]	명 공포 a horror movie 공포 영화	
860	**scent** [sent]	명 냄새, 향기 동 냄새 맡다 the scent of roses 장미 향기	유 smell
861	**scrub** [skrʌb]	동 문지르다	유 rub
862	**seize** [si:z]	동 붙잡다 seize the throne 왕위를 빼앗다	유 grab
863	**sensitivity** [sènsətívəti]	명 민감도, 감수성 her sensitivity to music 음악에 대한 그녀의 감수성	형 sensitive 민감한 유 susceptibility
864	**vow** [vau]	동 맹세하다 take a vow 맹세하다	참 bow 절하다
865	**embarrassing** [imbǽrəsiŋ]	형 당황케 하는, 난처한 an embarrassing situation 난처한 상황	동 embarrass 난처하게 하다
866	**regretful** [rigrétfəl]	형 후회하는 a regretful moment 후회스러운 순간	명 regretfulness 후회스러움
867	**abrupt** [əbrʌ́pt]	형 퉁명스러운 an abrupt manner 퉁명스러운 태도	명 abruptness 퉁명스러움 유 impolite
868	**communicable** [kəmjú:nikəbl]	형 전염성의 a communicable disease 전염병	유 contagious
869	**estimate** [éstəmèit]	동 평가하다, 어림잡다 명 평가, 견적 estimate by rule of thumb 주먹구구로 어림하다	명 estimation 판단
870	**instructive** [instrʌ́ktiv]	형 교훈적인, 유익한 an instructive experience 유익한 경험	명 instruction 교훈

✦ 주어진 우리말 문장에 맞도록 알맞은 단어를 넣어 문장을 완성하시오. 정답 p.207

People __________ food from companies that use harmful ingredients.
사람들은 해로운 성분을 사용한 회사의 식품은 사지 않는다.

The __________ image passed in my mind.
그 희미한 이미지가 마음속에 지나갔다.

It's illegal to dump __________ chemicals into the sea.
위험한 화학물을 바다에 버리는 것은 불법이다.

I don't like seeing __________ movies alone.
나는 공포영화를 혼자 보는 것을 좋아하지 않는다.

The room is filled with the __________ of coffee.
그 방은 커피 향으로 가득 차 있다.

__________ the floor with soap to make it clean.
깨끗이 하기 위해 바닥을 비누로 문질러라.

I __________ the chance to meet the celebrity.
나는 유명인사를 만날 기회를 잡았다.

I felt terribly annoyed by his lack of __________.
나는 그의 무신경함에 무척 화가 났다.

I have made a __________ not to gamble again.
나는 다시는 도박하지 않기로 맹세했다.

It was very __________ when the client pointed out several mistakes I had made.
고객이 내가 한 몇 가지 실수들을 지적해서 매우 난처했다.

He is deeply __________ for what he has done so far.
그는 그가 이제까지 해온 것에 대해 깊이 후회한다.

The man explained the situation in an __________ manner.
그 남자는 퉁명스러운 태도로 그 상황을 설명했다.

A __________ disease can exterminate an entire species.
전염병이 종 전체를 멸종시킬 수 있다.

The Medicare cost is __________ to be one million dollars.
노인 의료보험료는 어림잡아 백만 달러에 달한다.

I like books which are __________.
나는 교훈적인 책을 좋아한다.

DAY 30

DAY 30 표제어 듣기

871 **population** [papjuléiʃən]
명 인구 동 populate 살다, 거주하다
the entire population 전체 인구

872 **stake** [steik]
명 화형
burn at the stake 화형에 처하다

873 **contagious** [kəntéidʒəs]
형 전염성의 명 contagiousness 전염성
a contagious germ 전염성 있는 세균

874 **invalid** [ínvəlid]
형 무효의
an invalid warranty 무효가 된 보증서

875 **stomp** [stamp]
동 쿵쿵거리며 걷다
stomp one's feet 발을 쾅쾅 구르다

876 **flush** [flʌʃ]
동 쏟아져 나오다

877 **literate** [lítərət]
형 읽고 쓸 줄 아는 반 illiterate 문맹의
computer-literate 컴퓨터를 다룰 줄 아는

878 **rap** [ræp]
명 톡톡 두드림 동 톡톡 두드리다 유 knock

879 **terminal** [tə́:rmənl]
형 끝의, 최종의 동 terminate 종결시키다
a terminal (station) 종착역

880 **astronomy** [əstránəmi]
명 천문학 형 astronomical 천문학적인
know a lot about astronomy 천문학에 능통하다

881 **deadly** [dédli]
형 치명적인 유 fatal
a deadly disease 생명을 잃게 되는 병

882 **generate** [dʒénərèit]
동 발생시키다 명 generation 발생, 세대 유 produce
generate energy 에너지를 만들어내다

883 **metropolitan** [mètrəpálitən]
형 대도시의 유 urban
a metropolitan newspaper (대도시에서 발간되는) 중앙지

884 **renovate** [rénəvèit]
동 수리하다 명 renovation 수선, 혁신
renovate a building 건물을 보수하다

885 **trekking** [trékiŋ]
명 도보여행 동 trek 고단한 여행을 하다 유 hiking
go trekking 도보여행을 가다

✦ 주어진 우리말 문장에 맞도록 알맞은 단어를 넣어 문장을 완성하시오. 정답 p.207

The entire ______ of one city in China is more than that of three cities in Korea.
중국에 있는 한 도시의 전체 인구는 한국의 세 개 도시의 전체 인구보다 더 많다.

The witch was burned at the ______.
그 마녀는 화형에 처해졌다.

______ germs can be killed by washing your hands.
전염성이 있는 세균들은 손을 씻음으로써 제거될 수 있다.

The contract is ______ without a signature.
서명이 없으면 계약은 무효이다.

The men ______ through the snow in their heavy boots.
남자들이 두터운 부츠를 신고 눈을 헤치며 걸어갔다.

If you pull the chain, the water will ______.
당신이 줄을 잡아 당기면 물이 쏟아져 나올 것이다.

Still, there are many teenagers who are not ______.
아직도 읽고 쓸 줄 모르는 청소년들이 많다.

There was a ______ at the door.
문을 톡톡 두드리는 소리가 났다.

Now, we have to check for the ______ problem.
이제 우리는 최종적인 문제를 위해 확인해야 한다.

Mr. Kim has devoted his life to ______.
김씨는 그의 인생 전체를 천문학에 헌신하였다.

The person has been fighting a ______ disease for 3 years.
그 사람은 3년 동안 치명적인 질병과 싸워오고 있다.

This machine can ______ heat during the daytime.
이 기계는 낮 동안 열을 발생시킬 수 있다.

______ means belonging to a large busy city.
'대도시의'라는 말은 크고 혼잡한 도시에 속하는 것을 말한다.

This old cathedral should be ______.
이 낡은 대성당은 수리되어야 한다.

Our club is planning to go ______.
우리 동아리는 도보여행 가는 것을 계획하고 있다.

DAY 30

	Word	Meaning	Related
886	**bold** [bould]	형 대담한 a bold headline 대담한 표제	유 brave, fearless 참 bald 대머리의
887	**diagram** [dáiəgræ̀m]	명 도표 동 도표로 나타내다 draw a diagram 도표를 만들다	형 diagrammatic 도표의
888	**halfway** [hǽfwèi]	형 중간의 부 중도에서 a halfway point 중간 지점	
889	**sympathize** [símpəθàiz]	동 공감하다, 지지하다 sympathize with his proposal 그의 제안에 찬성하다	
890	**neutral** [njú:trəl]	형 중립의 a neutral nation 중립국	
891	**visually** [víʒuəli]	부 시각적으로, 외관상으로 a visually difficult book 겉보기에 어려운 책	형 visual 시각의
892	**childish** [tʃáildiʃ]	형 어린이 같은, 유치한 a childish idea 유치한 생각	명 child 어린이 참 childlike 순진한
893	**emerge** [imə́:rdʒ]	동 나오다 emerge from the water 물 속에서 나오다	명 emergence 출현 반 withdraw 철수하다
894	**adulthood** [ədʌ́lthùd]	명 성인 reach adulthood 성인이 되다	
895	**extension** [iksténʃən]	명 연장 a time extension 시간 연장	동 extend 연장하다
896	**prevail** [privéil]	동 이기다, 널리 보급되다 Truth will prevail. 진리는 승리한다.	형 prevalent 우세한
897	**ambitious** [æmbíʃəs]	형 야심적인 be ambitious of ~을 열망하고 있다	명 ambition 야망, 야심 반 unambitious 야심 없는
898	**satellite** [sǽtəlàit]	명 위성 an artificial satellite 인공위성	
899	**appoint** [əpɔ́int]	동 임명하다 appoint A B A를 B로 임명하다	명 appointment 임명, 지명 유 nominate
900	**costly** [kɔ́:stli]	형 값비싼 a costly product 비싼 상품	명 costliness 고가 반 cheap 값싼

1회독	월	일
2회독	월	일

✦ 주어진 우리말 문장에 맞도록 알맞은 단어를 넣어 문장을 완성하시오. 정답 p.207

I think it is a ________ venture to start a business which is not proved to be successful. 성공이 검증되지 않은 사업을 시작하는 것은 대담한 모험이라고 나는 생각한다.

You can see the results in ________ 4.
도표 4에서 그 결과를 볼 수 있다.

This is the ________ point.
여기가 중간 지점이다.

My mother ________ with my hope to become an actress.
엄마는 여배우가 되고 싶다는 나의 희망에 공감하셨다.

I don't like him taking a ________ attitude.
나는 그가 중립적인 태도를 취하는 것이 싫다.

________, the chair is very pleasing, but it's uncomfortable.
겉보기에 그 의자는 굉장히 편해 보이지만 불편하다.

Don't be ________ any more.
더 이상 유치하게 굴지 마라.

The Moon ________ from behind a cloud.
달이 구름 뒤에서 나왔다.

It takes time for a child to reach ________.
어린이가 성인이 되는 데는 시간이 걸린다.

The time ________ helped them to finish the project.
시간 연장이 그들이 프로젝트를 끝내는 데 도움이 되었다.

Good will always ________ against evil.
선은 언제나 악을 이긴다.

He is an ________ politician.
그는 야심이 많은 정치가이다.

The weather forecast information is sent through artificial ________.
일기예보 정보는 인공위성들을 통해 전달된다.

My father was ________ the president of his company.
나의 아빠는 회사 사장으로 임명되었다.

We can't afford to buy a new computer because it is too ________.
새 컴퓨터가 너무 비싸기 때문에 우리는 그것을 살 여유가 없다.

REVIEW TEST 15 DAY 29 ~ DAY 30

A 우리말과 같은 뜻이 되도록 빈칸에 들어갈 알맞은 단어를 적으시오.

1. an ________________ book (출석부)
2. take a ________________ (맹세하다)
3. a ________________ nation (중립국)
4. the entire ________________ (전체 인구)
5. the ________________ of roses (장미 향기)
6. an ________________ manner (퉁명스러운 태도)
7. a ________________ moment (후회스러운 순간)
8. ________________ one's feet (발을 쾅쾅 구르다)
9. an ________________ warranty (무효가 된 보증서)
10. ________________ with his proposal (그의 제안에 찬성하다)

B 다음 괄호 안의 지시대로 주어진 단어를 변형시키고 그 뜻을 적으시오.

		변형	뜻
1	courageous (명사형으로) →	________	________
2	abrupt (명사형으로) →	________	________
3	appoint (명사형으로) →	________	________
4	sensitivity (형용사형으로) →	________	________
5	loosen (형용사형으로) →	________	________
6	geographical (명사형으로) →	________	________
7	population (동사형으로) →	________	________
8	terminal (동사형으로) →	________	________
9	astronomy (형용사형으로) →	________	________
10	prevail (형용사형으로) →	________	________

정답 p.207

C 다음 영영풀이에 해당하는 단어를 보기에서 골라 적으시오.

보기				
extension	embarrassing	dim	neutral	contagious
emerge	adulthood	seize	childish	instructive

1. of, like, or befitting a child → ______________
2. to come forth into view or notice → ______________
3. to take hold of suddenly or forcibly; grasp → ______________
4. not bright; obscure from lack of light or emitted light → ______________
5. causing to feel ashamed or nervous → ______________
6. tending to spread from person to person → ______________
7. not aligned with or supporting any side or position in a controversy
   → ______________
8. the state of being fully grown or mature → ______________
9. an act or instance of extending → ______________
10. serving to instruct or inform; conveying instruction → ______________

D 우리말과 같은 뜻이 되도록 주어진 문장의 빈칸을 완성하시오.

1. 수업에 참석하는 것은 의무이다.
   → ______________ at class is compulsory.
2. 이 낡은 대성당은 수리되어야 한다.
   → This old cathedral should be ______________.
3. '대도시의'라는 말은 크고 혼잡한 도시에 속하는 것을 말한다.
   → ______________ means belonging to a large busy city.
4. 사회 인류학은 사회 과학의 한 영역이다.
   → Social ______________ is one of the social sciences.
5. 닭의 넓적다리는 아주 맛있다.
   → Chicken ______________ are very delicious.

⑥ 나는 공포영화를 혼자 보는 것을 좋아하지 않는다.

→ I don't like seeing ______________ movies alone.

⑦ 노인 의료보험료는 어림잡아 백만 달러에 달한다.

→ The Medicare cost is ______________ to be one million dollars.

⑧ 그 마녀는 화형에 처해졌다.

→ The witch was burned at the ______________.

⑨ 도표 4에서 그 결과를 볼 수 있다.

→ You can see the results in ______________ 4.

⑩ 여기가 중간 지점이다.

→ This is the ______________ point.

E 문장의 밑줄 친 부분에 해당하는 유의어 혹은 반의어를 보기에서 골라 적으시오.

보기				
modern	ban	obvious	produce	knock
devote	cheap	contagious	illiterate	fatal

① There was a rap at the door. 유의어 = ______________

② We can't afford to buy a new computer because it is too costly.

반의어 ↔ ______________

③ Still, there are many teenagers who are not literate. 반의어 ↔ ______________

④ Primitive people often lived in caves. 반의어 ↔ ______________

⑤ People boycott food from companies that use harmful ingredients.

유의어 = ______________

⑥ A communicable disease can exterminate an entire species.

유의어 = ______________

⑦ I would like to dedicate myself to playing instruments. 유의어 = ______________

⑧ The person has been fighting a deadly disease for 3 years. 유의어 = ______________

⑨ It is apparent that they are all true. 유의어 = ______________

⑩ This machine can generate heat during the daytime. 유의어 = ______________

F 영어발음을 듣고 영어단어를 적은 후, 우리말 뜻을 적으시오.

영어단어 듣고 쓰기 

	영어	우리말		영어	우리말
❶	________	________	❽	________	________
❷	________	________	❾	________	________
❸	________	________	❿	________	________
❹	________	________	⓫	________	________
❺	________	________	⓬	________	________
❻	________	________	⓭	________	________
❼	________	________	⓮	________	________

G 영어문장을 듣고 빈칸에 들어갈 단어를 채워 문장을 완성하시오.

영어문장 듣고 쓰기

❶ He is an ________ politician.

❷ The weather forecast information is sent through artificial ________.

❸ The room is filled with the ________ of coffee.

❹ Our club is planning to go ________.

❺ We have ________ for the babies as well.

❻ The contract is ________ without a signature.

❼ The men ________ through the snow in their heavy boots.

❽ Her ________ behavior is to be praised.

❾ The man explained the situation in an ________ manner.

❿ My father was ________ the president of his company.

⓫ I felt terribly annoyed by his lack of ________.

⓬ By degrees, her tongue became ________.

⓭ Many birds follow major ________ features.

⓮ Now, we have to check for the ________ problem.

⓯ Mr. Kim has devoted his life to ________.

⓰ Good will always ________ against evil.

3rd Edition

절대어휘 5100

③ 고등 내신 기본 900

ANSWER KEY

DAY 01

P. 11

001 abandoned
002 Commerce
003 equator
004 inscribed
005 political
006 Spouses
007 constitution
008 interrelated
009 stimulated
010 conveys
011 cope
012 correspondence
013 flaws
014 liable
015 quivered
016 temporary
017 assist
018 customized
019 gadget
020 melancholic
021 Relief
022 transforms
023 blended
024 destructive
025 guarantee
026 narrated
027 revolver
028 needy
029 urge
030 vacant

DAY 02

P. 15

031 ventilation
032 vigorous
033 Celsius
034 elderly
035 emission
036 cluster
037 simulate
038 colony
039 enthusiasm
040 initiate
041 Plows
042 spiral
043 administers
044 exhaustion
045 prescribed
046 alternate
047 fame
048 fatigue
049 feminine
050 leakage
051 qualifications
052 takeoff
053 aspiration
054 cruelties
055 fundamental
056 Maximizing
057 regulations
058 Toxic
059 bilingual
060 descend

REVIEW TEST 01

P. 18

A
❶ takeoff
❷ qualification
❸ plow
❹ prescribe
❺ interrelated
❻ destructive
❼ guarantee
❽ liable
❾ respect
❿ blend

B
❶ cruel 잔인한
❷ aspire 열망하다
❸ emit 방출하다
❹ famous 유명한
❺ commercial 상업상의
❻ customize 고객 맞춤화하다
❼ colonize 식민지화하다
❽ politics 정치 / politician 정치인
❾ leak 새다
❿ correspond 일치하다

C
❶ abandon
❷ fundamental
❸ exhaustion
❹ assist
❺ elderly
❻ quiver
❼ qualification
❽ bilingual
❾ urge
❿ vigorous

D
❶ administers
❷ stimulated
❸ constitution
❹ gadget
❺ ventilation
❻ equator
❼ prescribed
❽ Relief
❾ narrated
❿ enthusiasm

E
❶ ascend
❷ constructive
❸ help
❹ minimize
❺ permanent
❻ begin
❼ carry
❽ change
❾ defect
❿ gloomy

F
❶ spiral 나선형의
❷ needy 가난한
❸ cruelty 잔혹
❹ fame 명성
❺ colony 식민지
❻ leakage 누출
❼ administer 관리하다, 통치하다
❽ stimulate 자극하다
❾ constitution 구성, 조직
❿ gadget 부품
⓫ ventilation 통풍
⓬ equator 적도
⓭ prescribe 처방하다
⓮ relief 안도, 경감

G
❶ fatigue
❷ cluster
❸ vacant
❹ regulations
❺ cope
❻ Toxic
❼ alternate
❽ Celsius
❾ aspiration
❿ emission
⓫ Commerce
⓬ customized
⓭ political
⓮ correspondence

⑮ abandoned ⑯ fundamental

DAY 03

P. 23

061 gradual 062 mourned
063 reunification 064 union
065 roared 066 calculation
067 capitalism 068 carved
069 Caterpillars 070 efficiency
071 impressed 072 emphasis
073 collaborate 074 sin
075 enlarge 076 ingenious
077 physicists 078 span
079 Acupuncture 080 conscience
081 intention 082 steep
083 continual 084 irreversible
085 ivory 086 landlords
087 psychological 088 swift
089 aroma 090 crisis

DAY 04

P. 27

091 frustration 092 maneuvers
093 refining 094 tighten
095 barely 096 departure
097 glimmering 098 mortal
099 restless 100 unearthed
101 brutal 102 unloading
103 distasteful 104 disturbances
105 donation 106 drill
107 impair 108 outlook
109 inaugural 110 collaborative
111 sincerity 112 inflate
113 performed 114 snuggled
115 accurately 116 concerning
117 exceptional 118 precise
119 affirmative 120 faded

REVIEW TEST 02

P. 30

A ❶ intention ❷ span
❸ calculation ❹ departure
❺ efficiency ❻ donation
❼ emphasis ❽ psychological
❾ carve ❿ landlord

B ❶ mournful 슬퍼하는 ❷ reunify 재통일하다
❸ efficient 효율적인 ❹ enlargement 증대
❺ ingenuity 기발함 ❻ intend 의도하다
❼ continuance 연속 ❽ brutality 잔인성
❾ disturb 방해하다 ❿ precision 정확; 정밀한

C ❶ carve ❷ physicist
❸ steep ❹ crisis
❺ refine ❻ unload
❼ distasteful ❽ outlook
❾ exceptional ❿ drill

D ❶ sin ❷ ivory
❸ swift ❹ aroma
❺ frustration ❻ barely
❼ impair ❽ collaborative
❾ inflate ❿ performed

E ❶ cooperate ❷ reversible
❸ arrival ❹ fatal
❺ uneasy ❻ endowment
❼ inaccurately ❽ regarding
❾ negative ❿ vanish

F ❶ emphasis 강조 ❷ acupuncture 침술
❸ unearth 발굴하다 ❹ reunification 재통일
❺ ingenious 교묘한, 기발한
❻ brutal 잔인한 ❼ sin 죄
❽ ivory 상아 ❾ swift 빠른
❿ aroma 향기 ⓫ frustration 좌절, 실패
⓬ barely 간신히
⓭ impair 손상시키다, 약화시키다
⓮ collaborative 협조적인

G ❶ gradual ❷ union
❸ calculations ❹ capitalism
❺ span ❻ conscience
❼ maneuvers ❽ mourned
❾ efficiency ❿ enlarge
⓫ intention ⓬ continual
⓭ disturbances ⓮ precise

⑮ performed ⑯ carved

DAY 05

P. 35

121 privacy 122 profitable
123 promotion 124 superficial
125 archaeologist 126 crazed
127 friendliness 128 magnificent
129 recovery 130 throb
131 awakening 132 degradable
133 gladiators 134 modest
135 residence 136 unbeaten
137 breeze 138 discrimination
139 burped 140 hospitality
141 humid 142 identification
143 illusion 144 organisms
145 shabby 146 inclines
147 enchanted 148 willingness
149 peculiarities 150 slope

DAY 06

P. 39

151 academic 152 composition
153 evoked 154 integrity
155 stale 156 contemporary
157 investigated 158 strained
159 subconscious 160 sufficient
161 apprehended 162 courteous
163 frank 164 lottery
165 reaping 166 thrashed
167 attorney 168 defense
169 geological 170 misled
171 reproduce 172 tug
173 Brainstorm 174 dimple
175 hearty 176 disrespectful
177 notable 178 nutrients
179 odors 180 onlooker

REVIEW TEST 03

P. 42

A ❶ lottery ❷ defense
❸ humid ❹ identification
❺ enchanted ❻ modest
❼ frank ❽ willingness
❾ mislead ❿ reap

B ❶ enchantment 매혹 ❷ identify 확인하다
❸ investigation 조사 ❹ hospitable 환대하는
❺ breezy 산들바람의 ❻ promote 승진시키다
❼ discriminate 차별하다
❽ misleading 오해하기 쉬운
❾ heart 마음 ❿ illusory 착각의

C ❶ apprehend ❷ modest
❸ courteous ❹ attorney
❺ craze ❻ awakening
❼ shabby ❽ composition
❾ contemporary ❿ evoke

D ❶ residence ❷ academic
❸ Brainstorm ❹ integrity
❺ subconscious ❻ thrashed
❼ reproduce ❽ dimple
❾ notable ❿ organisms

E ❶ respectful ❷ profound
❸ insufficient ❹ offense
❺ publicity ❻ beneficial
❼ bystander ❽ feature
❾ healing ❿ reluctance

F ❶ friendliness 친절, 우정
❷ humid 습한
❸ identification (신원) 확인
❹ mislead 잘못 인도하다 ❺ residence 주거
❻ academic 학구적인
❼ brainstorm 브레인스토밍하다
❽ integrity 고결, 청렴
❾ subconscious 잠재의식의; 잠재의식
❿ thrash 때리다, 완패시키다
⓫ reproduce 재생하다, 복제하다
⓬ dimple 보조개; 보조개를 짓다
⓭ notable 주목할 만한, 뛰어난
⓮ organism 유기체

G ❶ stale ❷ magnificent
❸ frank ❹ nutrients

⑤ odors ⑥ enchanted
⑦ investigated ⑧ hospitality
⑨ breeze ⑩ promotion
⑪ discrimination ⑫ hearty
⑬ illusion ⑭ apprehended
⑮ courteous ⑯ attorney

DAY 07

P. 47

181 sentiment 182 wagged
183 inconvenience 184 enchanting
185 withheld 186 skeleton
187 absent 188 companions
189 eternally 190 insulated
191 portion 192 Adverse
193 extensive 194 preventable
195 amnesty 196 Antibiotic
197 appliances 198 counsel
199 folklore 200 loans
201 rash 202 testified
203 atlas 204 decayed
205 generosity 206 mighty
207 repetitive 208 tribute
209 boredom 210 digest

DAY 08

P. 51

211 hauled 212 natural
213 hobbled 214 scar
215 scoop 216 Seasonings
217 selfishness 218 vivid
219 chilly 220 incurable
221 enclosed 222 workforce
223 abide 224 commit
225 equivalent 226 insight
227 pollen 228 squeezed
229 constructed 230 interruption
231 stimulation 232 convicted
233 core 234 corridor
235 flexibility 236 likewise
237 quotient 238 tendency
239 assistance 240 damp

REVIEW TEST 04

P. 54

A ① decayed ② likewise
③ commit ④ folklore
⑤ wail ⑥ flexibility
⑦ generosity ⑧ preventable
⑨ scar ⑩ abide

B ① like ~ 같은 ② flexible 유연한
③ sentimental 감정적인 ④ repetition 반복
⑤ conviction 유죄 판결 ⑥ might 힘
⑦ adversely 반대로 ⑧ generous 관대한
⑨ skeletal 골격의 ⑩ prevention 예방

C ① haul ② withhold
③ inconvenience ④ extensive
⑤ testify ⑥ insight
⑦ stimulation ⑧ core
⑨ corridor ⑩ companion

D ① enclosed ② core
③ squeezed ④ Antibiotic
⑤ tribute ⑥ natural
⑦ workforce ⑧ pollen
⑨ quotient ⑩ Seasonings

E ① cautious ② destruct
③ present ④ equal
⑤ fascinating ⑥ inclination
⑦ moist ⑧ help
⑨ shivery ⑩ tedium

F ① rash 분별없는, 경솔한 ② construct 건설하다
③ absent 결석한; 결석하다 ④ equivalent 동등한
⑤ enchanting 매혹적인 ⑥ tendency 경향, 풍조
⑦ damp 축축한; 습기; 축축하게 하다, (기름) 꺼다
⑧ assistance 원조, 도움 ⑨ chilly 추운, 냉담한
⑩ boredom 지루함 ⑪ repetitive 반복적인
⑫ generosity 관용, 너그러움
⑬ commit 저지르다, 범하다
⑭ insulate 절연하다, 분리하다

G ① likewise ② flexibility
③ sentiment ④ convicted
⑤ mighty ⑥ Adverse

❼ skeleton
❽ preventable
❾ interruption
❿ scoop
⓫ wagged
⓬ amnesty
⓭ vivid
⓮ incurable
⓯ hauling
⓰ inconvenience

DAY 09

P. 59

241 Gambling
242 melody
243 religious
244 transparency
245 bless
246 detective
247 guard
248 narration
249 rhymes
250 negative
251 utensils
252 variations
253 vertical
254 violate
255 certified
256 elevate
257 Industrial
258 endurance
259 yearned
260 columns
261 lull
262 innocent
263 poetic
264 Spit
265 adolescents
266 expanse
267 prescription
268 altogether
269 famine
270 faucet

DAY 10

P. 63

271 feverish
272 leash
273 qualified
274 technical
275 assemble
276 crumble
277 furious
278 meantime
279 rejected
280 trackless
281 bound
282 deserved
283 greasy
284 multilayered
285 revealed
286 unity
287 rubbish
288 calmly
289 carbonated
290 casual
291 cathedral
292 efficient
293 Impulse
294 overacts
295 enhance
296 youthful
297 enlist
298 ingredients
299 pilgrims
300 specialists

REVIEW TEST 05

P. 66

A ❶ casual ❷ impulse ❸ column ❹ detective ❺ bound ❻ reveal ❼ calmly ❽ enhance ❾ reject ❿ famine

B ❶ melodious 선율적인 ❷ religion 종교 ❸ detect 탐색하다 ❹ industry 산업 ❺ innocence 결백 ❻ technic 기술 ❼ grease 기름 ❽ multilayer 다층 ❾ calm 고요한 ❿ overaction 과장

C ❶ gambling ❷ transparency ❸ certify ❹ endurance ❺ yearn ❻ prescription ❼ trackless ❽ unity ❾ qualify ❿ specialist

D ❶ enthusiastic ❷ bless ❸ variations ❹ violate ❺ elevate ❻ expanse ❼ assemble ❽ revealed ❾ Impulse ❿ enhance

E ❶ account ❷ positive ❸ horizontal ❹ juvenile ❺ tap ❻ angry ❼ accepted ❽ litter ❾ inefficient ❿ proved

F ❶ deserve ~할 만하다, ~을 받을 자격이 있다
❷ cathedral 대성당
❸ narration 이야기하기, 서술
❹ negative 부정적인 ❺ vertical 수직의, 세로의
❻ adolescent 청년기의; 청소년
❼ faucet 수도꼭지 ❽ furious 격노한, 맹렬한
❾ reject 거절하다 ❿ rubbish 쓰레기
⓫ efficient 효율적인 ⓬ youthful 젊은
⓭ religious 신앙심이 깊은 ⓮ technical 기술의

G ❶ columns ❷ famine ❸ leash ❹ meantime ❺ carbonated ❻ casual

⑦ pilgrims
⑧ altogether
⑨ melody
⑩ detective
⑪ Industrial
⑫ innocent
⑬ multilayered
⑭ calmly
⑮ overacts
⑯ poetic

DAY 11

P. 71

301 adapting
302 conservation
303 Interacting
304 steering
305 continuous
306 irrigated
307 kidneys
308 launched
309 pupils
310 symbolic
311 arrested
312 criticized
313 fulfill
314 mansion
315 Reforming
316 tiresome
317 baron
318 dependable
319 glimpse
320 moth
321 retail
322 Unethical
323 bulk
324 unnoticeable
325 distinct
326 diversion
327 doom
328 drips
329 imperialism
330 overall

DAY 12

P. 75

331 overhead
332 industrious
333 influenza
334 Periodic
335 socialize
336 acid
337 conference
338 exclamation
339 precision
340 agenda
341 faithfully
342 procedure
343 progressive
344 propelled
345 suppressed
346 validity
347 creativity
348 frowned
349 maintenance
350 rectangle
351 throng
352 bail
353 democracy
354 glamorous
355 mold
356 respectable
357 uncared
358 bribe
359 dishonest
360 bush

REVIEW TEST 06

P. 78

A
① retail ② baron
③ overhead ④ validity
⑤ moth ⑥ overall
⑦ bribe ⑧ irrigate
⑨ arrest ⑩ faithfully

B
① tire 싫증나게 하다 ② imperial 제국의
③ period 주기 ④ acidly 까다롭게
⑤ exclaim 외치다 ⑥ faithful 충실한
⑦ frowner 눈살을 찌푸리는 사람
⑧ democratic 민주주의의
⑨ respect 존경하다 ⑩ dishonesty 부정직

C
① adapt ② arrest
③ reform ④ diversion
⑤ conference ⑥ procedure
⑦ suppress ⑧ conservation
⑨ irrigate ⑩ influenza

D
① steering ② kidneys
③ launched ④ symbolic
⑤ mansion ⑥ unnoticeable
⑦ progressive ⑧ maintenance
⑨ bail ⑩ uncared

E
① continual ② student
③ praise ④ reliant
⑤ ethical ⑥ fate
⑦ diligent ⑧ exactness
⑨ pushed ⑩ originality

F
① moth 나방
② overall 종합적인, 전체의; 종합적으로
③ continuous 계속적인 ④ pupil 학생
⑤ criticize 비판하다
⑥ dependable 의존할 수 있는
⑦ unethical 비도덕적인 ⑧ doom 운명, 파멸
⑨ industrious 부지런한 ⑩ precision 정확; 정밀한
⑪ propel 추진하다 ⑫ creativity 창조성
⑬ imperialism 제국주의 ⑭ faithfully 충실하게, 굳게

G
① baron ② retail
③ drips ④ overhead

⑤ rectangle ⑥ throng
⑦ mold ⑧ bush
⑨ tiresome ⑩ Periodic
⑪ acid ⑫ exclamations
⑬ frowned ⑭ democracy
⑮ respectable ⑯ Interacting

DAY 13

P. 83

361 hounds	362 hunchback
363 idle	364 imagination
365 originality	366 shallow
367 overload	368 inevitable
369 perceived	370 slot
371 acceptable	372 comprehend
373 evolution	374 intellectual
375 stance	376 contends
377 investment	378 striking
379 subsequent	380 sufficiently
381 approval	382 arisen
383 fraud	384 lotuses
385 recalls	386 threatened
387 attraction	388 defensive
389 geometry	390 misty

DAY 14

P. 87

391 reptiles	392 twinkled
393 brass	394 directive
395 hesitated	396 dissatisfied
397 notion	398 objected
399 offended	400 orally
401 sequence	402 walkabout
403 overused	404 infant
405 skull	406 absorption
407 comparison	408 eternity
409 insulation	410 pose
411 advertisements	412 extinguished
413 Prevention	414 analogies
415 anxiety	416 applicable
417 counteract	418 craft
419 location	420 ratio

REVIEW TEST 07

P. 90

A ① notion ② imagination
③ twinkle ④ object
⑤ approval ⑥ sequence
⑦ applicable ⑧ arise
⑨ comprehend ⑩ pose

B ① inevitableness 불가피함
② comprehension 이해
③ contention 싸움
④ approve 찬성하다, 승인하다
⑤ fraudulent 속이는 ⑥ attract 끌다
⑦ geometric 기하학의 ⑧ eternal 영원한
⑨ analogous 유사한
⑩ counteraction 방해, 중화

C ① perceive ② evolution
③ investment ④ recall
⑤ directive ⑥ overuse
⑦ absorption ⑧ pose
⑨ advertisement ⑩ location

D ① hounds ② intellectual
③ striking ④ sufficiently
⑤ twinkled ⑥ hesitated
⑦ orally ⑧ skull
⑨ anxiety ⑩ ratio

E ① unemployed ② deep
③ following ④ intimidate
⑤ foggy ⑥ satisfy
⑦ upset ⑧ baby
⑨ contrast ⑩ put out

F ① stance 자세
② brass 놋쇠, 금관 악기; 금관 악기의
③ idle 한가한, 놀고 있는 ④ shallow 얕은
⑤ subsequent 그 후의
⑥ threaten 협박하다, 위협하다
⑦ misty 안개가 짙은
⑧ dissatisfy 불만을 느끼게 하다
⑨ offend 기분을 상하게 하다
⑩ infant 유아; 유아의, 초기의

⑪ comparison 비교 ⑫ extinguish 진화하다
⑬ craft 기술, 재주 ⑭ comprehend 이해하다

G ❶ hunchback ❷ overload
❸ lotuses ❹ reptiles
❺ sequence ❻ walkabout
❼ insulation ❽ inevitable
❾ contends ❿ approval
⑪ fraud ⑫ attraction
⑬ geometry ⑭ analogies
⑮ counteract ⑯ imagination

DAY 15

P. 95

421 thermometer 422 atomic
423 decibels 424 genre
425 migrate 426 reportedly
427 triumph 428 bounced
429 dignity 430 hardships
431 navigation 432 hoe
433 Scarce 434 scraps
435 secure 436 semiconductors
437 vocalist 438 chunk
439 painful 440 infection
441 abolished 442 commitment
443 erected 444 inspections
445 pollution 446 squid
447 constructive 448 interval
449 stimulus 450 convictions

DAY 16

P. 99

451 corporate 452 corruption
453 flourishes 454 foremost
455 rage 456 tender
457 association 458 dare
459 gazed 460 mentally
461 remarked 462 transplanted
463 blister 464 détente
465 guilty 466 narrative
467 ridge 468 neighborhood
469 utter 470 varnished
471 veteran 472 virtue
473 chamber 474 elevation
475 sheriff 476 inferior
477 Combat 478 envelope
479 innovate 480 poetry

REVIEW TEST 08

P. 102

A ❶ pollution ❷ squid
❸ commitment ❹ blister
❺ constructive ❻ secure
❼ veteran ❽ semiconductor
❾ migrate ❿ scarce

B ❶ migration 이주 ❷ report 보고
❸ hard 어려운, 힘든 ❹ scarcely 거의 ~ 아니다
❺ pollute 오염시키다 ❻ stimulate 자극하다
❼ convict 유죄를 증명하다 ❽ transplantation 이식
❾ elevate 올리다 ❿ innovative 혁신적인

C ❶ navigation ❷ foremost
❸ dignity ❹ secure
❺ infection ❻ inspection
❼ neighborhood ❽ envelope
❾ association ❿ narrative

D ❶ genre ❷ vocalist
❸ abolished ❹ interval
❺ corporate ❻ mentally
❼ détente ❽ varnished
❾ chamber ❿ poetry

E ❶ victory ❷ dedication
❸ built ❹ destructive
❺ thrive ❻ soft
❼ stare ❽ innocent
❾ absolute ❿ superior

F ❶ decibel 데시벨 ❷ triumph 승리
❸ commitment 헌신 ❹ erect 세우다; 똑바로 선
❺ constructive 건설적인, 구조적인
❻ flourish 번창하다 ❼ tender 부드러운
❽ gaze 응시하다 ❾ guilty 유죄의
❿ utter 전적의, 완전한
⑪ veteran 노련한; 베테랑, 전문가

⑫ virtue 미덕, 덕
⑬ inferior 하위의, 열등한
⑭ reportedly 보도에 의하면

G ❶ thermometer ❷ hoe
❸ semiconductors ❹ chunk
❺ squid ❻ ridge
❼ sheriff ❽ migrate
❾ hardships ❿ Scarce
⓫ pollution ⓬ stimulus
⓭ convictions ⓮ transplanted
⓯ innovative ⓰ bounced

DAY 17

P. 107

481 splinters
482 adoration
483 expose
484 presence
485 Amber
486 fare
487 feast
488 finite
489 legal
490 lineup
491 technological
492 assessment
493 curator
494 fusion
495 medication
496 relaxation
497 tragedy
498 biological
499 despair
500 grief
501 nagged
502 revolutionary
503 universal
504 sacred
505 capable
506 cardiac
507 catalog(ue)
508 caution
509 effortlessly
510 inactivity

DAY 18

P. 111

511 shifted
512 spent
513 enormous
514 inhabitants
515 pitiful
516 specializes
517 adequate
518 considerate
519 intermediate
520 sticky
521 contract
522 irritated
523 knitted / knit
524 laundry
525 purified
526 queasy
527 arrogant
528 crooks
529 functional
530 massive
531 refresh
532 tolerable
533 behalf
534 dependent
535 glowed
536 motivation
537 retained
538 uneven
539 bundle
540 untimely

REVIEW TEST 09

P. 114

A ❶ caution ❷ sacred
❸ behalf ❹ fare
❺ laundry ❻ considerate
❼ glow ❽ inhabitants
❾ bundle ❿ spend

B ❶ festal 축제의 ❷ technology 기술
❸ tragic 비극적인 ❹ biology 생물학
❺ revolution 혁명 ❻ capability 능력
❼ special 특별한 ❽ stick 붙다
❾ irritating 짜증나게 하는 / irritated 짜증이 난
❿ purification 정화

C ❶ assessment ❷ curator
❸ fusion ❹ universal
❺ contract ❻ laundry
❼ queasy ❽ arrogant
❾ motivation ❿ uneven

D ❶ adoration ❷ expose
❸ fare ❹ medication
❺ relaxation ❻ shifted
❼ pitiful ❽ intermediate
❾ functional ❿ refresh

E ❶ fragment ❷ infinite
❸ illegal ❹ hope
❺ sorrow ❻ huge
❼ suitable ❽ bend
❾ bearable ❿ independent

F ❶ caution 조심 ❷ spend 쓰다, 소비하다
❸ splinter 부서진 조각 ❹ finite 한정된
❺ legal 법률의 ❻ despair 절망
❼ grief 슬픔 ❽ enormous 거대한
❾ adequate 알맞은 ❿ crook 구부리다; 굽은 것
⓫ tolerable 참을 수 있는

⑫ dependent 의존하고 있는
⑬ tragedy 비극
⑭ specialize 전공하다, 전문으로 하다

G ① cardiac ② catalog(ue)
③ effortlessly ④ inactivity
⑤ knitted ⑥ glowed
⑦ bundle ⑧ untimely
⑨ feast ⑩ technological
⑪ biological ⑫ revolutionary
⑬ capable ⑭ sticky
⑮ irritated ⑯ purified

DAY 19

P. 119

541 distort 542 diversity
543 doubtless 544 dwells
545 impersonal 546 overcome
547 shivered 548 panic
549 informed 550 perish
551 sophisticated 552 acknowledge
553 confessed 554 executive
555 preference 556 aisle
557 fake 558 procession
559 prohibited 560 proportion
561 surgeon 562 aristocracy
563 creature 564 frozen
565 majestic 566 recurring
567 thrust 568 bare
569 demolish 570 glance

DAY 20

P. 123

571 momentary 572 respective
573 undiscovered 574 broke
575 dismissed 576 bustles
577 hub 578 hygiene
579 ignorance 580 imaginative
581 originated 582 shattered
583 shrinks 584 parallel
585 perception 586 snatch
587 accommodation 588 comprehensive
589 evolved 590 intense
591 staple 592 content
593 inward 594 stumbled
595 subtle 596 superiority
597 approximately 598 craftsman
599 freelance 600 loyalty

REVIEW TEST 10

P. 126

A ① bare ② staple
③ glance ④ prohibit
⑤ snatch ⑥ stumble
⑦ shatter ⑧ loyalty
⑨ thrust ⑩ demolish

B ① origin 기원, 시작
② impersonality 비인간성, 비정함
③ acknowledgement 인정
④ confession 고백 ⑤ proceed 나아가다
⑥ majesty 장엄 ⑦ moment 순간
⑧ snatchable 낚아챌 수 있는
⑨ comprehend 이해하다
⑩ approximate 대략의

C ① frozen ② distort
③ panic ④ inform
⑤ perish ⑥ preference
⑦ hub ⑧ hygiene
⑨ aisle ⑩ perception

D ① diversity ② overcome
③ shivered ④ surgeon
⑤ creature ⑥ broke
⑦ imaginative ⑧ shrinks
⑨ evolved ⑩ freelance

E ① real ② forbid
③ ratio ④ push
⑤ fired ⑥ rush
⑦ knowledge ⑧ satisfied
⑨ outward ⑩ inferiority

F ① accommodation 숙박시설
② fake 가짜의; 가짜 ③ prohibit 금지하다
④ proportion 비율, 비례 ⑤ thrust 밀다; 밀침

⑥ dismiss 해고시키다
⑦ bustle 분주하게 돌아다니다; 야단법석
⑧ ignorance 무지 ⑨ content 만족해 하는
⑩ inward 안의, 내적인 ⑪ superiority 우세, 우월
⑫ acknowledge 인정하다
⑬ majestic 장엄한
⑭ snatch 와락 붙잡다, 낚아채다

G ❶ doubtless ❷ sophisticated
❸ executive ❹ aristocracy
❺ recurring ❻ undiscovered
❼ stumbled ❽ craftsman
❾ loyalty ❿ originated
⓫ impersonal ⓬ confessed
⓭ procession ⓮ momentary
⓯ comprehensive ⓰ approximately

DAY 21

P. 131

601 reckless 602 thrifty
603 auditorium 604 definition
605 gigantic 606 mock
607 requirements 608 ultrasonic
609 breakdowns 610 disappointment
611 hijack 612 dissatisfied
613 numerals 614 occasions
615 offered 616 orbit
617 sermon 618 warfare
619 signature 620 participation
621 slack 622 abstract
623 competent 624 evenly
625 insulting 626 possesses
627 advisable 628 extraordinary
629 primary 630 analysis

DAY 22

P. 135

631 apologetic 632 applicant
633 counterbalance 634 foretell
635 logic 636 reaction
637 thermostat 638 attain
639 decorated 640 genuine
641 minimize 642 representative
643 troops 644 boundary
645 diligent 646 haste
647 near-sighted 648 horizontal
649 scattered 650 scratch
651 segment 652 sensation
653 vocation 654 circular
655 warm-hearted 656 particles
657 abounds 658 commonplace
659 errand 660 inspiration

REVIEW TEST 11

P. 138

A ❶ haste ❷ deliver
❸ occasions ❹ representative
❺ particle ❻ reckless
❼ evenly ❽ foretell
❾ reaction ❿ scratch

B ❶ circle 원 ❷ sermonize 설교하다
❸ recklessness 무모함 ❹ define 정의를 내리다
❺ occasional 이따금씩의 ❻ participate 참여하다
❼ apologetically 변명하여
❽ genuinely 진정으로
❾ sensational 감각의, 지각의
❿ logical 논리적인

C ❶ requirement ❷ disappointment
❸ numeral ❹ applicant
❺ attain ❻ diligent
❼ horizontal ❽ scatter
❾ warfare ❿ reaction

D ❶ thrifty ❷ gigantic
❸ mock ❹ orbit
❺ signature ❻ possesses
❼ primary ❽ decorated
❾ warm-hearted ❿ inspiration

E ❶ satisfied ❷ room
❸ concrete ❹ capable
❺ wise ❻ ordinary
❼ maximize ❽ long-sighted
❾ occupation ❿ rare

F ❶ sermon 설교 ❷ scratch 긁다, 할퀴다
❸ particle 입자
❹ dissatisfied 불만을 품은
❺ slack 느슨한, 꾸물거리는; 느슨함, 여유
❻ abstract 추상적인
❼ competent 자격이 있는, 유능한
❽ advisable 현명한, 바람직한
❾ extraordinary 비상한, 비범한
❿ minimize 최소화시키다 ⓫ near-sighted 근시안의
⓬ vocation 직업
⓭ commonplace 평범한 것; 평범한
⓮ occasion 경우

G ❶ ultrasonic ❷ breakdowns
❸ counterbalance ❹ thermostat
❺ segment ❻ abounds
❼ errand ❽ circular
❾ offered ❿ reckless
⓫ definition ⓬ participation
⓭ apologetic ⓮ sensation
⓯ logic ⓰ hijack

DAY 23

P. 143

661 populated 662 squished
663 consult 664 intricate
665 stung 666 coordinate
667 corporation 668 cosmetic
669 fluency 670 lining
671 ragged 672 tension
673 assumption 674 daylight
675 generalization 676 messy
677 Renaissance 678 treadmill
679 blockade 680 devastated
681 habitats 682 nationality
683 riot 684 neighboring
685 vacancies 686 ventilated
687 viewpoint 688 Visualizing
689 chaotic 690 (to) circulate

DAY 24

P. 147

691 weary 692 significance
693 Comet 694 equation
695 inquire 696 poked
697 spotless 698 adrenaline
699 exposure 700 preservation
701 ambition 702 fate
703 feedback 704 fistful
705 legend 706 quit
707 temper 708 asset
709 currency 710 fuss
711 meditate 712 reliable
713 tragic 714 blades
715 destiny 716 grim
717 nap 718 revolutionized
719 unlimited 720 sake

REVIEW TEST 12

P. 150

A ❶ blade ❷ daylight
❸ nap ❹ quit
❺ sake ❻ neighboring
❼ ventilate ❽ stung
❾ fistful ❿ fuss

B ❶ equational 균등한, 방정식의
❷ population 인구 ❸ consultation 상담
❹ coordination 조정 ❺ assume 가정하다
❻ devastation 황폐 ❼ significant 중요한
❽ cometary 혜성 같은 ❾ spotlessness 결백
❿ legendary 전설상의

C ❶ ragged ❷ blockade
❸ circulate ❹ expose
❺ ambition ❻ feedback
❼ currency ❽ corporation
❾ nationality ❿ riot

D ❶ fluency ❷ tension
❸ treadmill ❹ habitats
❺ vacancies ❻ inquire
❼ poked ❽ preservation
❾ asset ❿ meditate

E ❶ sunlight ❷ tidy

❸ tired ❹ adjoining
❺ disordered ❻ confer
❼ unreliable ❽ comedic
❾ limited ❿ fate

F ❶ daylight 일광, 햇빛, 낮 ❷ messy 어질러진
❸ Renaissance 문예부흥기, 르네상스
❹ neighboring 이웃의, 근접해 있는
❺ chaotic 혼돈된 ❻ quit 그만두다
❼ reliable 신뢰할 수 있는 ❽ tragic 비극의
❾ unlimited 제한 없는 ❿ destiny 운명
⓫ equation 동등, 등식, 방정식
⓬ consult 의견을 듣다, 상담하다
⓭ significance 중요성 ⓮ legend 전설

G ❶ squished ❷ cosmetic
❸ generalization ❹ Visualizing
❺ adrenaline ❻ fistful
❼ temper ❽ blades
❾ revolutionized ❿ fate
⓫ populated ⓬ coordinate
⓭ assumption ⓮ devastated
⓯ Comet ⓰ spotless

DAY 25

P. 155

721 cape 722 carefree
723 categorized 724 ceases
725 elaborate 726 citizenship
727 weird 728 simplify
729 ensure 730 inherited
731 plague 732 spectacular
733 adjustment 734 consistent
735 interpretation 736 stiff
737 controversy 738 itches
739 landfill 740 leadership
741 python 742 tact
743 ascended 744 crucial
745 fund 746 masterpieces
747 regulates 748 tolled
749 beware 750 depiction

DAY 26

P. 159

751 gorgeous 752 mount
753 retrospect 754 unidentifiable
755 bureau 756 unwilling
757 distribution 758 domestic
759 drawing 760 effective
761 impolite 762 civilization
763 wholesome 764 informed
765 physician 766 sowed
767 activated 768 confirmed
769 exert 770 preliminary
771 alertness 772 falsehood
773 professional 774 prominent
775 prospect 776 swarm
777 arithmetic 778 creek
779 fruitless 780 management

REVIEW TEST 13

P. 162

A ❶ fund ❷ domestic
❸ adjustment ❹ informed
❺ spectacular ❻ weird
❼ regulate ❽ masterpiece
❾ confirm ❿ effective

B ❶ inheritance 유산, 유전 ❷ effect 효과, 결과
❸ adjust 적응하다 ❹ consistency 일관성
❺ stiffen 뻣뻣해지다 ❻ controversial 논쟁의
❼ depict 묘사하다 ❽ domesticate 길들이다
❾ exertion 노력 ❿ prominence 현저함

C ❶ ensure ❷ elaborate
❸ simplify ❹ landfill
❺ tact ❻ toll
❼ mount ❽ activate
❾ falsehood ❿ management

D ❶ carefree ❷ ceases
❸ interpretation ❹ itches
❺ leadership ❻ ascended
❼ beware ❽ bureau
❾ wholesome ❿ sowed

E ❶ normal ❷ epidemic ❸ govern ❹ splendid ❺ prospect ❻ reluctant ❼ culture ❽ vigilance ❾ herd ❿ fruitful

F ❶ citizenship 시민권 ❷ drawing 그림 ❸ weird 기묘한, 이상한 ❹ plague 전염병 ❺ regulate 통제하다, 규정하다 ❻ gorgeous 멋진 ❼ retrospect 회고, 회상; 회고하다 ❽ unwilling 마지못해 하는 ❾ civilization 문명(화) ❿ alertness 방심하지 않음, 경각심 ⓫ swarm 떼 ⓬ fruitless 결실이 없는 ⓭ domestic 국내의 ⓮ categorize 분류하다

G ❶ cape ❷ python ❸ fund ❹ unidentifiable ❺ physician ❻ confirmed ❼ professional ❽ arithmetic ❾ inherited ❿ effective ⓫ adjustment ⓬ consistent ⓭ stiff ⓮ controversy ⓯ depiction ⓰ exert

DAY 27

P. 167

781 recyclable 782 tickling 783 barefoot 784 density 785 glaze 786 monks 787 respiration 788 undo 789 bruised 790 Dispose 791 cabinet 792 humble 793 hymn 794 illuminated 795 immigration 796 outlaw 797 civilize 798 wicked 799 perfection 800 sniffed 801 accumulate 802 compression 803 exaggerate 804 intensive 805 starry 806 context 807 irresistible 808 stunned 809 succession 810 superlative

DAY 28

P. 171

811 apt 812 crammed 813 frequencies 814 luxurious 815 reconciled 816 thrilling 817 auxiliary 818 defrost 819 glacier 820 moderate 821 resemble 822 unarmed 823 breed 824 disclosed 825 hired 826 dissimilar 827 numerous 828 odd 829 official 830 organic 831 session 832 eliminate 833 classification 834 Sleet 835 abused 836 completion 837 eventful 838 insured 839 precautions 840 affectionate

REVIEW TEST 14

P. 174

A ❶ monk ❷ humble ❸ barefoot ❹ disclose ❺ hymn ❻ insure ❼ thrilling ❽ classification ❾ unarmed ❿ defrost

B ❶ accumulation 축적 ❷ civilization 문명 ❸ complete 완성하다 ❹ contextual 문맥상의, 전후관계의 ❺ dense 조밀한 ❻ disposal 처분 ❼ frequent 자주 일어나는 ❽ insurance 보험 ❾ stunning 굉장히 멋진 / stunned 정신이 멍한 ❿ successive 연속적인

C ❶ abuse ❷ affectionate ❸ bruise ❹ cram ❺ eliminate ❻ illuminate ❼ recyclable ❽ wicked ❾ superlative ❿ monk

D ❶ compression ❷ eventful ❸ glacier ❹ glaze ❺ luxurious ❻ numerous

❼ odd
❽ resemble
❾ hymn
❿ sniffed

E ❶ reveal
❷ similar
❸ understate
❹ employ
❺ extensive
❻ overwhelming
❼ unofficial
❽ caution
❾ quarrel
❿ breath

F ❶ barefoot 맨발의
❷ perfection 완벽, 완전
❸ accumulate 모으다
❹ completion 완성
❺ stun 기절시키다
❻ bruise 타박상, 멍; 멍들게 하다
❼ superlative 최상급의, 최고의
❽ compression 압축
❾ eventful 사건이 많은, 다사다난한
❿ glacier 빙하
⓫ glaze 유약, 광택제
⓬ luxurious 화려한
⓭ numerous 매우 많은
⓮ odd 이상한

G ❶ apt
❷ humble
❸ immigration
❹ moderate
❺ organic
❻ outlaw
❼ starry
❽ undo
❾ civilize
❿ context
⓫ density
⓬ Dispose
⓭ frequencies
⓮ insured
⓯ succession
⓰ abused

DAY 29

P. 179

841 facilities
842 Primitive
843 anthropology
844 apparent
845 courageous
846 formulating
847 loosened
848 realization
849 thighs
850 Attendance
851 dedicate
852 geographical
853 minister
854 reproduction
855 trout
856 boycott
857 dim
858 hazardous
859 horror
860 scent
861 Scrub
862 seized
863 sensitivity
864 vow
865 embarrassing
866 regretful
867 abrupt
868 communicable
869 estimated
870 instructive

DAY 30

P. 183

871 population
872 stake
873 Contagious
874 invalid
875 stomped
876 flush
877 literate
878 rap
879 terminal
880 astronomy
881 deadly
882 generate
883 Metropolitan
884 renovated
885 trekking
886 bold
887 diagram
888 halfway
889 sympathized
890 neutral
891 Visually
892 childish
893 emerged
894 adulthood
895 extension
896 prevail
897 ambitious
898 satellites
899 appointed
900 costly

REVIEW TEST 15

P. 186

A ❶ attendance
❷ vow
❸ neutral
❹ population
❺ scent
❻ abrupt
❼ regretful
❽ stomp
❾ invalid
❿ sympathize

B ❶ courage 용기
❷ abruptness 퉁명스러움
❸ appointment 임명, 지명
❹ sensitive 민감한
❺ loose 헐거운
❻ geography 지리
❼ populate 살다, 거주하다
❽ terminate 종결시키다
❾ astronomical 천문학적인
❿ prevalent 우세한

C ❶ childish
❷ emerge
❸ seize
❹ dim
❺ embarrassing
❻ contagious
❼ neutral
❽ adulthood
❾ extension
❿ instructive

D ❶ Attendance ❷ renovated ❸ Metropolitan ❹ anthropology ❺ thighs ❻ horror ❼ estimated ❽ stake ❾ diagram ❿ halfway

E ❶ knock ❷ cheap ❸ illiterate ❹ modern ❺ ban ❻ contagious ❼ devote ❽ fatal ❾ obvious ❿ produce

F ❶ bold 대담한 ❷ vow 맹세하다 ❸ minister 성직자, 장관 ❹ population 인구 ❺ childish 어린이 같은, 유치한 ❻ seize 붙잡다 ❼ contagious 전염성의 ❽ extension 연장 ❾ attendance 참석 ❿ renovate 수리하다 ⓫ metropolitan 대도시의 ⓬ anthropology 인류학 ⓭ thigh 넓적다리 ⓮ horror 공포

G ❶ ambitious ❷ satellites ❸ scent ❹ trekking ❺ facilities ❻ invalid ❼ stomped ❽ courageous ❾ abrupt ❿ appointed ⓫ sensitivity ⓬ loosened ⓭ geographical ⓮ terminal ⓯ astronomy ⓰ prevail

3rd Edition

내신 · 수능 · 토플이 가벼워지는
Vocabulary master
5단계 시리즈

고등 내신 기본 900

WORKBOOK

DARAKWON

WORKBOOK

DAY 01

STEP 1
한국어 뜻 생각하며 외우기

월 일

✦ 해당 영어의 한국어 의미를 생각하면서 2번씩 적으시오.

01	가난한	**needy**	가난한	가난한
02	결점, 약점	**flaw**	결점, 약점	결점, 약점
03	고객 맞춤화된	**customized**	고객 맞춤화된	고객 맞춤화된
04	구성, 조직	**constitution**	구성, 조직	구성, 조직
05	나르다, 전달하다	**convey**	나르다, 전달하다	나르다, 전달하다
06	대처하다	**cope**	대처하다	대처하다
07	돕다	**assist**	돕다	돕다
08	떨다	**quiver**	떨다	떨다
09	배우자	**spouse**	배우자	배우자
10	변형시키다	**transform**	변형시키다	변형시키다
11	보증하다; 보증	**guarantee**	보증하다; 보증	보증하다; 보증
12	부품	**gadget**	부품	부품
13	비어 있는	**vacant**	비어 있는	비어 있는
14	상업	**commerce**	상업	상업
15	새기다	**inscribe**	새기다	새기다
16	서로 관계가 있는	**interrelated**	서로 관계가 있는	서로 관계가 있는
17	섞다	**blend**	섞다	섞다
18	안도	**relief**	안도	안도
19	연발 권총	**revolver**	연발 권총	연발 권총
20	우울한	**melancholic**	우울한	우울한
21	이야기하다	**narrate**	이야기하다	이야기하다
22	일시적인, 임시의	**temporary**	일시적인, 임시의	일시적인, 임시의
23	일치, 조화	**correspondence**	일치, 조화	일치, 조화
24	자극하다	**stimulate**	자극하다	자극하다
25	적도	**equator**	적도	적도
26	정치적인	**political**	정치적인	정치적인
27	책임 있는	**liable**	책임 있는	책임 있는
28	촉구하다	**urge**	촉구하다	촉구하다
29	파괴적인	**destructive**	파괴적인	파괴적인
30	포기하다	**abandon**	포기하다	포기하다

STEP 2 최종실력 점검하기

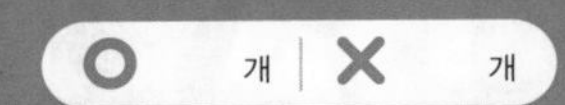

✦ 다음을 영어는 한국어로 한국어는 영어로 적으시오.

정답 p.65

01	abandon	
02	assist	
03	blend	
04	commerce	
05	constitution	
06	convey	
07	cope	
08	correspondence	
09	customized	
10	destructive	
11	equator	
12	flaw	
13	gadget	
14	guarantee	
15	inscribe	
16	interrelated	
17	liable	
18	melancholy	
19	narrate	
20	needy	
21	political	
22	quiver	
23	relief	
24	revolver	
25	spouse	
26	stimulate	
27	temporary	
28	transform	
29	urge	
30	vacant	

01	동 나르다, 전달하다	
02	동 대처하다	
03	동 돕다	
04	동 떨다	
05	동 변형시키다	
06	동 보증하다 명 보증	
07	동 새기다	
08	동 섞다	
09	동 이야기하다	
10	동 자극하다	
11	동 촉구하다	
12	동 포기하다	
13	명 결점, 약점	
14	명 구성, 조직	
15	명 배우자	
16	명 부품	
17	명 상업	
18	명 안도	
19	명 연발 권총	
20	명 일치, 조화	
21	명 적도	
22	형 가난한	
23	형 고객 맞춤화된	
24	형 비어 있는	
25	형 서로 관계가 있는	
26	형 우울한	
27	형 일시적인, 임시의	
28	형 정치적인	
29	형 책임 있는	
30	형 파괴적인	

DAY 02

STEP 1
한국어 뜻 생각하며 외우기

월 일

✦ 해당 영어의 한국어 의미를 생각하면서 2번씩 적으시오.

01	극대[최대]로 하다	maximize	극대[최대]로 하다	극대[최대]로 하다
02	관리하다	administer	관리하다	관리하다
03	교대시키다, 번갈아 하다	alternate	교대시키다, 번갈아 하다	교대시키다, 번갈아 하다
04	규제	regulation	규제	규제
05	극도의 피로	exhaustion	극도의 피로	극도의 피로
06	기본적인	fundamental	기본적인	기본적인
07	나선형의	spiral	나선형의	나선형의
08	나이가 지긋한	elderly	나이가 지긋한	나이가 지긋한
09	내려가다	descend	내려가다	내려가다
10	누출	leakage	누출	누출
11	독성의	toxic	독성의	독성의
12	2개 국어를 할 수 있는	bilingual	2개 국어를 할 수 있는	2개 국어를 할 수 있는
13	명성	fame	명성	명성
14	방출	emission	방출	방출
15	섭씨; 섭씨의	Celsius	섭씨; 섭씨의	섭씨; 섭씨의
16	송이, 무리	cluster	송이, 무리	송이, 무리
17	시작하다	initiate	시작하다	시작하다
18	식민지	colony	식민지	식민지
19	여자의, 여자 같은	feminine	여자의, 여자 같은	여자의, 여자 같은
20	열광	enthusiasm	열광	열광
21	열망, 포부	aspiration	열망, 포부	열망, 포부
22	원기 왕성한	vigorous	원기 왕성한	원기 왕성한
23	이륙, 출발	takeoff	이륙, 출발	이륙, 출발
24	자격	qualification	자격	자격
25	잔혹	cruelty	잔혹	잔혹
26	쟁기; (밭을) 갈다	plow	쟁기; (밭을) 갈다	쟁기; (밭을) 갈다
27	처방하다	prescribe	처방하다	처방하다
28	통풍	ventilation	통풍	통풍
29	피로	fatigue	피로	피로
30	흉내 내다	simulate	흉내 내다	흉내 내다

STEP 2
최종실력 점검하기

✦ 다음을 영어는 한국어로 한국어는 영어로 적으시오.

정답 p.65

01	**administer**
02	**alternate**
03	**aspiration**
04	**bilingual**
05	**Celsius**
06	**cluster**
07	**colony**
08	**cruelty**
09	**descend**
10	**elderly**
11	**emission**
12	**enthusiasm**
13	**exhaustion**
14	**fame**
15	**fatigue**
16	**feminine**
17	**fundamental**
18	**initiate**
19	**leakage**
20	**maximize**
21	**plow**
22	**prescribe**
23	**qualification**
24	**regulation**
25	**simulate**
26	**spiral**
27	**takeoff**
28	**toxic**
29	**ventilation**
30	**vigorous**

01	동 극대[최대]로 하다
02	동 관리하다
03	동 교대시키다, 번갈아 하다
04	동 내려가다
05	동 시작하다
06	동 처방하다
07	동 흉내 내다
08	명 규제
09	명 극도의 피로
10	명 누출
11	명 명성
12	명 방출
13	명 섭씨 형 섭씨의
14	명 송이, 무리
15	명 식민지
16	명 열광
17	명 열망, 포부
18	명 이륙, 출발
19	명 자격
20	명 잔혹
21	명 쟁기 동 (밭을) 갈다
22	명 통풍
23	명 피로
24	형 기본적인
25	형 나선형의
26	형 나이가 지긋한
27	형 독성의
28	형 2개 국어를 할 수 있는
29	형 여자의, 여자 같은
30	형 원기 왕성한

DAY 03 STEP 1 한국어 뜻 생각하며 외우기

월 일

✦ 해당 영어의 한국어 의미를 생각하면서 2번씩 적으시오.

01	(종교·도덕상의) 죄	**sin**	(종교·도덕상의) 죄	(종교·도덕상의) 죄
02	확대[증대]시키다	**enlarge**	확대[증대]시키다	확대[증대]시키다
03	가파른	**steep**	가파른	가파른
04	감명 깊은	**impressed**	감명 깊은	감명 깊은
05	강조	**emphasis**	강조	강조
06	결합, 조합	**union**	결합, 조합	결합, 조합
07	계산	**calculation**	계산	계산
08	계속적인	**continual**	계속적인	계속적인
09	교묘한, 기발한	**ingenious**	교묘한, 기발한	교묘한, 기발한
10	되돌릴 수 없는	**irreversible**	되돌릴 수 없는	되돌릴 수 없는
11	애벌레	**caterpillar**	애벌레	애벌레
12	물리학자	**physicist**	물리학자	물리학자
13	빠른	**swift**	빠른	빠른
14	상아	**ivory**	상아	상아
15	새기다, 조각하다	**carve**	새기다, 조각하다	새기다, 조각하다
16	애도하다, 슬퍼하다	**mourn**	애도하다, 슬퍼하다	애도하다, 슬퍼하다
17	심리적인	**psychological**	심리적인	심리적인
18	양심	**conscience**	양심	양심
19	위기	**crisis**	위기	위기
20	으르렁거리다; 포효	**roar**	으르렁거리다; 포효	으르렁거리다; 포효
21	의도	**intention**	의도	의도
22	자본주의	**capitalism**	자본주의	자본주의
23	재통일	**reunification**	재통일	재통일
24	점진적인	**gradual**	점진적인	점진적인
25	집주인	**landlord**	집주인	집주인
26	침술	**acupuncture**	침술	침술
27	한 뼘, 기간	**span**	한 뼘, 기간	한 뼘, 기간
28	향기	**aroma**	향기	향기
29	협력하다	**collaborate**	협력하다	협력하다
30	효율성	**efficiency**	효율성	효율성

✦ 다음을 영어는 한국어로 한국어는 영어로 적으시오.

정답 p.66

01	acupuncture	
02	aroma	
03	calculation	
04	capitalism	
05	carve	
06	caterpillar	
07	collaborate	
08	conscience	
09	continual	
10	crisis	
11	efficiency	
12	emphasis	
13	enlarge	
14	gradual	
15	impressed	
16	ingenious	
17	intention	
18	irreversible	
19	ivory	
20	landlord	
21	mourn	
22	physicist	
23	psychological	
24	reunification	
25	roar	
26	sin	
27	span	
28	steep	
29	swift	
30	union	

01	동 확대[증대]시키다	
02	동 새기다, 조각하다	
03	동 애도하다, 슬퍼하다	
04	동 으르렁거리다 명 포효	
05	동 협력하다	
06	명 결합, 조합	
07	명 (종교·도덕상의) 죄	
08	명 강조	
09	명 계산	
10	명 애벌레	
11	명 물리학자	
12	명 상아	
13	명 양심	
14	명 위기	
15	명 의도	
16	명 자본주의	
17	명 재통일	
18	명 집주인	
19	명 침술	
20	명 한 뼘, 기간	
21	명 향기	
22	명 효율성	
23	형 가파른	
24	형 감명 깊은	
25	형 계속적인	
26	형 교묘한, 기발한	
27	형 되돌릴 수 없는	
28	형 빠른	
29	형 심리적인	
30	형 점진적인	

DAY 04 STEP 1
한국어 뜻 생각하며 외우기

월 일

✦ 해당 영어의 한국어 의미를 생각하면서 2번씩 적으시오.

01	간신히	**barely**	간신히	간신히
02	~에 관하여	**concerning**	~에 관하여	~에 관하여
03	구멍을 뚫다	**drill**	구멍을 뚫다	구멍을 뚫다
04	정제하다	**refine**	정제하다	정제하다
05	전망, 시야	**outlook**	전망, 시야	전망, 시야
06	긍정적인	**affirmative**	긍정적인	긍정적인
07	기부	**donation**	기부	기부
08	끌어안다	**snuggle**	끌어안다	끌어안다
09	발굴하다	**unearth**	발굴하다	발굴하다
10	방해, 소동	**disturbance**	방해, 소동	방해, 소동
11	불쾌한	**distasteful**	불쾌한	불쾌한
12	사라지다	**fade**	사라지다	사라지다
13	성실, 진실성	**sincerity**	성실, 진실성	성실, 진실성
14	손상시키다	**impair**	손상시키다	손상시키다
15	예외적인	**exceptional**	예외적인	예외적인
16	이행하다	**perform**	이행하다	이행하다
17	잔인한	**brutal**	잔인한	잔인한
18	정확하게	**accurately**	정확하게	정확하게
19	정확한, 정밀한	**precise**	정확한	정확한
20	조작, 책략	**maneuver**	조작, 책략	조작, 책략
21	좌절	**frustration**	좌절	좌절
22	짐을 내리다	**unload**	짐을 내리다	짐을 내리다
23	출발	**departure**	출발	출발
24	취임의; 취임식	**inaugural**	취임의	취임의
25	치명적인, 죽을 운명의	**mortal**	치명적인	치명적인
26	팽창시키다	**inflate**	팽창시키다	팽창시키다
27	팽팽하게 치다	**tighten**	팽팽하게 치다	팽팽하게 치다
28	협조적인	**collaborative**	협조적인	협조적인
29	잠 못 이루는, 불안한	**restless**	잠 못 이루는, 불안한	잠 못 이루는, 불안한
30	희미한 빛, 기색	**glimmering**	희미한 빛, 기색	희미한 빛, 기색

정답 p.66

✦ 다음을 영어는 한국어로 한국어는 영어로 적으시오.

01	**accurately**	
02	**affirmative**	
03	**barely**	
04	**brutal**	
05	**collaborative**	
06	**concerning**	
07	**departure**	
08	**distasteful**	
09	**disturbance**	
10	**donation**	
11	**drill**	
12	**exceptional**	
13	**fade**	
14	**frustration**	
15	**glimmering**	
16	**impair**	
17	**inaugural**	
18	**inflate**	
19	**maneuver**	
20	**mortal**	
21	**outlook**	
22	**perform**	
23	**precise**	
24	**refine**	
25	**restless**	
26	**sincerity**	
27	**snuggle**	
28	**tighten**	
29	**unearth**	
30	**unload**	

01	[동] 구멍을 뚫다	
02	[동] 정제하다	
03	[동] 끌어안다	
04	[동] 발굴하다	
05	[동] 사라지다	
06	[동] 손상시키다	
07	[동] 이행하다	
08	[동] 짐을 내리다	
09	[동] 팽창시키다	
10	[동] 팽팽하게 치다	
11	[명] 전망, 시야	
12	[명] 기부	
13	[명] 방해, 소동	
14	[명] 성실, 진실성	
15	[부] 정확하게	
16	[명] 조작, 책략	
17	[명] 좌절	
18	[명] 출발	
19	[명] 희미한 빛, 기색	
20	[부] 간신히	
21	[전] ~에 관하여	
22	[형] 긍정적인	
23	[형] 불쾌한	
24	[형] 예외적인	
25	[형] 잔인한	
26	[형] 정확한, 정밀한	
27	[형] 취임의 [명] 취임식	
28	[형] 치명적인, 죽을 운명의	
29	[형] 협조적인	
30	[형] 잠 못 이루는, 불안한	

DAY 05 STEP 1 한국어 뜻 생각하며 외우기

월 일

✦ 해당 영어의 한국어 의미를 생각하면서 2번씩 적으시오.

01	매혹하다	**enchant**	매혹하다	매혹하다
02	검투사	**gladiator**	검투사	검투사
03	겸손한	**modest**	겸손한	겸손한
04	고고학자	**archaeologist**	고고학자	고고학자
05	기꺼이 하는 마음	**willingness**	기꺼이 하는 마음	기꺼이 하는 마음
06	깨닫게 하는; 각성	**awakening**	깨닫게 하는; 각성	깨닫게 하는; 각성
07	마음을 내키게 하다	**incline**	마음을 내키게 하다	마음을 내키게 하다
08	진 적이 없는, 무적의	**unbeaten**	진 적이 없는, 무적의	진 적이 없는, 무적의
09	맥박이 뛰다	**throb**	맥박이 뛰다	맥박이 뛰다
10	미치게 하다; 열광	**craze**	미치게 하다; 열광	미치게 하다; 열광
11	분해할 수 있는	**degradable**	분해할 수 있는	분해할 수 있는
12	비탈	**slope**	비탈	비탈
13	사생활	**privacy**	사생활	사생활
14	산들바람	**breeze**	산들바람	산들바람
15	습한	**humid**	습한	습한
16	승진	**promotion**	승진	승진
17	웅장한, 훌륭한	**magnificent**	웅장한, 훌륭한	웅장한, 훌륭한
18	유기체	**organism**	유기체	유기체
19	유익한, 이익이 되는	**profitable**	유익한, 이익이 되는	유익한, 이익이 되는
20	주거	**residence**	주거	주거
21	차별	**discrimination**	차별	차별
22	착각	**illusion**	착각	착각
23	초라한	**shabby**	초라한	초라한
24	친절	**friendliness**	친절	친절
25	트림하다; 트림	**burp**	트림하다; 트림	트림하다; 트림
26	특이한 성질	**peculiarity**	특이한 성질	특이한 성질
27	피상적인	**superficial**	피상적인	피상적인
28	(신원) 확인	**identification**	(신원) 확인	(신원) 확인
29	환대	**hospitality**	환대	환대
30	회복	**recovery**	회복	회복

정답 p.67

✦ 다음을 영어는 한국어로 한국어는 영어로 적으시오.

01	archaeologist	
02	awakening	
03	breeze	
04	burp	
05	craze	
06	degradable	
07	discriminate	
08	enchant	
09	friendliness	
10	gladiator	
11	hospitality	
12	humid	
13	identification	
14	illusion	
15	incline	
16	magnificent	
17	modest	
18	organism	
19	peculiarity	
20	privacy	
21	profitable	
22	promotion	
23	recovery	
24	residence	
25	shabby	
26	slope	
27	supernatural	
28	throb	
29	unbeaten	
30	willingness	

01	동 매혹하다	
02	동 마음을 내키게 하다	
03	동 맥박이 뛰다	
04	동 미치게 하다 명 열광	
05	명 차별	
06	명 검투사	
07	명 고고학자	
08	명 기꺼이 하는 마음	
09	명 비탈	
10	명 사생활	
11	명 산들바람	
12	명 승진	
13	명 유기체	
14	명 주거	
15	명 착각	
16	명 친절	
17	동 트림하다 명 트림	
18	명 특이한 성질	
19	명 (신원) 확인	
20	명 환대	
21	명 회복	
22	형 겸손한	
23	형 깨닫게 하는 명 각성	
24	형 진 적이 없는, 무적의	
25	형 분해할 수 있는	
26	형 습한	
27	형 웅장한, 훌륭한	
28	형 유익한, 이익이 되는	
29	형 초라한	
30	형 피상적인	

DAY 06 STEP 1 한국어 뜻 생각하며 외우기

월 일

✦ 해당 영어의 한국어 의미를 생각하면서 2번씩 적으시오.

01	완패시키다	**thrash**	완패시키다	완패시키다
02	고결, 청렴	**integrity**	고결, 청렴	고결, 청렴
03	구성, 작문	**composition**	구성, 작문	구성, 작문
04	냄새, 악취	**odor**	냄새, 악취	냄새, 악취
05	당기다	**tug**	당기다	당기다
06	동시대의; 같은 시대의 사람	**contemporary**	동시대의; 같은 시대의 사람	동시대의; 같은 시대의 사람
07	마음에서 우러난	**hearty**	마음에서 우러난	마음에서 우러난
08	무리하게 사용하다	**strain**	무리하게 사용하다	무리하게 사용하다
09	방관자	**onlooker**	방관자	방관자
10	방어	**defense**	방어	방어
11	변호사	**attorney**	변호사	변호사
12	보조개; 보조개를 짓다	**dimple**	보조개; 보조개를 짓다	보조개; 보조개를 짓다
13	복권, 추첨	**lottery**	복권, 추첨	복권, 추첨
14	브레인스토밍하다	**brainstorm**	브레인스토밍하다	브레인스토밍하다
15	재생하다, 복제하다	**reproduce**	재생하다, 복제하다	재생하다, 복제하다
16	솔직한	**frank**	솔직한	솔직한
17	수확하다	**reap**	수확하다	수확하다
18	무례한, 실례되는	**disrespectful**	무례한, 실례되는	무례한, 실례되는
19	양분, 영양소	**nutrient**	양분, 영양소	양분, 영양소
20	예의 바른, 공손한	**courteous**	예의 바른, 공손한	예의 바른, 공손한
21	일깨우다	**evoke**	일깨우다	일깨우다
22	잘못 인도하다	**mislead**	잘못 인도하다	잘못 인도하다
23	잠재의식의; 잠재의식	**subconscious**	잠재의식의; 잠재의식	잠재의식의; 잠재의식
24	조사하다	**investigate**	조사하다	조사하다
25	주목할 만한	**notable**	주목할 만한	주목할 만한
26	지질학의	**geological**	지질학의	지질학의
27	진부한; 진부하게 하다	**stale**	진부한; 진부하게 하다	진부한; 진부하게 하다
28	체포하다	**apprehend**	체포하다	체포하다
29	충분한	**sufficient**	충분한	충분한
30	학구적인	**academic**	학구적인	학구적인

✦ 다음을 영어는 한국어로 한국어는 영어로 적으시오.

정답 p.67

01	academic	
02	apprehend	
03	attorney	
04	brainstorm	
05	composition	
06	contemporary	
07	courteous	
08	defense	
09	dimple	
10	disrespectful	
11	evoke	
12	frank	
13	geological	
14	hearty	
15	integrity	
16	investigate	
17	lottery	
18	mislead	
19	notable	
20	nutrient	
21	odor	
22	onlooker	
23	reap	
24	reproduce	
25	stale	
26	strain	
27	subconscious	
28	sufficient	
29	thrash	
30	tug	

01	동 완패시키다	
02	동 당기다	
03	동 무리하게 사용하다	
04	동 브레인스토밍하다	
05	동 수확하다	
06	동 일깨우다	
07	동 잘못 인도하다	
08	동 조사하다	
09	동 체포하다	
10	명 고결, 청렴	
11	명 구성, 작문	
12	명 냄새, 악취	
13	명 방관자	
14	명 방어	
15	명 변호사	
16	명 보조개 동 보조개를 짓다	
17	명 복권, 추첨	
18	명 양분, 영양소	
19	형 동시대의 명 같은 시대의 사람	
20	형 마음에서 우러난	
21	동 재생하다, 복제하다	
22	형 솔직한	
23	형 무례한, 실례되는	
24	형 예의 바른, 공손한	
25	형 잠재의식의 명 잠재의식	
26	형 주목할 만한	
27	형 지질학의	
28	형 진부한 동 진부하게 하다	
29	형 충분한	
30	형 학구적인	

DAY 07 STEP 1 한국어 뜻 생각하며 외우기

월 일

✦ 해당 영어의 한국어 의미를 생각하면서 2번씩 적으시오.

01	(꼬리, 머리 등을) 흔들다	**wag**	(꼬리, 머리 등을) 흔들다	(꼬리, 머리 등을) 흔들다
02	언제나, 영원히	**eternally**	언제나, 영원히	언제나, 영원히
03	찬사, 감사의 표시	**tribute**	찬사, 감사의 표시	찬사, 감사의 표시
04	감정, 정서	**sentiment**	감정, 정서	감정, 정서
05	강력한	**mighty**	강력한	강력한
06	거스르는, 부정적인	**adverse**	거스르는, 부정적인	거스르는, 부정적인
07	결석한; 결석하다	**absent**	결석한; 결석하다	결석한; 결석하다
08	골격, 해골	**skeleton**	골격, 해골	골격, 해골
09	관용	**generosity**	관용	관용
10	광범위한	**extensive**	광범위한	광범위한
11	기구, 전기제품	**appliance**	기구, 전기제품	기구, 전기제품
12	대출	**loan**	대출	대출
13	동료	**companion**	동료	동료
14	막을 수 있는	**preventable**	막을 수 있는	막을 수 있는
15	매혹적인	**enchanting**	매혹적인	매혹적인
16	민속, 민간 전승	**folklore**	민속, 민간 전승	민속, 민간 전승
17	반복적인	**repetitive**	반복적인	반복적인
18	보류하다	**withhold**	보류하다	보류하다
19	부분	**portion**	부분	부분
20	썩은	**decayed**	썩은	썩은
21	분별없는, 경솔한	**rash**	분별없는, 경솔한	분별없는, 경솔한
22	불편	**inconvenience**	불편	불편
23	상담, 조언	**counsel**	상담, 조언	상담, 조언
24	소화하다	**digest**	소화하다	소화하다
25	절연하다	**insulate**	절연하다	절연하다
26	증명하다, 증언하다	**testify**	증명하다, 증언하다	증명하다, 증언하다
27	지도책	**atlas**	지도책	지도책
28	지루함	**boredom**	지루함	지루함
29	사면	**amnesty**	사면	사면
30	항생물질의; 항생물질	**antibiotic**	항생물질의; 항생물질	항생물질의; 항생물질

✦ 다음을 영어는 한국어로 한국어는 영어로 적으시오.

정답 p.68

01	**absent**	
02	**adverse**	
03	**amnesty**	
04	**antibiotic**	
05	**appliance**	
06	**atlas**	
07	**boredom**	
08	**companion**	
09	**counsel**	
10	**decayed**	
11	**digest**	
12	**enchanting**	
13	**eternally**	
14	**extensive**	
15	**folklore**	
16	**generosity**	
17	**inconvenience**	
18	**insulate**	
19	**loan**	
20	**mighty**	
21	**portion**	
22	**preventable**	
23	**rash**	
24	**repetitive**	
25	**sentiment**	
26	**skeleton**	
27	**testify**	
28	**tribute**	
29	**wag**	
30	**withhold**	

01	동 (꼬리, 머리 등을) 흔들다	
02	동 보류하다	
03	형 썩은	
04	동 소화하다	
05	동 절연하다	
06	동 증명하다, 증언하다	
07	명 찬사, 감사의 표시	
08	명 감정, 정서	
09	명 골격, 해골	
10	명 관용	
11	명 기구, 전기제품	
12	명 대출	
13	명 동료	
14	명 민속, 민간 전승	
15	명 부분	
16	명 불편	
17	명 상담, 조언	
18	명 지도책	
19	명 지루함	
20	명 사면	
21	부 언제나, 영원히	
22	형 강력한	
23	형 거스르는, 부정적인	
24	형 결석한; 결석하다	
25	형 광범위한	
26	형 막을 수 있는	
27	형 매혹적인	
28	형 반복적인	
29	형 분별없는, 경솔한	
30	형 항생물질의 명 항생물질	

DAY 08 STEP 1

한국어 뜻 생각하며 외우기

월 일

✦ 해당 영어의 한국어 의미를 생각하면서 2번씩 적으시오.

01	유죄를 선고하다	convict	유죄를 선고하다	유죄를 선고하다
02	(세게) 끌어당기다	haul	(세게) 끌어당기다	(세게) 끌어당기다
03	저지르다, 범하다	commit	저지르다, 범하다	저지르다, 범하다
04	건설하다	construct	건설하다	건설하다
05	경향	tendency	경향	경향
06	국자, 한 숟가락	scoop	국자, 한 숟가락	국자, 한 숟가락
07	꽃가루	pollen	꽃가루	꽃가루
08	(모든) 노동자	workforce	(모든) 노동자	(모든) 노동자
09	동등한	equivalent	동등한	동등한
10	둘러싸다, 동봉하다	enclose	둘러싸다, 동봉하다	둘러싸다, 동봉하다
11	마찬가지로	likewise	마찬가지로	마찬가지로
12	머물다	abide	머물다	머물다
13	방해	interruption	방해	방해
14	복도	corridor	복도	복도
15	불치의	incurable	불치의	불치의
16	생생한	vivid	생생한	생생한
17	축축한; (기를) 꺾다	damp	축축한; (기를) 꺾다	축축한; (기를) 꺾다
18	원조, 도움	assistance	원조, 도움	원조, 도움
19	융통성, 유연성	flexibility	융통성, 유연성	융통성, 유연성
20	이기적임, 이기심	selfishness	이기적임, 이기심	이기적임, 이기심
21	자극	stimulation	자극	자극
22	자연의	natural	자연의	자연의
23	절뚝거리며 걷다	hobble	절뚝거리며 걷다	절뚝거리며 걷다
24	조미료	seasoning	조미료	조미료
25	중심, 핵심	core	중심, 핵심	중심, 핵심
26	쥐어 짜다	squeeze	쥐어 짜다	쥐어 짜다
27	지수, 몫	quotient	지수, 몫	지수, 몫
28	추운	chilly	추운	추운
29	통찰력	insight	통찰력	통찰력
30	흉터; 상처를 내다	scar	흉터; 상처를 내다	흉터; 상처를 내다

정답 p.68

✦ 다음을 영어는 한국어로 한국어는 영어로 적으시오.

01	abide	
02	assistance	
03	chilly	
04	commit	
05	construct	
06	convict	
07	core	
08	corridor	
09	damp	
10	enclose	
11	equivalent	
12	flexibility	
13	haul	
14	hobble	
15	incurable	
16	insight	
17	interruption	
18	likewise	
19	naturalistic	
20	pollen	
21	quotient	
22	scar	
23	scoop	
24	seasoning	
25	selfishness	
26	squeeze	
27	stimulation	
28	tendency	
29	vivid	
30	workforce	

01	동 유죄를 선고하다	
02	동 (세게) 끌어당기다	
03	동 저지르다, 범하다	
04	동 건설하다	
05	동 둘러싸다, 동봉하다	
06	동 머물다	
07	동 절뚝거리며 걷다	
08	동 쥐어 짜다	
09	명 경향	
10	명 국자, 한 숟가락	
11	명 꽃가루	
12	명 (모든) 노동자	
13	명 방해	
14	명 복도	
15	형 축축한 동 (기를) 꺾다	
16	명 원조, 도움	
17	명 융통성, 유연성	
18	명 이기적임, 이기심	
19	명 자극	
20	명 조미료	
21	명 중심, 핵심	
22	명 지수, 몫	
23	명 통찰력	
24	명 흉터 동 상처를 내다	
25	형 동등한	
26	부 마찬가지로	
27	형 불치의	
28	형 생생한	
29	형 자연의	
30	형 추운	

DAY 09 STEP 1 한국어 뜻 생각하며 외우기

월 일

✦ 해당 영어의 한국어 의미를 생각하면서 2번씩 적으시오.

01	완전히	altogether	완전히	완전히
02	갈망하다	yearn	갈망하다	갈망하다
03	기구	utensil	기구	기구
04	기근	famine	기근	기근
05	기둥	column	기둥	기둥
06	넓게 펼쳐진 공간	expanse	넓게 펼쳐진 공간	넓게 펼쳐진 공간
07	높이다	elevate	높이다	높이다
08	도박	gambling	도박	도박
09	변화	variation	변화	변화
10	보호자, 감시인	guard	보호자, 감시인	보호자, 감시인
11	부정적인	negative	부정적인	부정적인
12	산업의	industrial	산업의	산업의
13	선율	melody	선율	선율
14	수도꼭지	faucet	수도꼭지	수도꼭지
15	수직의, 세로의	vertical	수직의, 세로의	수직의, 세로의
16	순진한, 결백한	innocent	순진한, 결백한	순진한, 결백한
17	시의, 시적인	poetic	시의, 시적인	시의, 시적인
18	(시의) 운	rhyme	(시의) 운	(시의) 운
19	신앙심이 깊은	religious	신앙심이 깊은	신앙심이 깊은
20	어기다, 위반하다	violate	어기다, 위반하다	어기다, 위반하다
21	이야기하기, 서술	narration	이야기하기, 서술	이야기하기, 서술
22	인내(심)	endurance	인내(심)	인내(심)
23	증명하다	certify	증명하다	증명하다
24	처방	prescription	처방	처방
25	청년기의; 청소년	adolescent	청년기의; 청소년	청년기의; 청소년
26	신의 은총을 빌다	bless	신의 은총을 빌다	신의 은총을 빌다
27	(침을) 뱉다	spit	(침을) 뱉다	(침을) 뱉다
28	탐정; 탐정의	detective	탐정; 탐정의	탐정; 탐정의
29	투명성	transparency	투명성	투명성
30	달래다	lull	달래다	달래다

O 개 | X 개

정답 p.69

✦ 다음을 영어는 한국어로 한국어는 영어로 적으시오.

01	**adolescent**	
02	**altogether**	
03	**bless**	
04	**certify**	
05	**column**	
06	**detective**	
07	**elevate**	
08	**endurance**	
09	**lull**	
10	**expanse**	
11	**famine**	
12	**faucet**	
13	**gambling**	
14	**guard**	
15	**industrial**	
16	**innocent**	
17	**melody**	
18	**narration**	
19	**negative**	
20	**poetic**	
21	**prescription**	
22	**religious**	
23	**rhyme**	
24	**spit**	
25	**transparency**	
26	**utensil**	
27	**variation**	
28	**vertical**	
29	**violate**	
30	**yearn**	

01	동 갈망하다	
02	동 높이다	
03	동 어기다, 위반하다	
04	동 증명하다	
05	동 (침을) 뱉다	
06	명 기구	
07	명 기근	
08	명 기둥	
09	명 넓게 펼쳐진 공간	
10	명 도박	
11	명 변화	
12	명 보호자, 감시인	
13	명 선율	
14	명 수도꼭지	
15	명 (시의) 운	
16	명 이야기하기, 서술	
17	명 인내(심)	
18	명 처방	
19	명 탐정 형 탐정의	
20	명 투명성	
21	부 완전히	
22	형 부정적인	
23	형 산업의	
24	형 수직의, 세로의	
25	형 순진한, 결백한	
26	형 시의, 시적인	
27	형 신앙심이 깊은	
28	형 청년기의 명 청소년	
29	동 신의 은총을 빌다	
30	동 달래다	

DAY 10

STEP 1 한국어 뜻 생각하며 외우기

월 일

✦ 해당 영어의 한국어 의미를 생각하면서 2번씩 적으시오.

01	자격을 부여하다	**qualify**	자격을 부여하다	자격을 부여하다
02	드러내다	**reveal**	드러내다	드러내다
03	~할 만하다	**deserve**	~할 만하다	~할 만하다
04	~행의	**bound**	~행의	~행의
05	거절하다	**reject**	거절하다	거절하다
06	격노한	**furious**	격노한	격노한
07	과장하여 행하다	**overact**	과장하여 행하다	과장하여 행하다
08	그동안	**meantime**	그동안	그동안
09	기름이 묻은	**greasy**	기름이 묻은	기름이 묻은
10	기술의	**technical**	기술의	기술의
11	높이다	**enhance**	높이다	높이다
12	능률적인	**efficient**	능률적인	능률적인
13	다층의	**multilayered**	다층의	다층의
14	대성당	**cathedral**	대성당	대성당
15	빻다, 부수다	**crumble**	빻다, 부수다	빻다, 부수다
16	사슬	**leash**	사슬	사슬
17	성분, 재료	**ingredient**	성분, 재료	성분, 재료
18	순례자	**pilgrim**	순례자	순례자
19	쓰레기	**rubbish**	쓰레기	쓰레기
20	열이 있는	**feverish**	열이 있는	열이 있는
21	입대하다	**enlist**	입대하다	입대하다
22	자취를 남기지 않은	**trackless**	자취를 남기지 않은	자취를 남기지 않은
23	전문가	**specialist**	전문가	전문가
24	젊은	**youthful**	젊은	젊은
25	조립하다	**assemble**	조립하다	조립하다
26	충동	**impulse**	충동	충동
27	침착하게	**calmly**	침착하게	침착하게
28	탄산가스로 포화시키다	**carbonate**	탄산가스로 포화시키다	탄산가스로 포화시키다
29	통일	**unity**	통일	통일
30	평상복; 평상복의	**casual**	평상복; 평상복의	평상복; 평상복의

정답 p.69

✦ 다음을 영어는 한국어로 한국어는 영어로 적으시오.

01	assemble	
02	bound	
03	calmly	
04	carbonate	
05	casual	
06	cathedral	
07	crumble	
08	deserve	
09	efficient	
10	enhance	
11	enlist	
12	feverish	
13	furious	
14	greasy	
15	impulse	
16	ingredient	
17	leash	
18	meantime	
19	multilayered	
20	overact	
21	pilgrim	
22	qualify	
23	reject	
24	reveal	
25	rubbish	
26	specialist	
27	technical	
28	trackless	
29	unity	
30	youthful	

01	동 자격을 부여하다	
02	동 드러내다	
03	동 ~할 만하다	
04	동 거절하다	
05	동 과장하여 행하다	
06	동 높이다	
07	동 빻다, 부수다	
08	동 입대하다	
09	동 조립하다	
10	명 그동안	
11	명 대성당	
12	명 사슬	
13	명 성분, 재료	
14	명 순례자	
15	명 쓰레기	
16	명 전문가	
17	명 충동	
18	부 침착하게	
19	동 탄산가스로 포화시키다	
20	명 통일	
21	명 평상복 형 평상복의	
22	형 ~행의	
23	형 격노한	
24	형 기름이 묻은	
25	형 기술의	
26	형 능률적인	
27	형 다층의	
28	형 열이 있는	
29	형 자취를 남기지 않은	
30	형 젊은	

DAY 11

STEP 1
한국어 뜻 생각하며 외우기

월 일

✦ 해당 영어의 한국어 의미를 생각하면서 2번씩 적으시오.

01	조종하다	**steer**	조종하다	조종하다
02	개혁하다	**reform**	개혁하다	개혁하다
03	계속적인	**continuous**	계속적인	계속적인
04	나방	**moth**	나방	나방
05	거물, ~왕	**baron**	거물, ~왕	거물, ~왕
06	대저택	**mansion**	대저택	대저택
07	뚜렷한, 명백한	**distinct**	뚜렷한, 명백한	뚜렷한, 명백한
08	뚝뚝 떨어지다; 물방울	**drip**	뚝뚝 떨어지다; 물방울	뚝뚝 떨어지다; 물방울
09	물을 대다	**irrigate**	물을 대다	물을 대다
10	보존	**conservation**	보존	보존
11	비도덕적인	**unethical**	비도덕적인	비도덕적인
12	비판하다	**criticize**	비판하다	비판하다
13	상징적인	**symbolic**	상징적인	상징적인
14	소매	**retail**	소매	소매
15	신장	**kidney**	신장	신장
16	운명, 파멸	**doom**	운명, 파멸	운명, 파멸
17	상호작용하다	**interact**	상호작용하다	상호작용하다
18	의존할 수 있는	**dependable**	의존할 수 있는	의존할 수 있는
19	이행하다	**fulfill**	이행하다	이행하다
20	적응하다	**adapt**	적응하다	적응하다
21	전환	**diversion**	전환	전환
22	제국주의	**imperialism**	제국주의	제국주의
23	종합적인; 종합적으로	**overall**	종합적인; 종합적으로	종합적인; 종합적으로
24	중요하지 않은	**unnoticeable**	중요하지 않은	중요하지 않은
25	지루한	**tiresome**	지루한	지루한
26	진수시키다, 발사하다	**launch**	진수시키다, 발사하다	진수시키다, 발사하다
27	체포하다; 체포	**arrest**	체포하다; 체포	체포하다; 체포
28	크기, 덩치	**bulk**	크기, 덩치	크기, 덩치
29	학생	**pupil**	학생	학생
30	흘깃 봄; 흘깃 보다	**glimpse**	흘깃 봄; 흘깃 보다	흘깃 봄; 흘깃 보다

✦ 다음을 영어는 한국어로 한국어는 영어로 적으시오.

정답 p.70

01	adapt	
02	arrest	
03	baron	
04	bulk	
05	conservation	
06	continuous	
07	criticize	
08	dependable	
09	distinct	
10	diversion	
11	doom	
12	drip	
13	fulfill	
14	glimpse	
15	imperialism	
16	interact	
17	irrigate	
18	kidney	
19	launch	
20	mansion	
21	moth	
22	overall	
23	pupil	
24	reform	
25	retail	
26	steer	
27	symbolic	
28	tiresome	
29	unethical	
30	unnoticeable	

01	동 조종하다	
02	동 개혁하다	
03	동 뚝뚝 떨어지다 명 물방울	
04	동 물을 대다	
05	동 비판하다	
06	동 상호작용하다	
07	동 이행하다	
08	동 진수시키다, 발사하다	
09	동 체포하다 명 체포	
10	명 나방	
11	명 거물, ~왕	
12	명 대저택	
13	명 보존	
14	명 소매	
15	명 운명, 파멸	
16	동 적응하다	
17	명 전환	
18	명 제국주의	
19	명 크기, 덩치	
20	명 학생	
21	명 흘깃 봄 동 흘깃 보다	
22	형 계속적인	
23	형 뚜렷한, 명백한	
24	형 비도덕적인	
25	형 상징적인	
26	형 신장	
27	형 의존할 수 있는	
28	형 종합적인 부 종합적으로	
29	형 중요하지 않은	
30	형 지루한	

DAY 12

STEP 1 한국어 뜻 생각하며 외우기

월 일

✦ 해당 영어의 한국어 의미를 생각하면서 2번씩 적으시오.

01	충실하게	**faithfully**	충실하게	충실하게
02	군중	**throng**	군중	군중
03	뇌물	**bribe**	뇌물	뇌물
04	눈살을 찌푸리다	**frown**	눈살을 찌푸리다	눈살을 찌푸리다
05	독감	**influenza**	독감	독감
06	관목, 덤불	**bush**	관목, 덤불	관목, 덤불
07	매혹적인	**glamorous**	매혹적인	매혹적인
08	머리 위의; 머리 위에	**overhead**	머리 위의; 머리 위에	머리 위의; 머리 위에
09	민주주의	**democracy**	민주주의	민주주의
10	보석(금)	**bail**	보석(금)	보석(금)
11	부정직한	**dishonest**	부정직한	부정직한
12	부지런한	**industrious**	부지런한	부지런한
13	교제하다	**socialize**	교제하다	교제하다
14	산성; 산성의	**acid**	산성; 산성의	산성; 산성의
15	손질하지 않는	**uncared**	손질하지 않는	손질하지 않는
16	진압하다	**suppress**	진압하다	진압하다
17	외침, 감탄	**exclamation**	외침, 감탄	외침, 감탄
18	유지, 정비	**maintenance**	유지, 정비	유지, 정비
19	유효성, 타당성	**validity**	유효성, 타당성	유효성, 타당성
20	절차	**procedure**	절차	절차
21	정확; 정밀한	**precision**	정확; 정밀한	정확; 정밀한
22	존경할 만한	**respectable**	존경할 만한	존경할 만한
23	주기적인	**periodic**	주기적인	주기적인
24	의제, 안건	**agenda**	의제, 안건	의제, 안건
25	직사각형	**rectangle**	직사각형	직사각형
26	진보적인, 점진적인	**progressive**	진보적인, 점진적인	진보적인, 점진적인
27	창조성	**creativity**	창조성	창조성
28	추진하다	**propel**	추진하다	추진하다
29	틀, 거푸집	**mold**	틀, 거푸집	틀, 거푸집
30	회담	**conference**	회담	회담

✦ 다음을 영어는 한국어로 한국어는 영어로 적으시오.

정답 p.70

01	acid	
02	agenda	
03	bail	
04	bribe	
05	bush	
06	conference	
07	creativity	
08	democracy	
09	dishonest	
10	exclamation	
11	faithfully	
12	frown	
13	glamorous	
14	industrious	
15	influenza	
16	maintenance	
17	mold	
18	overhead	
19	periodic	
20	precision	
21	procedure	
22	progressive	
23	propel	
24	rectangle	
25	respectable	
26	socialize	
27	suppress	
28	throng	
29	uncared	
30	validity	

01	동 눈살을 찌푸리다	
02	동 교제하다	
03	동 진압하다	
04	동 추진하다	
05	명 군중	
06	명 뇌물	
07	명 독감	
08	명 관목, 덤불	
09	명 민주주의	
10	명 보석(금)	
11	명 산성 형 산성의	
12	명 외침, 감탄	
13	명 유지, 정비	
14	명 유효성, 타당성	
15	명 절차	
16	명 정확 형 정밀한	
17	명 의제, 안건	
18	명 직사각형	
19	명 창조성	
20	명 틀, 거푸집	
21	명 회담	
22	부 충실하게	
23	형 매혹적인	
24	형 머리 위의 부 머리 위에	
25	형 부정직한	
26	형 부지런한	
27	형 손질하지 않는	
28	형 존경할 만한	
29	형 주기적인	
30	형 진보적인, 점진적인	

DAY 13 STEP 1 한국어 뜻 생각하며 외우기

월 일

✦ 해당 영어의 한국어 의미를 생각하면서 2번씩 적으시오.

01	충분히	**sufficiently**	충분히	충분히
02	그 후의	**subsequent**	그 후의	그 후의
03	기하학	**geometry**	기하학	기하학
04	길쭉한 구멍	**slot**	길쭉한 구멍	길쭉한 구멍
05	등이 굽은 사람	**hunchback**	등이 굽은 사람	등이 굽은 사람
06	끌어당김, 매력	**attraction**	끌어당김, 매력	끌어당김, 매력
07	독창성	**originality**	독창성	독창성
08	(식물) 연, 연꽃 무늬	**lotus**	(식물) 연, 연꽃 무늬	(식물) 연, 연꽃 무늬
09	발전, 진화	**evolution**	발전, 진화	발전, 진화
10	방어적인	**defensive**	방어적인	방어적인
11	사기	**fraud**	사기	사기
12	사냥개	**hound**	사냥개	사냥개
13	상기하다[시키다]	**recall**	상기하다[시키다]	상기하다[시키다]
14	상상(력)	**imagination**	상상(력)	상상(력)
15	수락할 수 있는	**acceptable**	수락할 수 있는	수락할 수 있는
16	안개가 짙은	**misty**	안개가 짙은	안개가 짙은
17	알아차리다	**perceive**	알아차리다	알아차리다
18	얕은	**shallow**	얕은	얕은
19	협박하다, 위협하다	**threaten**	협박하다, 위협하다	협박하다, 위협하다
20	이해하다	**comprehend**	이해하다	이해하다
21	일어나다	**arise**	일어나다	일어나다
22	자세	**stance**	자세	자세
23	주장하다, 다투다	**contend**	주장하다, 다투다	주장하다, 다투다
24	지적인	**intellectual**	지적인	지적인
25	(짐을) 너무 많이 싣다	**overload**	(짐을) 너무 많이 싣다	(짐을) 너무 많이 싣다
26	찬성, 승인	**approval**	찬성, 승인	찬성, 승인
27	투자	**investment**	투자	투자
28	파업 중인	**striking**	파업 중인	파업 중인
29	피할 수 없는, 당연한	**inevitable**	피할 수 없는, 당연한	피할 수 없는, 당연한
30	한가한, 놀고 있는	**idle**	한가한, 놀고 있는	한가한, 놀고 있는

✦ 다음을 영어는 한국어로 한국어는 영어로 적으시오.

정답 p.71

01	acceptable	
02	approval	
03	arise	
04	attraction	
05	comprehend	
06	contend	
07	defensive	
08	evolution	
09	fraud	
10	geometry	
11	hound	
12	hunchback	
13	idle	
14	imagination	
15	inevitable	
16	intellectual	
17	investment	
18	lotus	
19	misty	
20	originality	
21	overload	
22	perceive	
23	recall	
24	shallow	
25	slot	
26	stance	
27	striking	
28	subsequent	
29	sufficiently	
30	threaten	

01	동 상기하다[시키다]	
02	동 알아차리다	
03	동 협박하다, 위협하다	
04	동 이해하다	
05	동 일어나다	
06	동 주장하다, 다투다	
07	동 (짐을) 너무 많이 싣다	
08	명 기하학	
09	명 길쭉한 구멍	
10	명 등이 굽은 사람	
11	명 끌어당김, 매력	
12	명 독창성	
13	명 (식물) 연, 연꽃 무늬	
14	명 발전, 진화	
15	명 사기	
16	명 사냥개	
17	명 상상(력)	
18	명 자세	
19	명 찬성, 승인	
20	명 투자	
21	부 충분히	
22	형 그 후의	
23	형 방어적인	
24	형 수락할 수 있는	
25	형 안개가 짙은	
26	형 얕은	
27	형 지적인	
28	형 파업 중인	
29	형 피할 수 없는, 당연한	
30	형 한가한, 놀고 있는	

DAY 14 STEP 1 한국어 뜻 생각하며 외우기

월 일

✦ 해당 영어의 한국어 의미를 생각하면서 2번씩 적으시오.

01	구두로	**orally**	구두로	구두로
02	개념	**notion**	개념	개념
03	방해하다, 중화하다	**counteract**	방해하다, 중화하다	방해하다, 중화하다
04	걱정	**anxiety**	걱정	걱정
05	기분을 상하게 하다	**offend**	기분을 상하게 하다	기분을 상하게 하다
06	광고	**advertisement**	광고	광고
07	기술, 재주	**craft**	기술, 재주	기술, 재주
08	남용하다; 남용	**overuse**	남용하다; 남용	남용하다; 남용
09	놋쇠; 금관악기의	**brass**	놋쇠; 금관악기의	놋쇠; 금관악기의
10	도보여행, 민정 시찰	**walkabout**	도보여행, 민정 시찰	도보여행, 민정 시찰
11	반대하다; 물건	**object**	반대하다; 물건	반대하다; 물건
12	반짝반짝 빛나다	**twinkle**	반짝반짝 빛나다	반짝반짝 빛나다
13	불만을 느끼게 하다	**dissatisfy**	불만을 느끼게 하다	불만을 느끼게 하다
14	비교	**comparison**	비교	비교
15	비율	**ratio**	비율	비율
16	연속	**sequence**	연속	연속
17	영원	**eternity**	영원	영원
18	예방	**prevention**	예방	예방
19	위치	**location**	위치	위치
20	유사	**analogy**	유사	유사
21	유아; 초기의	**infant**	유아; 초기의	유아; 초기의
22	자세; 자세를 취하다	**pose**	자세; 자세를 취하다	자세; 자세를 취하다
23	적용할 수 있는	**applicable**	적용할 수 있는	적용할 수 있는
24	주저하다	**hesitate**	주저하다	주저하다
25	지시; 지시하는	**directive**	지시; 지시하는	지시; 지시하는
26	진화하다	**extinguish**	진화하다	진화하다
27	차단, 절연	**insulation**	차단, 절연	차단, 절연
28	파충류	**reptile**	파충류	파충류
29	해골	**skull**	해골	해골
30	흡수	**absorption**	흡수	흡수

✦ 다음을 영어는 한국어로 한국어는 영어로 적으시오.

정답 p.71

01	absorption	
02	advertisement	
03	analogy	
04	anxiety	
05	applicable	
06	brass	
07	comparison	
08	counteract	
09	craft	
10	directive	
11	dissatisfy	
12	eternity	
13	extinguish	
14	hesitate	
15	infant	
16	insulation	
17	location	
18	notion	
19	object	
20	offend	
21	orally	
22	overuse	
23	pose	
24	prevention	
25	ratio	
26	reptile	
27	sequence	
28	skull	
29	twinkle	
30	walkabout	

01	동 남용하다 명 남용	
02	동 방해하다, 중화하다	
03	동 기분을 상하게 하다	
04	동 반짝반짝 빛나다	
05	동 주저하다	
06	동 진화하다	
07	명 개념	
08	명 걱정	
09	명 광고	
10	명 기술, 재주	
11	명 놋쇠 형 금관악기의	
12	명 도보여행, 민정 시찰	
13	동 반대하다 명 물건	
14	동 불만을 느끼게 하다	
15	명 비교	
16	명 비율	
17	명 연속	
18	명 영원	
19	명 예방	
20	명 위치	
21	명 유사	
22	명 유아 형 초기의	
23	명 자세 동 자세를 취하다	
24	명 지시 형 지시하는	
25	명 차단, 절연	
26	명 파충류	
27	명 해골	
28	명 흡수	
29	부 구두로	
30	형 적용할 수 있는	

DAY 15 STEP 1

한국어 뜻 생각하며 외우기

월 일

✦ 해당 영어의 한국어 의미를 생각하면서 2번씩 적으시오.

01	보도에 의하면	**reportedly**	보도에 의하면	보도에 의하면
02	헌신	**commitment**	헌신	헌신
03	세우다; 똑바로 선	**erect**	세우다; 똑바로 선	세우다; 똑바로 선
04	간격, 중간 휴식 시간	**interval**	간격, 중간 휴식 시간	간격, 중간 휴식 시간
05	감염	**infection**	감염	감염
06	건설적인, 구조적인	**constructive**	건설적인, 구조적인	건설적인, 구조적인
07	고충, 곤란	**hardship**	고충, 곤란	고충, 곤란
08	괭이	**hoe**	괭이	괭이
09	데시벨	**decibel**	데시벨	데시벨
10	튀다; 튀어오름	**bounce**	튀다; 튀어오름	튀다; 튀어오름
11	반도체	**semiconductor**	반도체	반도체
12	보컬리스트, 가수	**vocalist**	보컬리스트, 가수	보컬리스트, 가수
13	부족한, 드문	**scarce**	부족한, 드문	부족한, 드문
14	상당한 양	**chunk**	상당한 양	상당한 양
15	승리	**triumph**	승리	승리
16	아픈, 힘드는	**painful**	아픈, 힘드는	아픈, 힘드는
17	안전한	**secure**	안전한	안전한
18	오염	**pollution**	오염	오염
19	오징어	**squid**	오징어	오징어
20	온도계	**thermometer**	온도계	온도계
21	원자의	**atomic**	원자의	원자의
22	유죄 판결	**conviction**	유죄 판결	유죄 판결
23	이주하다	**migrate**	이주하다	이주하다
24	자극	**stimulus**	자극	자극
25	장르	**genre**	장르	장르
26	정밀검사	**inspection**	정밀검사	정밀검사
27	조각	**scrap**	조각	조각
28	존엄	**dignity**	존엄	존엄
29	폐지하다	**abolish**	폐지하다	폐지하다
30	항해, 항공	**navigation**	항해, 항공	항해, 항공

STEP 2
최종실력 점검하기

O 개 | X 개

✦ 다음을 영어는 한국어로 한국어는 영어로 적으시오.

정답 p.72

01	abolish	
02	atomic	
03	bounce	
04	chunk	
05	commitment	
06	constructive	
07	conviction	
08	decibel	
09	dignity	
10	erect	
11	genre	
12	hardship	
13	hoe	
14	infection	
15	inspection	
16	interval	
17	migrate	
18	navigation	
19	painful	
20	pollution	
21	reportedly	
22	scarce	
23	scrap	
24	secure	
25	semiconductor	
26	squid	
27	stimulus	
28	thermometer	
29	triumph	
30	vocalist	

01	동 세우다 형 똑바로 선	
02	동 튀다 명 튀어오름	
03	동 이주하다	
04	동 폐지하다	
05	명 헌신	
06	명 간격, 중간 휴식 시간	
07	명 감염	
08	명 고충, 곤란	
09	명 괭이	
10	명 데시벨	
11	명 반도체	
12	명 보컬리스트, 가수	
13	명 상당한 양	
14	명 승리	
15	명 오염	
16	명 오징어	
17	명 온도계	
18	명 유죄 판결	
19	명 자극	
20	명 장르	
21	명 정밀검사	
22	명 조각	
23	명 존엄	
24	명 항해, 항공	
25	부 보도에 의하면	
26	형 건설적인, 구조적인	
27	형 부족한, 드문	
28	형 아픈, 힘드는	
29	형 안전한	
30	형 원자의	

DAY 16

STEP 1
한국어 뜻 생각하며 외우기

월 일

✦ 해당 영어의 한국어 의미를 생각하면서 2번씩 적으시오.

01	정신적으로	mentally	정신적으로	정신적으로
02	말하다; 논평	remark	말하다; 논평	말하다; 논평
03	감히 ~ 하다	dare	감히 ~ 하다	감히 ~ 하다
04	국제간 긴장 완화	detente	국제간 긴장 완화	국제간 긴장 완화
05	높이	elevation	높이	높이
06	니스를 칠하다; 니스	varnish	니스를 칠하다; 니스	니스를 칠하다; 니스
07	단체, 협회	association	단체, 협회	단체, 협회
08	덕, 미덕	virtue	덕, 미덕	덕, 미덕
09	맨 앞의	foremost	맨 앞의	맨 앞의
10	물집	blister	물집	물집
11	방, 회의실	chamber	방, 회의실	방, 회의실
12	번창하다	flourish	번창하다	번창하다
13	법인의	corporate	법인의	법인의
14	노련한; 전문가	veteran	노련한; 전문가	노련한; 전문가
15	보안관	sheriff	보안관	보안관
16	봉투	envelope	봉투	봉투
17	부드러운	tender	부드러운	부드러운
18	부패, 타락	corruption	부패, 타락	부패, 타락
19	분노; 격노하다	rage	분노; 격노하다	분노; 격노하다
20	시집	poetry	시집	시집
21	싸우다; 전투	combat	싸우다; 전투	싸우다; 전투
22	유죄의	guilty	유죄의	유죄의
23	융기, 산마루	ridge	융기, 산마루	융기, 산마루
24	응시하다	gaze	응시하다	응시하다
25	이식하다	transplant	이식하다	이식하다
26	이야기	narrative	이야기	이야기
27	이웃; 근처의	neighborhood	이웃; 근처의	이웃; 근처의
28	전적의, 완전한	utter	전적의, 완전한	전적의, 완전한
29	하위의, 열등한	inferior	하위의, 열등한	하위의, 열등한
30	혁신하다	innovate	혁신하다	혁신하다

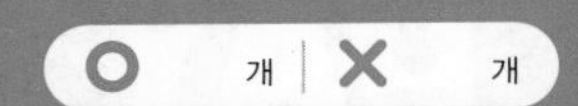

✦ 다음을 영어는 한국어로 한국어는 영어로 적으시오.

정답 p.72

01	association	
02	blister	
03	chamber	
04	combat	
05	corporate	
06	corruption	
07	dare	
08	detente	
09	elevation	
10	envelope	
11	flourish	
12	foremost	
13	gaze	
14	guilty	
15	inferior	
16	innovate	
17	mentally	
18	narrative	
19	neighborhood	
20	poetry	
21	rage	
22	remark	
23	ridge	
24	sheriff	
25	tender	
26	transplant	
27	utter	
28	varnish	
29	veteran	
30	virtue	

01	동 말하다 명 논평	
02	동 감히 ~ 하다	
03	동 니스를 칠하다 명 니스	
04	동 번창하다	
05	동 싸우다 명 전투	
06	동 응시하다	
07	동 이식하다	
08	동 혁신하다	
09	명 국제간 긴장 완화	
10	명 높이	
11	명 단체, 협회	
12	명 덕, 미덕	
13	명 물집	
14	명 방, 회의실	
15	형 노련한 명 전문가	
16	명 보안관	
17	명 봉투	
18	명 부패, 타락	
19	명 분노 동 격노하다	
20	명 시집	
21	명 융기, 산마루	
22	명 이야기	
23	명 이웃 형 근처의	
24	부 정신적으로	
25	형 맨 앞의	
26	형 법인의	
27	형 부드러운	
28	형 유죄의	
29	형 전적의, 완전한	
30	형 하위의, 열등한	

DAY 17

STEP 1
한국어 뜻 생각하며 외우기

월 일

✦ 해당 영어의 한국어 의미를 생각하면서 2번씩 적으시오.

01	쉽게	effortlessly	쉽게	쉽게
02	전시 책임자	curator	전시 책임자	전시 책임자
03	기술적인	technological	기술적인	기술적인
04	정렬, 사람의 줄	lineup	정렬, 사람의 줄	정렬, 사람의 줄
05	동경, 찬양	adoration	동경, 찬양	동경, 찬양
06	드러내다, 폭로하다	expose	드러내다, 폭로하다	드러내다, 폭로하다
07	목록	catalog(ue)	목록	목록
08	법률의	legal	법률의	법률의
09	보편적인	universal	보편적인	보편적인
10	부서진 조각	splinter	부서진 조각	부서진 조각
11	비극	tragedy	비극	비극
12	비활동, 부진	inactivity	비활동, 부진	비활동, 부진
13	생물학적인	biological	생물학적인	생물학적인
14	잔소리하다	nag	잔소리하다	잔소리하다
15	슬픔	grief	슬픔	슬픔
16	신성한	sacred	신성한	신성한
17	심장의	cardiac	심장의	심장의
18	약물 (치료)	medication	약물 (치료)	약물 (치료)
19	요금	fare	요금	요금
20	융합, 용해	fusion	융합, 용해	융합, 용해
21	유능한	capable	유능한	유능한
22	절망	despair	절망	절망
23	조심	caution	조심	조심
24	존재, 출석	presence	존재, 출석	존재, 출석
25	축하연	feast	축하연	축하연
26	평가	assessment	평가	평가
27	한정된	finite	한정된	한정된
28	혁명의	revolutionary	혁명의	혁명의
29	황갈색, 호박색	amber	황갈색, 호박색	황갈색, 호박색
30	휴식, 이완	relaxation	휴식, 이완	휴식, 이완

STEP 2 최종실력 점검하기

정답 p.73

✦ 다음을 영어는 한국어로 한국어는 영어로 적으시오.

01	**adoration**		01	[동] 드러내다, 폭로하다	
02	**amber**		02	[동] 잔소리하다	
03	**assessment**		03	[명] 전시 책임자	
04	**biological**		04	[명] 정렬, 사람의 줄	
05	**capable**		05	[명] 동경, 찬양	
06	**cardiac**		06	[명] 목록	
07	**catalog(ue)**		07	[명] 부서진 조각	
08	**caution**		08	[명] 비극	
09	**curator**		09	[명] 비활동, 부진	
10	**despair**		10	[명] 슬픔	
11	**effortlessly**		11	[명] 약물 (치료)	
12	**expose**		12	[명] 요금	
13	**fare**		13	[명] 융합, 용해	
14	**feast**		14	[명] 절망	
15	**finite**		15	[명] 조심	
16	**fusion**		16	[명] 존재, 출석	
17	**grief**		17	[명] 축하연	
18	**inactivity**		18	[명] 평가	
19	**legal**		19	[명] 황갈색, 호박색	
20	**lineup**		20	[명] 휴식, 이완	
21	**medication**		21	[부] 쉽게	
22	**nag**		22	[형] 기술적인	
23	**presence**		23	[형] 법률의	
24	**relaxation**		24	[형] 보편적인	
25	**revolutionary**		25	[형] 생물학적인	
26	**sacred**		26	[형] 신성한	
27	**splinter**		27	[형] 심장의	
28	**technological**		28	[형] 유능한	
29	**tragedy**		29	[형] 한정된	
30	**universal**		30	[형] 혁명의	

DAY 18

STEP 1
한국어 뜻 생각하며 외우기

월 일

✦ 해당 영어의 한국어 의미를 생각하면서 2번씩 적으시오.

01	(돈을) 쓰다	spend	(돈을) 쓰다	(돈을) 쓰다
02	구부리다; 굽은 것	crook	구부리다; 굽은 것	구부리다; 굽은 것
03	짜증나게 하다	irritate	짜증나게 하다	짜증나게 하다
04	위치를 바꾸다	shift	위치를 바꾸다	위치를 바꾸다
05	거대한	enormous	거대한	거대한
06	거만한	arrogant	거만한	거만한
07	계속 유지하다	retain	계속 유지하다	계속 유지하다
08	계약(서); 계약하다	contract	계약(서); 계약하다	계약(서); 계약하다
09	고르지 않는	uneven	고르지 않는	고르지 않는
10	기능의	functional	기능의	기능의
11	동기부여, 자극	motivation	동기부여, 자극	동기부여, 자극
12	때 아닌	untimely	때 아닌	때 아닌
13	뜨다, 짜다	knit	뜨다, 짜다	뜨다, 짜다
14	메스꺼운, 역겨운	queasy	메스꺼운, 역겨운	메스꺼운, 역겨운
15	묶음	bundle	묶음	묶음
16	불쌍한, 측은한	pitiful	불쌍한, 측은한	불쌍한, 측은한
17	빛나다	glow	빛나다	빛나다
18	빨래	laundry	빨래	빨래
19	상쾌하게 하다	refresh	상쾌하게 하다	상쾌하게 하다
20	알맞은	adequate	알맞은	알맞은
21	육중한, 엄청난	massive	육중한, 엄청난	육중한, 엄청난
22	의존하고 있는	dependent	의존하고 있는	의존하고 있는
23	인정 많은, 사려 깊은	considerate	인정 많은, 사려 깊은	인정 많은, 사려 깊은
24	편, 측, 이익	behalf	편, 측, 이익	편, 측, 이익
25	전공하다	specialize	전공하다	전공하다
26	정화하다	purify	정화하다	정화하다
27	주민	inhabitant	주민	주민
28	중간의; 중재하다	intermediate	중간의; 중재하다	중간의; 중재하다
29	끈적거리는	sticky	끈적거리는	끈적거리는
30	참을 수 있는	tolerable	참을 수 있는	참을 수 있는

STEP 2 최종실력 점검하기

O 개 | X 개

정답 p.73

✦ 다음을 영어는 한국어로 한국어는 영어로 적으시오.

01	adequate	
02	arrogant	
03	behalf	
04	bundle	
05	considerate	
06	contract	
07	crook	
08	dependent	
09	enormous	
10	functional	
11	glow	
12	inhabitant	
13	intermediate	
14	irritate	
15	knit	
16	laundry	
17	massive	
18	motivation	
19	pitiful	
20	purify	
21	queasy	
22	refresh	
23	retain	
24	shift	
25	specialize	
26	spend	
27	sticky	
28	tolerable	
29	uneven	
30	untimely	

01	동 (돈을) 쓰다	
02	동 구부리다 명 굽은 것	
03	동 짜증나게 하다	
04	동 위치를 바꾸다	
05	동 계속 유지하다	
06	동 뜨다, 짜다	
07	동 빛나다	
08	동 상쾌하게 하다	
09	동 전공하다	
10	동 정화하다	
11	명 계약(서) 동 계약하다	
12	명 동기부여, 자극	
13	형 메스꺼운, 역겨운	
14	명 묶음	
15	명 빨래	
16	명 편, 측, 이익	
17	명 주민	
18	형 거대한	
19	형 거만한	
20	형 고르지 않는	
21	형 기능의	
22	형 때 아닌	
23	형 불쌍한, 측은한	
24	형 알맞은	
25	형 육중한, 엄청난	
26	형 의존하고 있는	
27	형 인정 많은, 사려 깊은	
28	형 중간의 동 중재하다	
29	형 끈적거리는	
30	형 참을 수 있는	

DAY 19

STEP 1
한국어 뜻 생각하며 외우기

월 일

✦ 해당 영어의 한국어 의미를 생각하면서 2번씩 적으시오.

01	가짜의; 가짜	**fake**	가짜의; 가짜	가짜의; 가짜
02	비인격적인, 객관적인	**impersonal**	비인격적인, 객관적인	비인격적인, 객관적인
03	경영진; 집행의	**executive**	경영진; 집행의	경영진; 집행의
04	고백하다	**confess**	고백하다	고백하다
05	공포	**panic**	공포	공포
06	귀족정치	**aristocracy**	귀족정치	귀족정치
07	극복하다	**overcome**	극복하다	극복하다
08	금지하다	**prohibit**	금지하다	금지하다
09	다양성	**diversity**	다양성	다양성
10	더 좋아함	**preference**	더 좋아함	더 좋아함
11	떨다; 떨림	**shiver**	떨다; 떨림	떨다; 떨림
12	밀다; 밀침	**thrust**	밀다; 밀침	밀다; 밀침
13	발가벗은	**bare**	발가벗은	발가벗은
14	비율, 비례	**proportion**	비율, 비례	비율, 비례
15	살다, 깃들다	**dwell**	살다, 깃들다	살다, 깃들다
16	세련된	**sophisticated**	세련된	세련된
17	알리다	**inform**	알리다	알리다
18	언, 냉동의	**frozen**	언, 냉동의	언, 냉동의
19	왜곡하다	**distort**	왜곡하다	왜곡하다
20	외과 의사	**surgeon**	외과 의사	외과 의사
21	의심 없는; 확실히	**doubtless**	의심 없는; 확실히	의심 없는; 확실히
22	인정하다	**acknowledge**	인정하다	인정하다
23	장엄한	**majestic**	장엄한	장엄한
24	재발하다	**recur**	재발하다	재발하다
25	죽다	**perish**	죽다	죽다
26	창조물	**creature**	창조물	창조물
27	통로	**aisle**	통로	통로
28	행진, 행렬, 진행	**procession**	행진, 행렬, 진행	행진, 행렬, 진행
29	헐다, 파괴하다	**demolish**	헐다, 파괴하다	헐다, 파괴하다
30	힐끗 보다; 힐끗 봄	**glance**	힐끗 보다; 힐끗 봄	힐끗 보다; 힐끗 봄

O 개 | X 개

✦ 다음을 영어는 한국어로 한국어는 영어로 적으시오.

정답 p.74

01	acknowledge	
02	aisle	
03	aristocracy	
04	bare	
05	confess	
06	creature	
07	demolish	
08	distort	
09	diversity	
10	doubtless	
11	dwell	
12	executive	
13	fake	
14	frozen	
15	glance	
16	impersonal	
17	inform	
18	majestic	
19	overcome	
20	panic	
21	perish	
22	preference	
23	procession	
24	prohibit	
25	proportion	
26	recur	
27	shiver	
28	sophisticated	
29	surgeon	
30	thrust	

01	동 고백하다	
02	동 극복하다	
03	동 금지하다	
04	동 떨다 명 떨림	
05	동 밀다 명 밀침	
06	동 살다, 깃들다	
07	동 알리다	
08	동 왜곡하다	
09	동 인정하다	
10	동 재발하다	
11	동 죽다	
12	동 헐다, 파괴하다	
13	동 힐끗 보다 명 힐끗 봄	
14	명 경영진 형 집행의	
15	명 공포	
16	명 귀족정치	
17	명 다양성	
18	명 더 좋아함	
19	명 비율, 비례	
20	명 외과 의사	
21	명 창조물	
22	명 통로	
23	명 행진, 행렬, 진행	
24	형 가짜의 명 가짜	
25	형 비인격적인, 객관적인	
26	형 발가벗은	
27	형 세련된	
28	형 언, 냉동의	
29	형 의심 없는 부 확실히	
30	형 장엄한	

DAY 20 STEP 1 한국어 뜻 생각하며 외우기

월 일

✦ 해당 영어의 한국어 의미를 생각하면서 2번씩 적으시오.

01	대략	**approximately**	대략	대략
02	각각의	**respective**	각각의	각각의
03	강렬한, 극심한	**intense**	강렬한, 극심한	강렬한, 극심한
04	넘어지다; 비틀거림	**stumble**	넘어지다; 비틀거림	넘어지다; 비틀거림
05	만족해 하는	**content**	만족해 하는	만족해 하는
06	무지	**ignorance**	무지	무지
07	민감한	**subtle**	민감한	민감한
08	발견되지 않은	**undiscovered**	발견되지 않은	발견되지 않은
09	분주히 돌아다니다	**bustle**	분주히 돌아다니다	분주히 돌아다니다
10	산산이 부수다	**shatter**	산산이 부수다	산산이 부수다
11	상상력이 풍부한	**imaginative**	상상력이 풍부한	상상력이 풍부한
12	수축하다	**shrink**	수축하다	수축하다
13	숙박시설	**accommodation**	숙박시설	숙박시설
14	순식간의	**momentary**	순식간의	순식간의
15	시작되다	**originate**	시작되다	시작되다
16	안의, 내적인	**inward**	안의, 내적인	안의, 내적인
17	와락 붙잡다, 낚아채다	**snatch**	와락 붙잡다, 낚아채다	와락 붙잡다, 낚아채다
18	우세, 우월	**superiority**	우세, 우월	우세, 우월
19	위생	**hygiene**	위생	위생
20	장인	**craftsman**	장인	장인
21	주요한; 주요 상품	**staple**	주요한; 주요 상품	주요한; 주요 상품
22	중심	**hub**	중심	중심
23	지각	**perception**	지각	지각
24	진화하다	**evolve**	진화하다	진화하다
25	충성	**loyalty**	충성	충성
26	파산한	**broke**	파산한	파산한
27	평행의; 평행선	**parallel**	평행의; 평행선	평행의; 평행선
28	포괄적인	**comprehensive**	포괄적인	포괄적인
29	프리랜서로 일하는	**freelance**	프리랜서로 일하는	프리랜서로 일하는
30	해고시키다	**dismiss**	해고시키다	해고시키다

정답 p.74

✦ 다음을 영어는 한국어로 한국어는 영어로 적으시오.

01	accommodation	
02	approximately	
03	broke	
04	bustle	
05	comprehensive	
06	content	
07	craftsman	
08	dismiss	
09	evolve	
10	freelance	
11	hub	
12	hygiene	
13	ignorance	
14	imaginative	
15	intense	
16	inward	
17	loyalty	
18	momentary	
19	originate	
20	parallel	
21	perception	
22	respective	
23	shatter	
24	shrink	
25	snatch	
26	staple	
27	stumble	
28	subtle	
29	superiority	
30	undiscovered	

01	동 넘어지다 명 비틀거림	
02	동 분주히 돌아다니다	
03	동 산산이 부수다	
04	동 수축하다	
05	동 시작되다	
06	동 와락 붙잡다, 낚아채다	
07	동 진화하다	
08	동 해고시키다	
09	명 무지	
10	명 숙박시설	
11	명 우세, 우월	
12	명 위생	
13	명 장인	
14	형 주요한 명 주요 상품	
15	명 중심	
16	명 지각	
17	명 충성	
18	형 프리랜서로 일하는	
19	부 대략	
20	형 각각의	
21	형 강렬한, 극심한	
22	형 만족해 하는	
23	형 민감한	
24	형 발견되지 않은	
25	형 상상력이 풍부한	
26	형 순식간의	
27	형 안의, 내적인	
28	형 파산한	
29	형 평행의 명 평행선	
30	형 포괄적인	

STEP 1
한국어 뜻 생각하며 외우기

월 일

✦ 해당 영어의 한국어 의미를 생각하면서 2번씩 적으시오.

01	(기계의) 고장	**breakdown**	(기계의) 고장	(기계의) 고장
02	공평히	**evenly**	공평히	공평히
03	자격이 있는, 유능한	**competent**	자격이 있는, 유능한	자격이 있는, 유능한
04	불만을 품은	**dissatisfied**	불만을 품은	불만을 품은
05	모방하다; 흉내	**mock**	모방하다; 흉내	모방하다; 흉내
06	강당	**auditorium**	강당	강당
07	거대한	**gigantic**	거대한	거대한
08	검소한, 절약하는	**thrifty**	검소한, 절약하는	검소한, 절약하는
09	경우	**occasion**	경우	경우
10	공중 납치하다	**hijack**	공중 납치하다	공중 납치하다
11	궤도	**orbit**	궤도	궤도
12	기본의, 주된	**primary**	기본의, 주된	기본의, 주된
13	느슨한; 느슨함, 여유	**slack**	느슨한; 느슨함, 여유	느슨한; 느슨함, 여유
14	모욕적인	**insulting**	모욕적인	모욕적인
15	무모한	**reckless**	무모한	무모한
16	분석	**analysis**	분석	분석
17	비상한, 비범한	**extraordinary**	비상한, 비범한	비상한, 비범한
18	서명	**signature**	서명	서명
19	설교	**sermon**	설교	설교
20	소유하다	**possess**	소유하다	소유하다
21	숫자	**numeral**	숫자	숫자
22	실망	**disappointment**	실망	실망
23	요구	**requirement**	요구	요구
24	전투	**warfare**	전투	전투
25	정의	**definition**	정의	정의
26	제공하다; 제공	**offer**	제공하다; 제공	제공하다; 제공
27	참여	**participation**	참여	참여
28	초음파의	**ultrasonic**	초음파의	초음파의
29	추상적인	**abstract**	추상적인	추상적인
30	현명한, 바람직한	**advisable**	현명한, 바람직한	현명한, 바람직한

정답 p.75

✦ 다음을 영어는 한국어로 한국어는 영어로 적으시오.

01	abstract	
02	advisable	
03	analysis	
04	auditorium	
05	breakdown	
06	competent	
07	definition	
08	disappointment	
09	dissatisfied	
10	evenly	
11	extraordinary	
12	gigantic	
13	hijack	
14	insulting	
15	mock	
16	numeral	
17	occasion	
18	offer	
19	orbit	
20	participation	
21	possess	
22	primary	
23	reckless	
24	requirement	
25	sermon	
26	signature	
27	slack	
28	thrifty	
29	ultrasonic	
30	warfare	

01	형 불만을 품은	
02	동 모방하다 명 흉내	
03	동 공중 납치하다	
04	동 소유하다	
05	동 제공하다 명 제공	
06	명 (기계의) 고장	
07	명 강당	
08	명 경우	
09	명 궤도	
10	명 분석	
11	명 서명	
12	명 설교	
13	명 숫자	
14	명 실망	
15	명 요구	
16	명 전투	
17	명 정의	
18	명 참여	
19	부 공평히	
20	형 자격이 있는, 유능한	
21	형 거대한	
22	형 검소한, 절약하는	
23	형 기본의, 주된	
24	형 느슨한 명 느슨함, 여유	
25	형 모욕적인	
26	형 무모한	
27	형 비상한, 비범한	
28	형 초음파의	
29	형 추상적인	
30	형 현명한, 바람직한	

DAY 22

STEP 1
한국어 뜻 생각하며 외우기

월 일

✦ 해당 영어의 한국어 의미를 생각하면서 2번씩 적으시오.

01	감각, 느낌	**sensation**	감각, 느낌	감각, 느낌
02	경계	**boundary**	경계	경계
03	구획, 단편	**segment**	구획, 단편	구획, 단편
04	군대, 병력	**troop**	군대, 병력	군대, 병력
05	근시안의	**near-sighted**	근시안의	근시안의
06	긁다, 할퀴다	**scratch**	긁다, 할퀴다	긁다, 할퀴다
07	급함, 서두름	**haste**	급함, 서두름	급함, 서두름
08	논리학, 논리	**logic**	논리학, 논리	논리학, 논리
09	달성하다	**attain**	달성하다	달성하다
10	대표자	**representative**	대표자	대표자
11	마음이 따뜻한	**warm-hearted**	마음이 따뜻한	마음이 따뜻한
12	많이 있다, 풍부하다	**abound**	많이 있다, 풍부하다	많이 있다, 풍부하다
13	반응	**reaction**	반응	반응
14	부지런한	**diligent**	부지런한	부지런한
15	사과의; 변명	**apologetic**	사과의; 변명	사과의; 변명
16	상쇄하다	**counterbalance**	상쇄하다	상쇄하다
17	수평의; 수평물	**horizontal**	수평의; 수평물	수평의; 수평물
18	심부름	**errand**	심부름	심부름
19	영감, 격려	**inspiration**	영감, 격려	영감, 격려
20	예측하다, 예언하다	**foretell**	예측하다, 예언하다	예측하다, 예언하다
21	온도 조절 장치	**thermostat**	온도 조절 장치	온도 조절 장치
22	원의	**circular**	원의	원의
23	입자	**particle**	입자	입자
24	장식하다	**decorate**	장식하다	장식하다
25	지원자	**applicant**	지원자	지원자
26	직업	**vocation**	직업	직업
27	진짜의	**genuine**	진짜의	진짜의
28	최소화하다	**minimize**	최소화하다	최소화하다
29	평범한 것; 평범한	**commonplace**	평범한 것; 평범한	평범한 것; 평범한
30	흩어버리다	**scatter**	흩어버리다	흩어버리다

정답 p.75

✦ 다음을 영어는 한국어로 한국어는 영어로 적으시오.

01	abound	
02	apologetic	
03	applicant	
04	attain	
05	boundary	
06	circular	
07	commonplace	
08	counterbalance	
09	decorate	
10	diligent	
11	errand	
12	foretell	
13	genuine	
14	haste	
15	horizontal	
16	inspiration	
17	logic	
18	minimize	
19	near-sighted	
20	particle	
21	reaction	
22	representative	
23	scatter	
24	scratch	
25	segment	
26	sensation	
27	thermostat	
28	troop	
29	vocation	
30	warm-hearted	

01	동 긁다, 할퀴다	
02	동 달성하다	
03	동 많이 있다, 풍부하다	
04	동 상쇄하다	
05	동 예측하다, 예언하다	
06	동 장식하다	
07	동 최소화하다	
08	동 흩어버리다	
09	명 감각, 느낌	
10	명 경계	
11	명 구획, 단편	
12	명 군대, 병력	
13	형 근시안의	
14	명 급함, 서두름	
15	명 논리학, 논리	
16	명 대표자	
17	명 반응	
18	명 심부름	
19	명 영감, 격려	
20	명 온도 조절 장치	
21	명 입자	
22	명 지원자	
23	명 직업	
24	명 평범한 것 형 평범한	
25	형 마음이 따뜻한	
26	형 부지런한	
27	형 사과의 명 변명	
28	형 수평의 명 수평물	
29	형 원의	
30	형 진짜의	

DAY 23 STEP 1 한국어 뜻 생각하며 외우기

월 일

✦ 해당 영어의 한국어 의미를 생각하면서 2번씩 적으시오.

01	거주하다	**populate**	거주하다	거주하다
02	의견을 듣다	**consult**	의견을 듣다	의견을 듣다
03	가정	**assumption**	가정	가정
04	견해	**viewpoint**	견해	견해
05	국적	**nationality**	국적	국적
06	긴장	**tension**	긴장	긴장
07	남루한, 초라한	**ragged**	남루한, 초라한	남루한, 초라한
08	문예부흥기, 르네상스	**Renaissance**	문예부흥기, 르네상스	문예부흥기, 르네상스
09	러닝머신	**treadmill**	러닝머신	러닝머신
10	빈자리, 빈방	**vacancy**	빈자리, 빈방	빈자리, 빈방
11	서식지	**habitat**	서식지	서식지
12	순환하다	**circulate**	순환하다	순환하다
13	시각화하다	**visualize**	시각화하다	시각화하다
14	안감	**lining**	안감	안감
15	어질러진	**messy**	어질러진	어질러진
16	얽힌, 복잡한	**intricate**	얽힌, 복잡한	얽힌, 복잡한
17	유창함	**fluency**	유창함	유창함
18	이웃의	**neighboring**	이웃의	이웃의
19	일광, 햇빛, 낮	**daylight**	일광, 햇빛, 낮	일광, 햇빛, 낮
20	일반화	**generalization**	일반화	일반화
21	조정하다	**coordinate**	조정하다	조정하다
22	주식회사	**corporation**	주식회사	주식회사
23	쏘다, 찌르다	**sting**	쏘다, 찌르다	쏘다, 찌르다
24	찌부러뜨리다	**squish**	찌부러뜨리다	찌부러뜨리다
25	봉쇄; 봉쇄하다	**blockade**	봉쇄; 봉쇄하다	봉쇄; 봉쇄하다
26	폭동	**riot**	폭동	폭동
27	혼돈된	**chaotic**	혼돈된	혼돈된
28	화장의	**cosmetic**	화장의	화장의
29	환기시키다	**ventilate**	환기시키다	환기시키다
30	황폐시키다	**devastate**	황폐시키다	황폐시키다

STEP 2 최종실력 점검하기

정답 p.76

✦ 다음을 영어는 한국어로 한국어는 영어로 적으시오.

01	assumption	
02	blockade	
03	chaotic	
04	circulate	
05	consult	
06	coordinate	
07	corporation	
08	cosmetic	
09	daylight	
10	devastate	
11	fluency	
12	generalization	
13	habitat	
14	intricate	
15	lining	
16	messy	
17	nationality	
18	neighboring	
19	populate	
20	ragged	
21	Renaissance	
22	riot	
23	squish	
24	sting	
25	tension	
26	treadmill	
27	vacancy	
28	ventilate	
29	viewpoint	
30	visualize	

01	동 거주하다	
02	동 의견을 듣다	
03	동 순환하다	
04	동 시각화하다	
05	동 조정하다	
06	동 쏘다, 찌르다	
07	동 찌부러뜨리다	
08	동 환기시키다	
09	동 황폐시키다	
10	명 가정	
11	명 견해	
12	명 국적	
13	명 긴장	
14	명 문예부흥기, 르네상스	
15	명 러닝머신	
16	명 빈자리, 빈방	
17	명 서식지	
18	명 안감	
19	명 유창함	
20	명 일광, 햇빛, 낮	
21	명 일반화	
22	명 주식회사	
23	명 봉쇄 동 봉쇄하다	
24	명 폭동	
25	형 남루한, 초라한	
26	형 어질러진	
27	형 얽힌, 복잡한	
28	형 이웃의	
29	형 혼돈된	
30	형 화장의	

DAY 24 STEP 1 한국어 뜻 생각하며 외우기

월 일

✦ 해당 영어의 한국어 의미를 생각하면서 2번씩 적으시오.

01	자산	**asset**	자산	자산
02	쿡쿡 찌르다; 찌르기	**poke**	쿡쿡 찌르다; 찌르기	쿡쿡 찌르다; 찌르기
03	결백한, 흠 없는	**spotless**	결백한, 흠 없는	결백한, 흠 없는
04	그만두다	**quit**	그만두다	그만두다
05	기질, 성질	**temper**	기질, 성질	기질, 성질
06	낮잠	**nap**	낮잠	낮잠
07	노출, 발각	**exposure**	노출, 발각	노출, 발각
08	대변혁을 일으키다	**revolutionize**	대변혁을 일으키다	대변혁을 일으키다
09	동등, 등식, 방정식	**equation**	동등, 등식, 방정식	동등, 등식, 방정식
10	명상하다	**meditate**	명상하다	명상하다
11	문의하다	**inquire**	문의하다	문의하다
12	보존	**preservation**	보존	보존
13	비극의	**tragic**	비극의	비극의
14	신뢰할 수 있는	**reliable**	신뢰할 수 있는	신뢰할 수 있는
15	아드레날린	**adrenaline**	아드레날린	아드레날린
16	야단법석	**fuss**	야단법석	야단법석
17	야망	**ambition**	야망	야망
18	엄한, 엄숙한	**grim**	엄한, 엄숙한	엄한, 엄숙한
19	운명, 비운	**fate**	운명, 비운	운명, 비운
20	운명	**destiny**	운명	운명
21	이익, 목적	**sake**	이익, 목적	이익, 목적
22	전설	**legend**	전설	전설
23	제한 없는	**unlimited**	제한 없는	제한 없는
24	중요성	**significance**	중요성	중요성
25	칼날	**blade**	칼날	칼날
26	통화	**currency**	통화	통화
27	피곤한	**weary**	피곤한	피곤한
28	피드백, 반응	**feedback**	피드백, 반응	피드백, 반응
29	한 주먹, 다수	**fistful**	한 주먹, 다수	한 주먹, 다수
30	혜성	**comet**	혜성	혜성

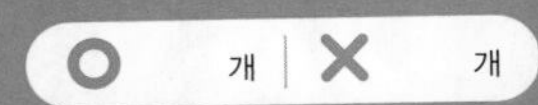

정답 p.76

✦ 다음을 영어는 한국어로 한국어는 영어로 적으시오.

01	adrenaline	
02	ambition	
03	asset	
04	blade	
05	comet	
06	currency	
07	destiny	
08	equation	
09	exposure	
10	fate	
11	feedback	
12	fistful	
13	fuss	
14	grim	
15	inquire	
16	legend	
17	meditate	
18	nap	
19	poke	
20	preservation	
21	quit	
22	reliable	
23	revolutionize	
24	sake	
25	significance	
26	spotless	
27	temper	
28	tragic	
29	unlimited	
30	weary	

01	동 쿡쿡 찌르다 명 찌르기	
02	동 그만두다	
03	동 대변혁을 일으키다	
04	동 명상하다	
05	동 문의하다	
06	명 기질, 성질	
07	명 낮잠	
08	명 노출, 발각	
09	명 동등, 등식, 방정식	
10	명 보존	
11	명 아드레날린	
12	명 야단법석	
13	명 야망	
14	명 운명, 비운	
15	명 운명	
16	명 이익, 목적	
17	명 전설	
18	명 중요성	
19	명 칼날	
20	명 통화	
21	명 피드백, 반응	
22	명 한 주먹, 다수	
23	명 혜성	
24	명 자산	
25	형 결백한, 흠 없는	
26	형 비극의	
27	형 신뢰할 수 있는	
28	형 엄한, 엄숙한	
29	형 제한 없는	
30	형 피곤한	

DAY 25

STEP 1 한국어 뜻 생각하며 외우기

월 일

✦ 해당 영어의 한국어 의미를 생각하면서 2번씩 적으시오.

01	(종·시계를) 울리다	**toll**	(종·시계를) 울리다	(종·시계를) 울리다
02	확실히 하다, 지키다	**ensure**	확실히 하다, 지키다	확실히 하다, 지키다
03	가렵다	**itch**	가렵다	가렵다
04	간단히 하다	**simplify**	간단히 하다	간단히 하다
05	걸작	**masterpiece**	걸작	걸작
06	공들인	**elaborate**	공들인	공들인
07	구렁이	**python**	구렁이	구렁이
08	근심이 없는	**carefree**	근심이 없는	근심이 없는
09	기금; 자금을 대다	**fund**	기금; 자금을 대다	기금; 자금을 대다
10	기묘한, 이상한	**weird**	기묘한, 이상한	기묘한, 이상한
11	논쟁	**controversy**	논쟁	논쟁
12	망토	**cape**	망토	망토
13	매립식 쓰레기 처리	**landfill**	매립식 쓰레기 처리	매립식 쓰레기 처리
14	묘사, 서술	**depiction**	묘사, 서술	묘사, 서술
15	분류하다	**categorize**	분류하다	분류하다
16	뻣뻣한, 딱딱한	**stiff**	뻣뻣한, 딱딱한	뻣뻣한, 딱딱한
17	상속하다	**inherit**	상속하다	상속하다
18	시민권	**citizenship**	시민권	시민권
19	오르다, 올라가다	**ascend**	오르다, 올라가다	오르다, 올라가다
20	일관된	**consistent**	일관된	일관된
21	장관인, 볼 만한	**spectacular**	장관인, 볼 만한	장관인, 볼 만한
22	재치, 요령	**tact**	재치, 요령	재치, 요령
23	적응	**adjustment**	적응	적응
24	전염병	**plague**	전염병	전염병
25	조심하다	**beware**	조심하다	조심하다
26	중요한	**crucial**	중요한	중요한
27	중지하다	**cease**	중지하다	중지하다
28	지도력	**leadership**	지도력	지도력
29	통제하다, 규정하다	**regulate**	통제하다, 규정하다	통제하다, 규정하다
30	해석, 이해	**interpretation**	해석, 이해	해석, 이해

STEP 2 최종실력 점검하기

✦ 다음을 영어는 한국어로 한국어는 영어로 적으시오.

정답 p.77

01	adjustment	
02	ascend	
03	beware	
04	cape	
05	carefree	
06	categorize	
07	cease	
08	citizenship	
09	consistent	
10	controversy	
11	crucial	
12	depiction	
13	elaborate	
14	ensure	
15	fund	
16	inherit	
17	interpretation	
18	itch	
19	landfill	
20	leadership	
21	masterpiece	
22	plague	
23	python	
24	regulate	
25	simplify	
26	spectacular	
27	stiff	
28	tact	
29	toll	
30	weird	

01	동 (종·시계를) 울리다	
02	동 확실히 하다, 지키다	
03	동 가렵다	
04	동 간단히 하다	
05	동 분류하다	
06	동 상속하다	
07	동 오르다, 올라가다	
08	동 조심하다	
09	동 중지하다	
10	동 통제하다, 규정하다	
11	명 걸작	
12	명 구렁이	
13	명 기금 동 자금을 대다	
14	명 논쟁	
15	명 망토	
16	명 매립식 쓰레기 처리	
17	명 묘사, 서술	
18	명 시민권	
19	명 재치, 요령	
20	명 적응	
21	명 전염병	
22	명 지도력	
23	명 해석, 이해	
24	형 공들인	
25	형 근심이 없는	
26	형 기묘한, 이상한	
27	형 뻣뻣한, 딱딱한	
28	형 일관된	
29	형 장관인, 볼 만한	
30	형 중요한	

월 일

✦ 해당 영어의 한국어 의미를 생각하면서 2번씩 적으시오.

01	(관청의) 국, 안내소	bureau	(관청의) 국, 안내소	(관청의) 국, 안내소
02	건강에 좋은	wholesome	건강에 좋은	건강에 좋은
03	결실이 없는	fruitless	결실이 없는	결실이 없는
04	경영	management	경영	경영
05	국내의	domestic	국내의	국내의
06	그림	drawing	그림	그림
07	시내, 지류	creek	시내, 지류	시내, 지류
08	내과 의사	physician	내과 의사	내과 의사
09	눈에 띄는, 중요한	prominent	눈에 띄는, 중요한	눈에 띄는, 중요한
10	떼	swarm	떼	떼
11	마지못해 하는	unwilling	마지못해 하는	마지못해 하는
12	멋진	gorgeous	멋진	멋진
13	문명(화)	civilization	문명(화)	문명(화)
14	발휘하다	exert	발휘하다	발휘하다
15	방심하지 않음, 경각심	alertness	방심하지 않음, 경각심	방심하지 않음, 경각심
16	분배, 분포	distribution	분배, 분포	분배, 분포
17	오르다	mount	오르다	오르다
18	산수; 산수상의	arithmetic	산수; 산수상의	산수; 산수상의
19	식별불능의	unidentifiable	식별불능의	식별불능의
20	씨를 뿌리다	sow	씨를 뿌리다	씨를 뿌리다
21	예비의; 준비	preliminary	예비의; 준비	예비의; 준비
22	예의 없는	impolite	예의 없는	예의 없는
23	전망	prospect	전망	전망
24	전문적인	professional	전문적인	전문적인
25	정보통의, 유식한	informed	정보통의, 유식한	정보통의, 유식한
26	허위	falsehood	허위	허위
27	확실히 하다, 확인하다	confirm	확실히 하다, 확인하다	확실히 하다, 확인하다
28	활성화하다	activate	활성화하다	활성화하다
29	회고, 회상; 회고하다	retrospect	회고, 회상; 회고하다	회고, 회상; 회고하다
30	효과적인	effective	효과적인	효과적인

정답 p.77

✦ 다음을 영어는 한국어로 한국어는 영어로 적으시오.

01	activate	
02	alertness	
03	arithmetic	
04	bureau	
05	civilization	
06	confirm	
07	creek	
08	distribution	
09	domestic	
10	drawing	
11	effective	
12	exert	
13	falsehood	
14	fruitless	
15	gorgeous	
16	impolite	
17	informed	
18	management	
19	mount	
20	physician	
21	preliminary	
22	professional	
23	prominent	
24	prospect	
25	retrospect	
26	sow	
27	swarm	
28	unidentifiable	
29	unwilling	
30	wholesome	

01	동 발휘하다	
02	동 씨를 뿌리다	
03	동 확실히 하다, 확인하다	
04	동 활성화하다	
05	명 (관청의) 국, 안내소	
06	명 경영	
07	명 그림	
08	명 시내, 지류	
09	명 내과 의사	
10	명 떼	
11	명 문명(화)	
12	명 방심하지 않음, 경각심	
13	명 분배, 분포	
14	동 오르다	
15	명 산수 형 산수상의	
16	명 전망	
17	명 허위	
18	명 회고, 회상 동 회고하다	
19	형 건강에 좋은	
20	형 결실이 없는	
21	형 국내의	
22	형 눈에 띄는, 중요한	
23	형 마지못해 하는	
24	형 멋진	
25	형 식별불능의	
26	형 예비의 명 준비	
27	형 예의 없는	
28	형 전문적인	
29	형 정보통의, 유식한	
30	형 효과적인	

DAY 27 STEP 1 한국어 뜻 생각하며 외우기

월 일

✦ 해당 영어의 한국어 의미를 생각하면서 2번씩 적으시오.

01	과장해서 말하다	**exaggerate**	과장해서 말하다	과장해서 말하다
02	간지럽히다; 간지럼	**tickle**	간지럽히다; 간지럼	간지럽히다; 간지럼
03	개화시키다	**civilize**	개화시키다	개화시키다
04	겸손한	**humble**	겸손한	겸손한
05	기절시키다	**stun**	기절시키다	기절시키다
06	맨발의	**barefoot**	맨발의	맨발의
07	모으다	**accumulate**	모으다	모으다
08	무법자	**outlaw**	무법자	무법자
09	문맥	**context**	문맥	문맥
10	밀도	**density**	밀도	밀도
11	밝게 하다	**illuminate**	밝게 하다	밝게 하다
12	별이 많은	**starry**	별이 많은	별이 많은
13	수도자, 성직자	**monk**	수도자, 성직자	수도자, 성직자
14	악한	**wicked**	악한	악한
15	압축	**compression**	압축	압축
16	연속	**succession**	연속	연속
17	완벽, 완전	**perfection**	완벽, 완전	완벽, 완전
18	원상태로 되돌리다	**undo**	원상태로 되돌리다	원상태로 되돌리다
19	유약, 광택제	**glaze**	유약, 광택제	유약, 광택제
20	이민	**immigration**	이민	이민
21	재활용할 수 있는	**recyclable**	재활용할 수 있는	재활용할 수 있는
22	저항할 수 없는	**irresistible**	저항할 수 없는	저항할 수 없는
23	진열장	**cabinet**	진열장	진열장
24	집중적인	**intensive**	집중적인	집중적인
25	찬송가	**hymn**	찬송가	찬송가
26	처리하다	**dispose**	처리하다	처리하다
27	최상급의, 최고의	**superlative**	최상급의, 최고의	최상급의, 최고의
28	코를 킁킁거리다	**sniff**	코를 킁킁거리다	코를 킁킁거리다
29	멍; 멍들게 하다	**bruise**	멍; 멍들게 하다	멍; 멍들게 하다
30	호흡	**respiration**	호흡	호흡

✦ 다음을 영어는 한국어로 한국어는 영어로 적으시오.

정답 p.78

01	accumulate	
02	barefoot	
03	bruise	
04	cabinet	
05	civilize	
06	compression	
07	context	
08	density	
09	dispose	
10	exaggerate	
11	glaze	
12	humble	
13	hymn	
14	illuminate	
15	immigration	
16	intensive	
17	irresistible	
18	monk	
19	outlaw	
20	perfection	
21	recyclable	
22	respiration	
23	sniff	
24	starry	
25	stun	
26	succession	
27	superlative	
28	tickle	
29	undo	
30	wicked	

01	동 과장해서 말하다	
02	동 간지럽히다 명 간지럼	
03	동 개화시키다	
04	동 기절시키다	
05	동 모으다	
06	동 밝게 하다	
07	동 원상태로 되돌리다	
08	동 처리하다	
09	동 코를 킁킁거리다	
10	명 무법자	
11	명 문맥	
12	명 밀도	
13	명 수도자, 성직자	
14	명 압축	
15	명 연속	
16	명 완벽, 완전	
17	명 유약, 광택제	
18	명 이민	
19	명 진열장	
20	명 찬송가	
21	명 멍 동 멍들게 하다	
22	명 호흡	
23	형 겸손한	
24	형 맨발의	
25	형 별이 많은	
26	형 악한	
27	형 재활용할 수 있는	
28	형 저항할 수 없는	
29	형 집중적인	
30	형 최상급의, 최고의	

STEP 1 한국어 뜻 생각하며 외우기

월 일

✦ 해당 영어의 한국어 의미를 생각하면서 2번씩 적으시오.

01	보험을 들다	**insure**	보험을 들다	보험을 들다
02	다른	**dissimilar**	다른	다른
03	닮다	**resemble**	닮다	닮다
04	화해시키다	**reconcile**	화해시키다	화해시키다
05	~ 하기 쉬운, 적절한	**apt**	~ 하기 쉬운, 적절한	~ 하기 쉬운, 적절한
06	고용하다	**hire**	고용하다	고용하다
07	공식적인	**official**	공식적인	공식적인
08	남용하다; 남용	**abuse**	남용하다; 남용	남용하다; 남용
09	떨리는	**thrilling**	떨리는	떨리는
10	매우 많은	**numerous**	매우 많은	매우 많은
11	무기를 지니지 않은	**unarmed**	무기를 지니지 않은	무기를 지니지 않은
12	밝히다, 폭로하다	**disclose**	밝히다, 폭로하다	밝히다, 폭로하다
13	보조의	**auxiliary**	보조의	보조의
14	분류	**classification**	분류	분류
15	빈번, 빈도, 주파수	**frequency**	빈번, 빈도, 주파수	빈번, 빈도, 주파수
16	빙하	**glacier**	빙하	빙하
17	사건이 많은	**eventful**	사건이 많은	사건이 많은
18	수업, 학기	**session**	수업, 학기	수업, 학기
19	알맞은	**moderate**	알맞은	알맞은
20	애정이 깊은	**affectionate**	애정이 깊은	애정이 깊은
21	양육하다	**breed**	양육하다	양육하다
22	억지로 채워 넣다	**cram**	억지로 채워 넣다	억지로 채워 넣다
23	얼음을 제거하다	**defrost**	얼음을 제거하다	얼음을 제거하다
24	완성	**completion**	완성	완성
25	유기체의	**organic**	유기체의	유기체의
26	이상한	**odd**	이상한	이상한
27	제거하다	**eliminate**	제거하다	제거하다
28	조심	**precaution**	조심	조심
29	진눈깨비	**sleet**	진눈깨비	진눈깨비
30	화려한	**luxurious**	화려한	화려한

STEP 2 최종실력 점검하기

O 개 | X 개

정답 p.78

✦ 다음을 영어는 한국어로 한국어는 영어로 적으시오.

01	abuse	
02	affectionate	
03	apt	
04	auxiliary	
05	breed	
06	classification	
07	completion	
08	cram	
09	defrost	
10	disclose	
11	dissimilar	
12	eliminate	
13	eventful	
14	frequency	
15	glacier	
16	hire	
17	insure	
18	luxurious	
19	moderate	
20	numerous	
21	odd	
22	official	
23	organic	
24	precaution	
25	reconcile	
26	resemble	
27	session	
28	sleet	
29	thrilling	
30	unarmed	

01	동 보험을 들다	
02	동 닮다	
03	동 화해시키다	
04	동 고용하다	
05	동 남용하다 명 남용	
06	동 밝히다, 폭로하다	
07	동 양육하다	
08	동 억지로 채워 넣다	
09	동 얼음을 제거하다	
10	동 제거하다	
11	명 진눈깨비	
12	명 분류	
13	명 빈번, 빈도, 주파수	
14	명 빙하	
15	명 수업, 학기	
16	명 완성	
17	명 조심	
18	형 다른	
19	형 ~ 하기 쉬운, 적절한	
20	형 공식적인	
21	형 떨리는	
22	형 매우 많은	
23	형 무기를 지니지 않은	
24	형 보조의	
25	형 사건이 많은	
26	형 알맞은	
27	형 애정이 깊은	
28	형 유기체의	
29	형 이상한	
30	형 화려한	

DAY 29

STEP 1
한국어 뜻 생각하며 외우기

월 일

✦ 해당 영어의 한국어 의미를 생각하면서 2번씩 적으시오.

01	~을 사지 않다; 불매 동맹	boycott	~을 사지 않다; 불매 동맹	~을 사지 않다; 불매 동맹
02	공포	horror	공포	공포
03	교훈적인, 유익한	instructive	교훈적인, 유익한	교훈적인, 유익한
04	깨달음	realization	깨달음	깨달음
05	냄새, 향기	scent	냄새, 향기	냄새, 향기
06	넓적다리	thigh	넓적다리	넓적다리
07	당황케 하는, 난처한	embarrassing	당황케 하는, 난처한	당황케 하는, 난처한
08	맹세하다	vow	맹세하다	맹세하다
09	명확하게 말하다	formulate	명확하게 말하다	명확하게 말하다
10	문지르다	scrub	문지르다	문지르다
11	민감도, 감수성	sensitivity	민감도, 감수성	민감도, 감수성
12	바치다	dedicate	바치다	바치다
13	분명한	apparent	분명한	분명한
14	붙잡다	seize	붙잡다	붙잡다
15	설비, 시설	facility	설비, 시설	설비, 시설
16	성직자, 장관	minister	성직자, 장관	성직자, 장관
17	송어; 송어를 낚다	trout	송어; 송어를 낚다	송어; 송어를 낚다
18	어렴풋한, 희미한	dim	어렴풋한, 희미한	어렴풋한, 희미한
19	용기 있는	courageous	용기 있는	용기 있는
20	원시의	primitive	원시의	원시의
21	위험한	hazardous	위험한	위험한
22	인류학	anthropology	인류학	인류학
23	재생, 재현	reproduction	재생, 재현	재생, 재현
24	전염성의	communicable	전염성의	전염성의
25	지리적인	geographical	지리적인	지리적인
26	참석	attendance	참석	참석
27	퉁명스러운	abrupt	퉁명스러운	퉁명스러운
28	평가하다; 견적	estimate	평가하다; 견적	평가하다; 견적
29	풀다, 늦추다	loosen	풀다, 늦추다	풀다, 늦추다
30	후회하는	regretful	후회하는	후회하는

STEP 2 최종실력 점검하기

정답 p.79

✦ 다음을 영어는 한국어로 한국어는 영어로 적으시오.

01	abrupt	
02	anthropology	
03	apparent	
04	attendance	
05	boycott	
06	communicable	
07	courageous	
08	dedicate	
09	dim	
10	embarrassing	
11	estimate	
12	facility	
13	formulate	
14	geographical	
15	hazardous	
16	horror	
17	instructive	
18	loosen	
19	minister	
20	primitive	
21	realization	
22	regretful	
23	reproduction	
24	scent	
25	scrub	
26	seize	
27	sensitivity	
28	thigh	
29	trout	
30	vow	

01	동 ~을 사지 않다 명 불매 동맹	
02	동 맹세하다	
03	동 명확하게 말하다	
04	동 문지르다	
05	동 바치다	
06	동 붙잡다	
07	동 평가하다 명 견적	
08	동 풀다, 늦추다	
09	명 공포	
10	명 깨달음	
11	명 냄새, 향기	
12	명 넓적다리	
13	명 민감도, 감수성	
14	명 설비, 시설	
15	명 성직자, 장관	
16	명 송어 동 송어를 낚다	
17	형 위험한	
18	명 인류학	
19	명 재생, 재현	
20	명 참석	
21	형 교훈적인, 유익한	
22	형 당황케 하는, 난처한	
23	형 분명한	
24	형 어렴풋한, 희미한	
25	형 용기 있는	
26	형 원시의	
27	형 전염성의	
28	형 지리적인	
29	형 퉁명스러운	
30	형 후회하는	

STEP 1 한국어 뜻 생각하며 외우기

월 일

✦ 해당 영어의 한국어 의미를 생각하면서 2번씩 적으시오.

01	시각적으로	visually	시각적으로	시각적으로
02	임명하다	appoint	임명하다	임명하다
03	값비싼	costly	값비싼	값비싼
04	끝의, 최종의	terminal	끝의, 최종의	끝의, 최종의
05	나오다	emerge	나오다	나오다
06	대담한	bold	대담한	대담한
07	대도시의	metropolitan	대도시의	대도시의
08	도보여행	trekking	도보여행	도보여행
09	도표; 도표로 나타내다	diagram	도표; 도표로 나타내다	도표; 도표로 나타내다
10	무효의	invalid	무효의	무효의
11	쿵쿵거리며 걷다	stomp	쿵쿵거리며 걷다	쿵쿵거리며 걷다
12	발생시키다	generate	발생시키다	발생시키다
13	성인	adulthood	성인	성인
14	수리하다	renovate	수리하다	수리하다
15	쏟아져 나오다	flush	쏟아져 나오다	쏟아져 나오다
16	야심적인	ambitious	야심적인	야심적인
17	어린이 같은, 유치한	childish	어린이 같은, 유치한	어린이 같은, 유치한
18	연장	extension	연장	연장
19	위성	satellite	위성	위성
20	이기다, 널리 보급하다	prevail	이기다, 널리 보급하다	이기다, 널리 보급하다
21	인구	population	인구	인구
22	읽고 쓸 줄 아는	literate	읽고 쓸 줄 아는	읽고 쓸 줄 아는
23	공감하다	sympathize	공감하다	공감하다
24	전염성의	contagious	전염성의	전염성의
25	중간의; 중도에서	halfway	중간의; 중도에서	중간의; 중도에서
26	중립의	neutral	중립의	중립의
27	천문학	astronomy	천문학	천문학
28	치명적인	deadly	치명적인	치명적인
29	톡톡 두드림	rap	톡톡 두드림	톡톡 두드림
30	화형	stake	화형	화형

✦ 다음을 영어는 한국어로 한국어는 영어로 적으시오.

정답 p.79

01	adulthood	
02	ambitious	
03	appoint	
04	astronomy	
05	bold	
06	childish	
07	contagious	
08	costly	
09	deadly	
10	diagram	
11	emerge	
12	extension	
13	flush	
14	generate	
15	halfway	
16	invalid	
17	literate	
18	metropolitan	
19	sympathize	
20	neutral	
21	population	
22	prevail	
23	rap	
24	renovate	
25	satellite	
26	stake	
27	stomp	
28	terminal	
29	trekking	
30	visually	

01	동 임명하다	
02	동 나오다	
03	동 발생시키다	
04	동 수리하다	
05	동 쏟아져 나오다	
06	동 이기다, 널리 보급하다	
07	명 도보여행	
08	명 도표 동 도표로 나타내다	
09	동 쿵쿵거리며 걷다	
10	명 성인	
11	명 연장	
12	명 위성	
13	명 인구	
14	명 천문학	
15	명 톡톡 두드림	
16	명 화형	
17	부 시각적으로	
18	형 값비싼	
19	형 끝의, 최종의	
20	형 대담한	
21	형 대도시의	
22	형 무효의	
23	형 야심적인	
24	형 어린이 같은, 유치한	
25	형 읽고 쓸 줄 아는	
26	동 공감하다	
27	형 전염성의	
28	형 중간의 부 중도에서	
29	형 중립의	
30	형 치명적인	

3rd Edition

절대어휘 5100

3 고등 내신 기본 900

---

* WORKBOOK ANSWER KEY

WORKBOOK
ANSWER KEY

DAY 01

P. 4

01 동 포기하다
02 동 돕다
03 동 섞다
04 명 상업
05 명 구성, 조직
06 동 나르다, 전달하다
07 동 대처하다
08 명 일치, 조화
09 형 고객 맞춤화된
10 형 파괴적인
11 명 적도
12 명 결점, 약점
13 명 부품
14 동 보증하다 명 보증
15 동 새기다
16 형 서로 관계가 있는
17 형 책임 있는
18 형 우울한
19 동 이야기하다
20 형 가난한
21 형 정치적인
22 동 떨다
23 명 안도
24 명 연발 권총
25 명 배우자
26 동 자극하다
27 형 일시적인, 임시의
28 동 변형시키다
29 동 촉구하다
30 형 비어 있는

01 convey
02 cope
03 assist
04 quiver
05 transform
06 guarantee
07 inscribe
08 blend
09 narrate
10 stimulate
11 urge
12 abandon
13 flaw
14 constitution
15 spouse
16 gadget
17 commerce
18 relief
19 revolver
20 correspondence
21 equator
22 needy
23 customized
24 vacant
25 interrelated
26 melancholy
27 temporary
28 political
29 liable
30 destructive

DAY 02

P. 6

01 동 관리하다
02 동 교대시키다, 번갈아 하다
03 명 열망, 포부
04 형 2개 국어를 할 수 있는
05 명 섭씨 형 섭씨의
06 명 송이, 무리
07 명 식민지
08 명 잔혹
09 동 내려가다
10 형 나이가 지긋한
11 명 방출
12 명 열광
13 명 극도의 피로
14 명 명성
15 명 피로
16 형 여자의, 여자 같은
17 형 기본적인
18 동 시작하다
19 명 누출
20 동 극대[최대]로 하다
21 명 쟁기 동 (밭을) 갈다
22 동 처방하다
23 명 자격
24 명 규제
25 동 흉내 내다
26 형 나선형의
27 명 이륙, 출발
28 형 독성의
29 명 통풍
30 형 원기 왕성한

01 maximize
02 administer
03 alternate
04 descend
05 initiate
06 prescribe
07 simulate
08 regulation
09 exhaustion
10 leakage
11 fame
12 emission
13 Celsius
14 cluster
15 colony
16 enthusiasm
17 aspiration
18 takeoff
19 qualification
20 cruelty
21 plow
22 ventilation
23 fatigue
24 fundamental
25 spiral
26 elderly
27 toxic
28 bilingual
29 feminine
30 vigorous

DAY 03

P. 8

01 명 침술
02 명 향기
03 명 계산
04 명 자본주의
05 동 새기다, 조각하다
06 명 애벌레
07 동 협력하다
08 명 양심
09 형 계속적인
10 명 위기
11 명 효율성
12 명 강조
13 동 확대[증대]시키다
14 형 점진적인
15 형 감명 깊은
16 형 교묘한, 기발한
17 명 의도
18 형 되돌릴 수 없는
19 명 상아
20 명 집주인
21 동 애도하다, 슬퍼하다
22 명 물리학자
23 형 심리적인
24 명 재통일
25 동 으르렁거리다 명 포효
26 명 (종교·도덕상의) 죄
27 명 한 뼘, 기간
28 형 가파른
29 형 빠른
30 명 결합, 조합

01 enlarge
02 carve
03 mourn
04 roar
05 collaborate
06 union
07 sin
08 emphasis
09 calculation
10 caterpillar
11 physicist
12 ivory
13 conscience
14 crisis
15 intention
16 capitalism
17 reunification
18 landlord
19 acupuncture
20 span
21 aroma
22 efficiency
23 steep
24 impressed
25 continual
26 ingenious
27 irreversible
28 swift
29 psychological
30 gradual

DAY 04

P. 10

01 부 정확하게
02 형 긍정적인
03 부 간신히
04 형 잔인한
05 형 협조적인
06 전 ~에 관하여
07 명 출발
08 형 불쾌한
09 명 방해, 소동
10 명 기부
11 동 구멍을 뚫다
12 형 예외적인
13 동 사라지다
14 명 좌절
15 명 희미한 빛, 기색
16 동 손상시키다
17 형 취임의 명 취임식
18 동 팽창시키다
19 명 조작, 책략
20 형 치명적인, 죽을 운명의
21 명 전망, 시야
22 동 이행하다
23 형 정확한, 정밀한
24 동 정제하다
25 형 잠 못 이루는, 불안한
26 명 성실, 진실성
27 동 끌어안다
28 동 팽팽하게 치다
29 동 발굴하다
30 동 짐을 내리다

01 drill
02 refine
03 snuggle
04 unearth
05 fade
06 impair
07 perform
08 unload
09 inflate
10 tighten
11 outlook
12 donation
13 disturbance
14 sincerity
15 accurately
16 maneuver
17 frustration
18 departure
19 glimmering
20 barely
21 concerning
22 affirmative
23 distasteful
24 exceptional
25 brutal
26 precise
27 inaugural
28 mortal
29 collaborative
30 restless

DAY 05

P. 12

01 명 고고학자
02 형 깨닫게 하는 명 각성
03 명 산들바람
04 동 트림하다 명 트림
05 동 미치게 하다 명 열광
06 형 분해할 수 있는
07 명 차별
08 동 매혹하다
09 명 친절
10 명 검투사
11 명 환대
12 형 습한
13 명 (신원) 확인
14 명 착각
15 동 마음을 내키게 하다
16 형 웅장한, 훌륭한
17 형 겸손한
18 명 유기체
19 명 특이한 성질
20 명 사생활
21 형 유익한, 이익이 되는
22 명 승진
23 명 회복
24 명 주거
25 형 초라한
26 명 비탈
27 형 피상적인
28 동 맥박이 뛰다
29 형 진 적이 없는, 무적의
30 명 기꺼이 하는 마음

01 enchant
02 incline
03 throb
04 craze
05 discriminate
06 gladiator
07 archaeologist
08 willingness
09 slope
10 privacy
11 breeze
12 promotion
13 organism
14 residence
15 illusion
16 friendliness
17 burp
18 peculiarity
19 identification
20 hospitality
21 recovery
22 modest
23 awakening
24 unbeaten
25 degradable
26 humid
27 magnificent
28 profitable
29 shabby
30 supernatural

DAY 06

P. 14

01 형 학구적인
02 동 체포하다
03 명 변호사
04 동 브레인스토밍하다
05 명 구성, 작문
06 형 동시대의 명 같은 시대의 사람
07 형 예의 바른, 공손한
08 명 방어
09 명 보조개 동 보조개를 짓다
10 형 무례한, 실례되는
11 동 일깨우다
12 형 솔직한
13 형 지질학의
14 형 마음에서 우러난
15 명 고결, 청렴
16 동 조사하다
17 명 복권, 추첨
18 동 잘못 인도하다
19 형 주목할 만한
20 명 양분, 영양소
21 명 냄새, 악취
22 명 방관자
23 동 수확하다
24 동 재생하다
25 형 진부한 동 진부하게 하다
26 동 무리하게 사용하다
27 형 잠재의식의 명 잠재의식
28 형 충분한
29 동 완패시키다
30 동 당기다

01 thrash
02 tug
03 strain
04 brainstorm
05 reap
06 evoke
07 mislead
08 investigate
09 apprehend
10 integrity
11 composition
12 odor
13 onlooker
14 defense
15 attorney
16 dimple
17 lottery
18 nutrient
19 contemporary
20 hearty
21 reproductive
22 frank
23 disrespectful
24 courteous
25 subconscious
26 notable
27 geological
28 stale
29 sufficient
30 academic

DAY 07

P. 16

01 형 결석한 동 결석하다
02 형 거스르는, 부정적인
03 명 사면
04 형 항생물질의 명 항생물질
05 명 기구, 전기제품
06 명 지도책
07 명 지루함
08 명 동료
09 명 상담, 조언
10 형 썩은
11 동 소화하다
12 형 매혹적인
13 부 언제나, 영원히
14 형 광범위한
15 명 민속, 민간 전승
16 명 관용
17 명 불편
18 동 절연하다
19 명 대출
20 형 강력한
21 명 부분
22 형 막을 수 있는
23 형 분별없는, 경솔한
24 형 반복적인
25 명 감정, 정서
26 명 골격, 해골
27 동 증명하다, 증언하다
28 명 찬사, 감사의 표시
29 동 (꼬리, 머리 등을) 흔들다
30 동 보류하다

01 wag
02 withhold
03 decayed
04 digest
05 insulate
06 testify
07 tribute
08 sentiment
09 skeleton
10 generosity
11 appliance
12 loan
13 companion
14 folklore
15 portion
16 inconvenience
17 counsel
18 atlas
19 boredom
20 amnesty
21 eternally
22 mighty
23 adverse
24 absent
25 extensive
26 preventable
27 enchanting
28 repetitive
29 rash
30 antibiotic

DAY 08

P. 18

01 동 머물다
02 명 원조, 도움
03 형 추운
04 동 저지르다, 범하다
05 동 건설하다
06 동 유죄를 선고하다
07 명 중심, 핵심
08 명 복도
09 형 축축한 동 (기를) 꺾다
10 동 둘러싸다, 동봉하다
11 형 동등한
12 명 융통성, 유연성
13 동 (세게) 끌어당기다
14 동 절뚝거리며 걷다
15 형 불치의
16 명 통찰력
17 명 방해
18 부 마찬가지로
19 형 자연의
20 명 꽃가루
21 명 지수, 몫
22 명 흉터 동 상처를 내다
23 명 국자, 한 숟갈
24 명 조미료
25 명 이기적임, 이기심
26 동 쥐어 짜다
27 명 자극
28 명 경향
29 형 생생한
30 명 (모든) 노동자

01 convict
02 haul
03 commit
04 construct
05 enclose
06 abide
07 hobble
08 squeeze
09 tendency
10 scoop
11 pollen
12 workforce
13 interruption
14 corridor
15 damp
16 assistance
17 flexibility
18 selfishness
19 stimulation
20 seasoning
21 core
22 quotient
23 insight
24 scar
25 equivalent
26 likewise
27 incurable
28 vivid
29 natural
30 chilly

DAY 09

P. 20

01 형 청년기의 명 청소년
02 부 완전히
03 동 신의 은총을 빌다
04 동 증명하다
05 명 기둥
06 명 탐정 형 탐정의
07 동 높이다
08 명 인내(심)
09 동 달래다
10 명 넓게 펼쳐진 공간
11 명 기근
12 명 수도꼭지
13 명 도박
14 명 보호자, 감시인
15 형 산업의
16 형 순진한, 결백한
17 명 선율
18 명 이야기하기, 서술
19 형 부정적인
20 형 시의, 시적인
21 명 처방
22 형 신앙심이 깊은
23 명 (시의) 운
24 동 (침을) 뱉다
25 명 투명성
26 명 기구
27 명 변화
28 형 수직의, 세로의
29 동 어기다, 위반하다
30 동 갈망하다

01 yearn
02 elevate
03 violate
04 certify
05 spit
06 utensil
07 famine
08 column
09 expanse
10 gambling
11 variation
12 guard
13 melody
14 faucet
15 rhyme
16 narration
17 endurance
18 prescription
19 detective
20 transparency
21 altogether
22 negative
23 industrial
24 vertical
25 innocent
26 poetic
27 religious
28 adolescent
29 bless
30 lull

DAY 10

P. 22

01 동 조립하다
02 형 ~행의
03 부 침착하게
04 동 탄산가스로 포화시키다
05 명 평상복 형 평상복의
06 명 대성당
07 동 빻다, 부수다
08 동 ~할 만하다
09 형 능률적인
10 동 높이다
11 동 입대하다
12 형 열이 있는
13 형 격노한
14 형 기름이 묻은
15 명 충동
16 명 성분, 재료
17 명 사슬
18 명 그동안
19 형 다층의
20 동 과장하여 행하다
21 명 순례자
22 동 자격을 부여하다
23 동 거절하다
24 동 드러내다
25 명 쓰레기
26 명 전문가
27 형 기술의
28 형 자취를 남기지 않은
29 명 통일
30 형 젊은

01 qualify
02 reveal
03 deserve
04 reject
05 overact
06 enhance
07 crumble
08 enlist
09 assemble
10 meantime
11 cathedral
12 leash
13 ingredient
14 pilgrim
15 rubbish
16 specialist
17 impulse
18 calmly
19 carbonate
20 unity
21 casual
22 bound
23 furious
24 greasy
25 technical
26 efficient
27 multilayered
28 feverish
29 trackless
30 youthful

WORKBOOK
ANSWER KEY

DAY 11

P. 24

01	동 적응하다	01	steer
02	동 체포하다 명 체포	02	reform
03	명 거물, ~왕	03	drip
04	명 크기, 덩치	04	irrigate
05	명 보존	05	criticize
06	형 계속적인	06	interact
07	동 비판하다	07	fulfill
08	형 의존할 수 있는	08	launch
09	형 뚜렷한, 명백한	09	arrest
10	명 전환	10	moth
11	명 운명, 파멸	11	baron
12	동 뚝뚝 떨어지다 명 물방울	12	mansion
13	동 이행하다	13	conservation
14	명 흘깃 봄 동 흘깃 보다	14	retail
15	명 제국주의	15	doom
16	동 상호작용하다	16	adapt
17	동 물을 대다	17	diversion
18	형 신장	18	imperialism
19	동 진수시키다, 발사하다	19	bulk
20	명 대저택	20	pupil
21	명 나방	21	glimpse
22	형 종합적인 부 종합적으로	22	continuous
23	명 학생	23	distinct
24	동 개혁하다	24	unethical
25	명 소매	25	symbolic
26	동 조종하다	26	kidney
27	형 상징적인	27	dependable
28	형 지루한	28	overall
29	형 비도덕적인	29	unnoticeable
30	형 중요하지 않은	30	tiresome

DAY 12

P. 26

01	명 산성 형 산성의	01	frown
02	명 의제, 안건	02	socialize
03	명 보석(금)	03	suppress
04	명 뇌물	04	propel
05	명 관목, 덤불	05	throng
06	명 회담	06	bribe
07	명 창조성	07	influenza
08	명 민주주의	08	bush
09	형 부정직한	09	democracy
10	명 외침, 감탄	10	bail
11	부 충실하게	11	acid
12	동 눈살을 찌푸리다	12	exclamation
13	형 매혹적인	13	maintenance
14	형 부지런한	14	validity
15	명 독감	15	procedure
16	명 유지, 정비	16	precision
17	명 틀, 거푸집	17	agenda
18	형 머리 위의 부 머리 위에	18	rectangle
19	형 주기적인	19	creativity
20	명 정확 형 정밀한	20	mold
21	명 절차	21	conference
22	형 진보적인, 점진적인	22	faithfully
23	동 추진하다	23	glamorous
24	명 직사각형	24	overhead
25	형 존경할 만한	25	dishonest
26	동 교제하다	26	industrious
27	동 진압하다	27	uncared
28	명 군중	28	respectable
29	형 손질하지 않는	29	periodic
30	명 유효성, 타당성	30	progressive

DAY 13

P. 28

01	형 수락할 수 있는	01	recall
02	명 찬성, 승인	02	perceive
03	동 일어나다	03	threaten
04	명 끌어당김, 매력	04	comprehend
05	동 이해하다	05	arise
06	동 주장하다, 다투다	06	contend
07	형 방어적인	07	overload
08	명 발전, 진화	08	geometry
09	명 사기	09	slot
10	명 기하학	10	hunchback
11	명 사냥개	11	attraction
12	명 등이 굽은 사람	12	originality
13	형 한가한, 놀고 있는	13	lotus
14	명 상상(력)	14	evolution
15	형 피할 수 없는, 당연한	15	fraud
16	형 지적인	16	hound
17	명 투자	17	imagination
18	명 (식물) 연, 연꽃 무늬	18	stance
19	형 안개가 짙은	19	approval
20	명 독창성	20	investment
21	동 (짐을) 너무 많이 싣다	21	sufficiently
22	동 알아차리다	22	subsequent
23	동 상기하다[시키다]	23	defensive
24	형 얕은	24	acceptable
25	명 길쭉한 구멍	25	misty
26	명 자세	26	shallow
27	형 파업 중인	27	intellectual
28	형 그 후의	28	striking
29	부 충분히	29	inevitable
30	동 협박하다, 위협하다	30	idle

DAY 14

P. 30

01	명 흡수	01	overuse
02	명 광고	02	counteract
03	명 유사	03	offend
04	명 걱정	04	twinkle
05	형 적용할 수 있는	05	hesitate
06	명 놋쇠 형 금관악기의	06	extinguish
07	명 비교	07	notion
08	동 방해하다, 중화하다	08	anxiety
09	명 기술, 재주	09	advertisement
10	명 지시 형 지시하는	10	craft
11	명 불만족	11	brass
12	명 영원	12	walkabout
13	동 진화하다	13	object
14	동 주저하다	14	dissatisfy
15	명 유아 형 초기의	15	comparison
16	명 차단, 절연	16	ratio
17	명 위치	17	sequence
18	명 개념	18	eternity
19	동 반대하다 명 물건	19	prevention
20	동 기분을 상하게 하다	20	location
21	부 구두로	21	analogy
22	동 남용하다 명 남용	22	infant
23	명 자세 동 자세를 취하다	23	pose
24	명 예방	24	directive
25	명 비율	25	insulation
26	명 파충류	26	reptile
27	명 연속	27	skull
28	명 해골	28	absorption
29	동 반짝반짝 빛나다	29	orally
30	명 도보여행, 민정 시찰	30	applicable

DAY 15

P. 32

01	동 폐지하다	01	erect
02	형 원자의	02	bounce
03	동 튀다 명 튀어오름	03	migrate
04	명 상당한 양	04	abolish
05	명 헌신	05	commitment
06	형 건설적인, 구조적인	06	interval
07	명 유죄 판결	07	infection
08	명 데시벨	08	hardship
09	명 존엄	09	hoe
10	동 세우다 형 똑바로 선	10	decibel
11	명 장르	11	semiconductor
12	명 고충, 곤란	12	vocalist
13	명 괭이	13	chunk
14	명 감염	14	triumph
15	명 정밀검사	15	pollution
16	명 간격, 중간 휴식 시간	16	squid
17	동 이주하다	17	thermometer
18	명 항해, 항공	18	conviction
19	형 아픈, 힘드는	19	stimulus
20	명 오염	20	genre
21	부 보도에 의하면	21	inspection
22	형 부족한, 드문	22	scrap
23	명 조각	23	dignity
24	형 안전한	24	navigation
25	명 반도체	25	reportedly
26	명 오징어	26	constructive
27	명 자극	27	scarce
28	명 온도계	28	painful
29	명 승리	29	secure
30	명 보컬리스트, 가수	30	atomic

DAY 16

P. 34

01	명 단체, 협회	01	remark
02	명 물집	02	dare
03	명 방, 회의실	03	varnish
04	동 싸우다 명 전투	04	flourish
05	형 법인의	05	combat
06	명 부패, 타락	06	gaze
07	동 감히 ~ 하다	07	transplant
08	명 국제간 긴장 완화	08	innovate
09	명 높이	09	détente
10	명 봉투	10	elevation
11	동 번창하다	11	association
12	형 맨 앞의	12	virtue
13	동 응시하다	13	blister
14	형 유죄의	14	chamber
15	형 하위의, 열등한	15	veteran
16	동 혁신하다	16	sheriff
17	부 정신적으로	17	envelope
18	명 이야기	18	corruption
19	명 이웃 형 근처의	19	rage
20	명 시집	20	poetry
21	명 분노 동 격노하다	21	ridge
22	동 말하다 명 논평	22	narrative
23	명 융기, 산마루	23	neighborhood
24	명 보안관	24	mentally
25	형 부드러운	25	foremost
26	동 이식하다	26	corporate
27	형 전적의, 완전한	27	tender
28	동 니스를 칠하다 명 니스	28	guilty
29	형 노련한 명 전문가	29	utter
30	명 덕, 미덕	30	inferior

DAY 17

P. 36

01 명 동경, 찬양	01 expose
02 명 황갈색, 호박색	02 nag
03 명 평가	03 curator
04 형 생물학적인	04 lineup
05 형 유능한	05 adoration
06 형 심장의	06 catalog(ue)
07 명 목록	07 splinter
08 명 조심	08 tragedy
09 명 전시 책임자	09 inactivity
10 명 절망	10 grief
11 부 쉽게	11 medication
12 동 드러내다	12 fare
13 명 요금	13 fusion
14 명 축하연	14 despair
15 형 한정된	15 caution
16 명 융합, 용해	16 presence
17 명 슬픔	17 feast
18 명 비활동, 부진	18 assessment
19 형 법률의	19 amber
20 명 정렬, 사람의 줄	20 relaxation
21 명 약물 (치료)	21 effortlessly
22 동 잔소리하다	22 technological
23 명 존재, 출석	23 legal
24 명 휴식, 이완	24 universal
25 형 혁명의	25 biological
26 형 신성한	26 sacred
27 명 부서진 조각	27 cardiac
28 형 기술적인	28 capable
29 명 비극	29 finite
30 형 보편적인	30 revolutionary

DAY 18

P. 38

01 형 알맞은	01 spend
02 형 거만한	02 crook
03 명 편, 측, 이익	03 irritate
04 명 묶음	04 shift
05 형 인정 많은, 사려 깊은	05 retain
06 명 계약(서) 동 계약하다	06 knit
07 동 구부리다 명 굽은 것	07 glow
08 형 의존하고 있는	08 refresh
09 형 거대한	09 specialize
10 형 기능의	10 purify
11 동 빛나다	11 contract
12 명 주민	12 motivation
13 형 중간의 동 중재하다	13 queasy
14 동 짜증나게 하다	14 bundle
15 동 뜨다, 짜다	15 laundry
16 명 빨래	16 behalf
17 형 육중한, 엄청난	17 inhabitant
18 명 동기부여, 자극	18 enormous
19 형 불쌍한, 측은한	19 arrogant
20 동 정화하다	20 uneven
21 형 메스꺼운, 역겨운	21 functional
22 동 상쾌하게 하다	22 untimely
23 동 계속 유지하다	23 pitiful
24 동 위치를 바꾸다	24 adequate
25 동 전공하다	25 massive
26 동 (돈을) 쓰다	26 dependent
27 형 끈적거리는	27 considerate
28 형 참을 수 있는	28 intermediate
29 형 고르지 않는	29 sticky
30 형 때 아닌	30 tolerable

DAY 19

P. 40

01	동 인정하다	01	confess
02	명 통로	02	overcome
03	명 귀족정치	03	prohibit
04	형 발가벗은	04	shiver
05	동 고백하다	05	thrust
06	명 창조물	06	dwell
07	동 헐다, 파괴하다	07	inform
08	동 왜곡하다	08	distort
09	명 다양성	09	acknowledge
10	형 의심 없는 부 확실히	10	recur
11	동 살다, 깃들다	11	perish
12	명 경영진 형 집행의	12	demolish
13	형 가짜의 명 가짜	13	glance
14	형 언, 냉동의	14	executive
15	동 힐끗 보다 명 힐끗 봄	15	panic
16	형 비인격적인, 객관적인	16	aristocracy
17	동 알리다	17	diversity
18	형 장엄한	18	preference
19	동 극복하다	19	proportion
20	명 공포	20	surgeon
21	동 죽다	21	creature
22	명 더 좋아함	22	aisle
23	명 행진, 행렬, 진행	23	procession
24	동 금지하다	24	fake
25	명 비율, 비례	25	impersonal
26	동 재발하다	26	bare
27	동 떨다 명 떨림	27	sophisticated
28	형 세련된	28	frozen
29	명 외과 의사	29	doubtless
30	동 밀다 명 밀침	30	majestic

DAY 20

P. 42

01	명 숙박시설	01	stumble
02	부 대략	02	bustle
03	형 파산한	03	shatter
04	동 분주히 돌아다니다	04	shrink
05	형 포괄적인	05	originate
06	형 만족해 하는	06	snatch
07	명 장인	07	evolve
08	동 해고시키다	08	dismiss
09	동 진화하다	09	ignorance
10	형 프리랜서로 일하는	10	accommodation
11	명 중심	11	superiority
12	명 위생	12	hygiene
13	명 무지	13	craftsman
14	형 상상력이 풍부한	14	staple
15	형 강렬한	15	hub
16	형 안의, 내적인	16	perception
17	명 충성	17	loyalty
18	형 순식간의	18	freelance
19	동 시작되다	19	approximately
20	형 평행의 명 평행선	20	respective
21	명 지각	21	intense
22	형 각각의	22	content
23	동 산산이 부수다	23	subtle
24	동 수축하다	24	undiscovered
25	동 와락 붙잡다, 낚아채다	25	imaginative
26	형 주요한 명 주요 상품	26	momentary
27	동 넘어지다 명 비틀거림	27	inward
28	형 민감한	28	broke
29	명 우세, 우월	29	parallel
30	형 발견되지 않은	30	comprehensive

DAY 21

P. 44

01	형 추상적인	01	dissatisfied
02	형 현명한, 바람직한	02	mock
03	명 분석	03	hijack
04	명 강당	04	possess
05	명 (기계의) 고장	05	offer
06	형 자격이 있는, 유능한	06	breakdown
07	명 정의	07	auditorium
08	명 실망	08	occasion
09	형 불만을 품은	09	orbit
10	부 공평히	10	analysis
11	형 비상한, 비범한	11	signature
12	형 거대한	12	sermon
13	동 공중 납치하다	13	numeral
14	형 모욕적인	14	disappointment
15	동 모방하다 명 흉내	15	requirement
16	명 숫자	16	warfare
17	명 경우	17	definition
18	동 제공하다 명 제공	18	participation
19	명 궤도	19	evenly
20	명 참여	20	competent
21	동 소유하다	21	gigantic
22	형 기본의, 주된	22	thrifty
23	형 무모한	23	primary
24	명 요구	24	slack
25	명 설교	25	insulting
26	명 서명	26	reckless
27	형 느슨한 명 느슨함, 여유	27	extraordinary
28	형 검소한, 절약하는	28	ultrasonic
29	형 초음파의	29	abstract
30	명 전투	30	advisable

DAY 22

P. 46

01	동 많이 있다, 풍부하다	01	scratch
02	형 사과의 명 변명	02	attain
03	명 지원자	03	abound
04	동 달성하다	04	counterbalance
05	명 경계	05	foretell
06	형 원의	06	decorate
07	명 평범한 것 형 평범한	07	minimize
08	동 상쇄하다	08	scatter
09	동 장식하다	09	sensation
10	형 부지런한	10	boundary
11	명 심부름	11	segment
12	동 예측하다, 예언하다	12	troop
13	형 진짜의	13	near-sighted
14	명 급함, 서두름	14	haste
15	형 수평의 명 수평물	15	logic
16	명 영감, 격려	16	representative
17	명 논리학, 논리	17	reaction
18	동 최소화하다	18	errand
19	형 근시안의	19	inspiration
20	명 입자	20	thermostat
21	명 반응	21	particle
22	명 대표자	22	applicant
23	동 흩어버리다	23	vocation
24	동 긁다, 할퀴다	24	commonplace
25	명 구획, 단편	25	warm-hearted
26	명 감각, 느낌	26	diligent
27	명 온도 조절 장치	27	apologetic
28	명 군대, 병력	28	horizontal
29	명 직업	29	circular
30	형 마음이 따뜻한	30	genuine

DAY 23

P. 48

01 명 가정
02 명 봉쇄 동 봉쇄하다
03 형 혼돈된
04 동 순환하다
05 동 의견을 듣다
06 동 조정하다
07 명 주식회사
08 형 화장의
09 명 일광, 햇빛, 낮
10 동 황폐시키다
11 명 유창함
12 명 일반화
13 명 서식지
14 형 얽힌, 복잡한
15 명 안감
16 형 어질러진
17 명 국적
18 형 이웃의
19 동 거주하다
20 형 남루한, 초라한
21 명 문예부흥기, 르네상스
22 명 폭동
23 동 찌부러뜨리다
24 동 찌르다
25 명 긴장
26 명 러닝머신
27 명 빈자리, 빈방
28 동 환기시키다
29 명 견해
30 동 시각화하다

01 populate
02 consult
03 circulate
04 visualize
05 coordinate
06 sting
07 squish
08 ventilate
09 devastate
10 assumption
11 viewpoint
12 nationality
13 tension
14 Renaissance
15 treadmill
16 vacancy
17 habitat
18 lining
19 fluency
20 daylight
21 generalization
22 corporation
23 blockade
24 riot
25 ragged
26 messy
27 intricate
28 neighboring
29 chaotic
30 cosmetic

DAY 24

P. 50

01 명 아드레날린
02 명 야망
03 명 자산
04 명 칼날
05 명 혜성
06 명 통화
07 명 운명
08 명 동등, 등식, 방정식
09 명 노출, 발각
10 명 운명, 비운
11 명 피드백, 반응
12 명 한 주먹, 다수
13 명 야단법석
14 형 엄한, 엄숙한
15 동 문의하다
16 명 전설
17 동 명상하다
18 명 낮잠
19 동 쿡쿡 찌르다 명 찌르기
20 명 보존
21 동 그만두다
22 형 신뢰할 수 있는
23 동 대변혁을 일으키다
24 명 이익, 목적
25 명 중요성
26 형 결백한, 흠 없는
27 명 기질, 성질
28 형 비극의
29 형 제한 없는
30 형 피곤한

01 poke
02 quit
03 revolutionize
04 meditate
05 inquire
06 temper
07 nap
08 exposure
09 equation
10 preservation
11 adrenaline
12 fuss
13 ambition
14 fate
15 destiny
16 sake
17 legend
18 significance
19 blade
20 currency
21 feedback
22 fistful
23 comet
24 asset
25 spotless
26 tragic
27 reliable
28 grim
29 unlimited
30 weary

DAY 25

P. 52

01 명 적응
02 동 오르다, 올라가다
03 동 조심하다
04 명 망토
05 형 근심이 없는
06 동 분류하다
07 동 중지하다
08 명 시민권
09 형 일관된
10 명 논쟁
11 형 중요한
12 명 묘사, 서술
13 형 공들인
14 동 확실히 하다, 지키다
15 명 기금 동 자금을 대다
16 동 상속하다
17 명 해석, 이해
18 동 가렵다
19 명 매립식 쓰레기 처리
20 명 지도력
21 명 걸작
22 명 전염병
23 명 구렁이
24 동 통제하다, 규정하다
25 동 간단히 하다
26 형 장관인, 볼 만한
27 형 뻣뻣한, 딱딱한
28 명 재치, 요령
29 동 (종·시계를) 울리다
30 형 기묘한, 이상한

01 toll
02 ensure
03 itch
04 simplify
05 categorize
06 inherit
07 ascend
08 beware
09 cease
10 regulate
11 masterpiece
12 python
13 fund
14 controversy
15 cape
16 landfill
17 depiction
18 citizenship
19 tact
20 adjustment
21 plague
22 leadership
23 interpretation
24 elaborate
25 carefree
26 weird
27 stiff
28 consistent
29 spectacular
30 crucial

DAY 26

P. 54

01 동 활성화하다
02 명 방심하지 않음, 경각심
03 명 산수 형 산수상의
04 명 (관청의) 국, 안내소
05 명 문명(화)
06 동 확실히 하다, 확인하다
07 명 시내, 지류
08 명 분배, 분포
09 형 국내의
10 명 그림
11 형 효과적인
12 동 발휘하다
13 명 허위
14 형 결실이 없는
15 형 멋진
16 형 예의 없는
17 형 정보통의, 유식한
18 명 경영
19 동 오르다
20 명 내과 의사
21 형 예비의 명 준비
22 형 전문적인
23 형 눈에 띄는, 중요한
24 명 전망
25 명 회고, 회상 동 회고하다
26 동 씨를 뿌리다
27 명 떼
28 형 식별불능의
29 형 마지못해 하는
30 형 건강에 좋은

01 exert
02 sow
03 confirm
04 activate
05 bureau
06 management
07 drawing
08 creek
09 physician
10 swarm
11 civilization
12 alertness
13 distribution
14 mount
15 arithmetic
16 prospect
17 falsehood
18 retrospect
19 wholesome
20 fruitless
21 domestic
22 prominent
23 unwilling
24 gorgeous
25 unidentifiable
26 preliminary
27 impolite
28 professional
29 informed
30 effective

WORKBOOK ANSWER KEY

DAY 27

P. 56

01	동 모으다	01	exaggerate
02	형 맨발의	02	tickle
03	명 멍 동 멍들게 하다	03	civilize
04	명 진열장	04	stun
05	동 개화시키다	05	accumulate
06	명 압축	06	illuminate
07	명 문맥	07	undo
08	명 밀도	08	dispose
09	동 처리하다	09	sniff
10	동 과장해서 말하다	10	outlaw
11	명 유약, 광택제	11	context
12	형 겸손한	12	density
13	명 찬송가	13	monk
14	동 밝게 하다	14	compression
15	명 이민	15	succession
16	형 집중적인	16	perfection
17	형 저항할 수 없는	17	glaze
18	명 수도자, 성직자	18	immigration
19	명 무법자	19	cabinet
20	명 완벽, 완전	20	hymn
21	형 재활용할 수 있는	21	bruise
22	명 호흡	22	respiration
23	동 코를 킁킁거리다	23	humble
24	형 별이 많은	24	barefoot
25	동 기절시키다	25	starry
26	명 연속	26	wicked
27	형 최상급의, 최고의	27	recyclable
28	동 간지럽히다	28	irresistible
29	동 원상태로 되돌리다	29	intensive
30	형 악한	30	superlative

DAY 28

P. 58

01	동 남용하다 명 남용	01	insure
02	형 애정이 깊은	02	resemble
03	형 ~ 하기 쉬운, 적절한	03	reconcile
04	형 보조의	04	hire
05	동 양육하다	05	abuse
06	명 분류	06	disclose
07	명 완성	07	breed
08	동 억지로 채워 넣다	08	cram
09	동 얼음을 제거하다	09	defrost
10	동 밝히다, 폭로하다	10	eliminate
11	형 다른	11	sleet
12	동 제거하다	12	classification
13	형 사건이 많은	13	frequency
14	명 빈번, 빈도, 주파수	14	glacier
15	명 빙하	15	session
16	동 고용하다	16	completion
17	동 보험을 들다	17	precaution
18	형 화려한	18	dissimilar
19	형 알맞은	19	apt
20	형 매우 많은	20	official
21	형 이상한	21	thrilling
22	형 공식적인	22	numerous
23	형 유기체의	23	unarmed
24	명 조심	24	auxiliary
25	동 화해시키다	25	eventful
26	동 닮다	26	moderate
27	명 수업, 학기	27	affectionate
28	명 진눈깨비	28	organic
29	형 떨리는	29	odd
30	형 무기를 지니지 않은	30	luxurious

DAY 29

P. 60

01 형 통명스러운
02 명 인류학
03 형 분명한
04 명 참석
05 동 ~을 사지 않다 명 불매 동맹
06 형 전염성의
07 형 용기 있는
08 동 바치다
09 형 어렴풋한, 희미한
10 형 당황한, 난처한
11 동 평가하다
12 명 설비, 시설
13 동 명확하게 말하다
14 형 지리적인
15 형 위험한
16 명 공포
17 형 교훈적인, 유익한
18 동 풀다, 늦추다
19 명 성직자, 장관
20 형 원시의
21 명 깨달음
22 형 후회하는
23 명 재생, 재현
24 명 냄새, 향기
25 동 문지르다
26 동 붙잡다
27 명 민감도, 감수성
28 명 넓적다리
29 명 송어 동 송어를 낚다
30 동 맹세하다

01 boycott
02 vow
03 formulate
04 scrub
05 dedicate
06 seize
07 estimate
08 loosen
09 horror
10 realization
11 scent
12 thigh
13 sensitivity
14 facility
15 minister
16 trout
17 hazardous
18 anthropology
19 reproduction
20 attendance
21 instructive
22 embarrassing
23 apparent
24 dim
25 courageous
26 primitive
27 communicable
28 geographical
29 abrupt
30 regretful

DAY 30

P. 62

01 명 성인
02 형 야심적인
03 동 임명하다
04 명 천문학
05 형 대담한
06 형 어린이 같은
07 형 전염성의
08 형 값비싼
09 형 치명적인
10 명 도표 동 도표로 나타내다
11 동 나오다
12 명 연장
13 동 쏟아져 나오다
14 동 발생시키다
15 형 중간의 부 중도에서
16 형 무효의
17 형 읽고 쓸 줄 아는
18 형 대도시의
19 동 공감하다
20 형 중립의
21 명 인구
22 동 이기다, 널리 보급하다
23 명 톡톡 두드림
24 동 수리하다
25 명 위성
26 명 화형
27 동 쿵쿵거리며 걷다
28 형 끝의, 최종의
29 명 도보여행
30 부 시각적으로

01 appoint
02 emerge
03 generate
04 renovate
05 flush
06 prevail
07 trekking
08 diagram
09 stomp
10 adulthood
11 extension
12 satellite
13 population
14 astronomy
15 rap
16 stake
17 visually
18 costly
19 terminal
20 bold
21 metropolitan
22 invalid
23 ambitious
24 childish
25 literate
26 sympathize
27 contagious
28 halfway
29 neutral
30 deadly

5100개의 절대어휘만 외워도 내신·수능·토플이 쉬워진다.

- ▶ 단계별 30일 구성의 계획적인 어휘 학습
- ▶ 단어 ➔ 어구 ➔ 문장의 효과적인 암기 프로세스
- ▶ 유의어, 반의어, 파생어를 통한 어휘력 확장
- ▶ QR코드를 통해 남녀 원어민 발음 바로 듣기
- ▶ 일일테스트와 누적테스트로 단어 반복 학습 강화

절대어휘 5100 Vocabulary master 5단계 시리즈

절대어휘 5100 ①	900 단어	중등 내신 기본 영단어
절대어휘 5100 ②	900 단어	중등 내신 필수 영단어
절대어휘 5100 ③	**900 단어**	**고등 내신 기본 영단어**
절대어휘 5100 ④	1200 단어	수능 필수 영단어
절대어휘 5100 ⑤	1200 단어	수능 고난도·토플 영단어

절대어휘 5100 시리즈 구성

본책 + 워크북 + MP3 + 문제출제프로그램 제공

QR코드를 통해 본 교재의 상세정보와
부가학습 자료를 이용할 수 있습니다.